M. L.

REA

ACPL ITEM
DISC

3 1833 00

D0762058

DO NOT REMOVE
CARDS FROM POCKET

306.48 B41w   2208588
BELL, MICHAEL J. 1947-
THE WORLD FROM BROWN'S
LOUNGE :

ALLEN COUNTY PUBLIC LIBRARY

FORT WAYNE, INDIANA 46802

You may return this book to any agency, branch,
or bookmobile of the Allen County Public Library.

DEMCO

The World from Brown's Lounge

THE WORLD FROM BROWN'S LOUNGE

An Ethnography of Black Middle-Class Play

Michael J. Bell

UNIVERSITY OF ILLINOIS PRESS

Urbana Chicago London

Allen County Public Library
Ft. Wayne, Indiana

© 1983 by the Board of Trustees of the University of Illinois
Manufactured in the United States of America

This book is printed on acid-free paper.

For permission to reprint copyrighted materials, the author is indebted to: the California Folklore Society for portions of his essay, "Tending Bar at Brown's: Occupational Role as Artistic Performance," published in *Western Folklore*, 25 (1976): 93–107; the editors of the *Southern Folklore Quarterly* for "The Kinesics of Performance: An Example Described," published in volume 41 (1977): 17–31; and the editors of *Sub-Stance* for "Social Control/ Social Order/Social Art," published in volume 22 (1979): 49–65.

Library of Congress Cataloging in Publication Data

Bell, Michael J. (Michael Joseph), 1947–
    The world from Brown's Lounge.

    Bibliography: p.
    1. Afro-Americans—Social life and customs.
2. Afro-Americans—Folklore.   I. Title.
E185.86.B378   306'.48'0880622   82–4732
ISBN 0–252–00956–8   AACR2

2208588

For Karen and Joshua

Contents

Preface

This is a study of black American folklore. Yet the term folklore does not appear, except once, in its pages because its use is open to debate. The study of folklore has undergone extended and profound changes in the last twenty-five years. From a discipline originally concerned with recovering the anonymous traditions of recognizable folk communities, folk studies have broadened their perspectives and concerns to include not only the traditional past but also the immediate present. Folklore is now understood to be the artistic communication created and used by ordinary people to order and direct their lives. It is the art of ordinary life, to be studied both for the ways in which it links us to the past and also for the ways in which its performance links us together in our day-to-day interactions. As the data of folk studies have changed, so, too, have the methods for their collection. Today folklore is studied in context. Folkloric performances are understood best when they are examined ethnographically, in terms of what they do to and for the people who do them at the moment they are done. And, accordingly, the meaning of folklore can only be grasped in light of the original network of information that made sense of it to its audience.

Still, for all these changes and widened perspectives, this work pushes at the boundaries of the discipline. It contains none of the traditional forms of folklore that might be expected in such a study. It deals with a segment of the population not usually included within the meaning of "folk." And it draws the boundaries of that group in novel ways. Traditional folklore was not a part of the life of Brown's Lounge. People did not tell jokes. It was considered inappropriate to do so. They did not do toasts. They belonged in contexts other than Brown's. There were plenty of stories told, but they were personal narratives, not traditional legends or tall tales. Instead, the patrons of Brown's did other things. They talked, they played with talk, they talked about talk, building out of these interactions enormously creative and artful communications that went to the heart of what was occurring and that expressed ideas and feelings which reached far beyond these individual moments of relationship. Moreover, these performances were unlikely to ever become traditional. They were innovative, performed to fit the moment and not to survive beyond it.

If the data are not traditional, neither are the informants. Folklorists no longer search for the "folk" on the margins of society or outside of the formal institutions of culture. Everyone is a member of the folk in so far as they can be or are a participant in the creation or communication of art in face-to-face interactions. The middle class remains, however, a largely uncharted territory. They have been thought too sophisticated, too caught up in the shifting currents of elite and popular experience, too concerned with the trendy and the novel, to continue traditional practices or to practice tradition. The complexity of their lives and life-styles, therefore, has worked against their being considered as a folk group.

Finally, this study focuses on this group in an unusual way. Folklorists have tended to draw the boundaries of their studies in terms of specific groups, studying the folklore of an age group, of an occupation, or of an ethnicity. The boundaries of my research were those of a place. I did not begin with the patrons of Brown's as an established group and then examine their interactions in a single context. Rather, I began with the bar and examined the group and the interactions that were created by its existence. The bar, then, was the determining factor. It made the group and determined how the other parameters of age, occupation, class, neighborhood, and the like would be fixed. Moreover, though I began my fieldwork in order to study folklore, I made no attempt during my time in the field to collect folklore or to discover what folklore my informants knew. Instead, I waited to see if folklore would happen. I am sure that those who used Brown's knew all sorts of traditional lore and that they would have been willing to allow me to collect it. I am sure also, because I witnessed it, that many of them interacted in other contexts and situations where this type of material was very much a part of the expected pattern of interaction. My interest, however, was not what my informants might know or what they might do (information that would have been extremely relevant if the group had been the focus of research); my interest was in what the patrons of Brown's actually did, given the environment they were in and the people they were with.

It is for these reasons that I have avoided entering into arguments over whether or not the contents of this book are folklore. That debate and the theoretical arguments on which it is based are better left for the technical journals and scholarly audiences to whom they are directly relevant. This book describes the world I saw and experienced, and those data are too important to worry here about their scholarly classification.

I am indebted to many individuals for their help and encouragement at all stages of this project. My research was supported by a National Institute of Mental Health U.S. Public Health Grant, No. MH 17-216, administered by the Center for Urban Ethnography at the University of Pennsylvania. I would like to thank all the members of the Department of Folklore and Folklife at the University of Pennsylvania, especially Kenneth S. Goldstein, John Szwed, and Dan Ben-Amos, who were extremely generous with their time and their ideas at the time when I was struggling to turn what I had heard and seen into a meaningful ethnography. Also, at Pennsylvania, I benefited from the criticisms of Ray Birdwhistell and Dell Hymes, each of whom read and criticized portions of my research. Dan Rose, Roger Renwick, and Sally Yerkovitch helped at critical moments, listening to me as I pieced this work together, providing encouragement when I became stuck or panicked, and sharing ideas when I needed to find a way out of or into my data. If they see their ideas in this work, I hope they will not mind that I borrowed them so freely.

I owe a special debt to Roger Abrahams. My earliest interest in Afro-American culture was kindled by his class on Afro-American folklore. It was also he who convinced me that ethnography was possible and that I could do it. Since that time, he has remained a constant source of ideas and my most intense critic. He read every portion of the final manuscript, and his insights and responses have affected every page of this work. We have not always agreed, but without his help I might never have taken the stands that I have.

I am also deeply in the debt of my colleagues at Wayne State University. Folklorists in English departments often complain that their literary colleagues understand little of what they do and show little interest in learning. This has never been my experience at Wayne State. The members of my department have been deeply interested in and supportive of my work from my earliest days at Detroit. They have wanted to know what I was doing. They were interested in establishing connections between my focus on aesthetic creativity in ordinary life and their own more literary interests. It was they who sought over and over to show me how our interests were connected not in literature but as a genuine merging of literary and anthropological perspectives. I would like to thank especially Charles Baxter, Leonard Tennenhouse, Edward Hirsch, Arden Reed, Jeanne Flood, Arthur Marotti, and John Franzosa, each of whom read and criticized my original manuscript.

My greatest debt is to my informants. They allowed me to enter their lives, to record their experiences, and to recount them in this work. Because it was their wish, I have not identified any of them by their correct names or nicknames. All references to persons, locations, and establishments, therefore, are pseudonymous. Though I cannot thank them by name, I can state categorically that without their concern and commitment this book would not have existed. It is a commonplace to say that fieldwork experiences affect the data that can be presented. I can say of mine that they also have affected how I will do fieldwork for the rest of my career. No amount of thanks can repay my informants for what they gave me and for what they taught me.

Finally, I thank my wife, Karen, who alternatively *kvetched* and *kvelled* this work into existence.

Introduction

This book is an ethnography of middle-class black Americans at play. It describes the social organization — the life and order created by its patrons — of Brown's Lounge, a black bar in Philadelphia. Its aim is to discover what is black about the black middle class, in what ways middle-class blacks express their blackness, and what their particular style of blackness says about the cultural and bicultural status of the black middle class. Because its author is white, it is necessary to introduce this work with a brief account of its origin.

I first came to know Brown's Lounge, then the Nassau Inn, while I was working in Philadelphia. One afternoon, Rick Clark, a black co-worker, and I left work early in search of a drink. We ended up at Ray's, a bar not far from the hospital where we worked. The next afternoon Rick suggested that we go to a bar closer to his home. He said that he didn't like the atmosphere at Ray's and that he didn't feel comfortable there. I drove him home, and we walked down to the corner and into the Nassau Inn. The Nassau Inn was a typical neighborhood tavern. Its customers were drawn from the surrounding area, and some had been coming to the bar since it had opened in the late 1930s. All of the patrons were male; most were white, and most were working class, reflecting the socioeconomic makeup of the neighborhood as it had been for the past twenty years. In recent years there had been an influx of black working and middle class into the neighborhood, and a few of those new residents such as Rick had taken to frequenting the bar. They came because it was close to their homes, because it was a way to express their rightful participation in the neighborhood, and, for the convenience, they were willing to act as if the Uncle Tomism forced upon them by the regular white customers was the joke it pretended to be.

As I was leaving the bar one Saturday about two months after my first visit, I called out to Jimmy, the owner, that I would see him the following week. He laughed and said that I wouldn't because he had sold the place. He explained that he was tired of being robbed, that his wife feared for his safety, and that he just didn't need the trouble anymore. A black man had made him an offer, and he had decided to get out while he could. More than a bit curious, I went by on Monday. The door was locked, and the Nassau Inn sign was gone. The next day the Nassau Inn had become Brown's Lounge.

Brown's Lounge was quite different from the Nassau Inn. The bright, open, television-dominated room of the Nassau was gone; in its place was a dimly lit, music-filled room presided over by a black bartender. Suddenly I felt very white and very out of place, though this feeling was diminished somewhat by the presence of Rick at the bar. Uncomfortably, I made my way to a stool next to his, and he and I began to talk while the bar began to fill up with other black customers, male and female, known to Rick but unknown to me. After about five minutes of casual talk, Rick said quietly but intensely in terms of our conversation at that moment: "You know, I feel very comfortable here." More out of friendship than understanding, I replied that I felt the same way.

I grew more relaxed and assured about my feelings in part by observing the reactions of other white patrons of the Nassau who entered the bar that afternoon. For those who came expecting to find the Nassau, the experience was visibly shocking. Most actually recoiled before turning away; some did not merely leave but turned and fled out the door. A few white patrons who had known that the bar had changed owners also came to look. They tended to stand in the doorway, looking and nodding until, unwilling to enter, they left. Though painful to watch, their behavior seemed to make sense. The Nassau was now a black bar, and it was obvious that none of its former white patrons knew or wanted to know how to behave there.

About an hour after I had arrived, one of the regular black customers came in. He, too, did a double take at the changes in the bar. Then he relaxed, ordered a drink, and began talking to the bartender, peppering his conversation with expletives. The bartender explained that such language was not allowed with ladies present and asked him to stop. He did, but not for long; soon he had shifted back to the old way of speaking which had been acceptable at the Nassau Inn. Again he was reminded, and again he stopped for a time. When he lapsed the third time, the bartender told him loudly and forcefully either to stop using such language or to leave. Rick, who had been half-following this interaction, intervened, saying: "I'll take care of this. He hasn't figured out the changes yet," and he took the offending customer to the back booths for a private talk.

That a black customer would not automatically know what was appropriate in what was to me a black bar was unexpected and compelling. I had assumed that in the now "exclusively black" Brown's Lounge blacks would know how to behave, while other whites and I would not. I was wrong. The black character of the bar that the other whites and I had found so obvious was, in fact, not something which could be taken for granted by anyone. In place of the seemingly solid world I had been seeing, it appeared that, at any moment in the course of action, it was possible for a number of distinct realities to exist side by side. This ambiguity and the uncertainty it represented were all too clear examples of the fact that the cultural identity of Brown's and its patrons was not the fixed universe I had been assuming but a reality that needed to be discovered and rediscovered each time it was experienced. Confronted with an example of the problematic quality of social relations, more vivid than any textbook or classroom exposition, I decided to make the world of Brown's Lounge the focus of my research.

The problematic nature of this social life became even more evident when I attempted to find descriptions in the literature for the kinds of behavior I had been observing. Since 1964, in large measure as a response to the tensions and pressures created by social action in the black community [Tumin, 1969, pp. 254–59], a great deal has been written on Afro-American life. The work of social scientists in this area has had a continuous and enduring effect on the civil rights movement for which so many have acted as ideological theorists. The most productive of these scholars and researchers have seen the solution to the problem of racism in the reeducation of whites and blacks to the acceptance of the viability of social patterns in black life. "Black life . . . [is] not suffused with dysfunction but with meaningful organizations and communications systems, not with institutional life in decay but with a set of ordering devices that are tenacious and successful and . . . blacks themselves are not a group of shattered and depressed people but a vibrant and creative set of individuals" [Abrahams, 1970b, p. 10]. Despite this concern, those interested in Afro-American life have concentrated their energy almost exclusively on the behavior and life-style of poor black America. This focus on the most politically visible segment of the black community has led to a serious distortion in the scholarly and popular understanding of the nature and scope of Afro-American

culture in the United States. By ignoring mainstream black Americans — working and middle class — responsible scholars have unnec-
essarily limited public understanding of how extensive and pervasive
are the patterns that their researches have uncovered. Such scholars
have made it possible for some to assert that Afro-American culture
is exclusively urban or exclusively poor. Indeed, given what the
present literature has to say about it, the most surprising fact about
the black middle class is that it exists at all.

Economic and statistical summaries of the black condition in
North America aside, there are few major studies of the life-style of
the black middle class. Of these, six — John Dollard's *Caste and
Class in a Small Southern Town*, Gunnar Myrdal's *An American
Dilemma*, St. Clair Drake and Horace Cayton's *Black Metropolis*,
E. Franklin Frazier's *The Black Bourgeoisie*, Nathan Hare's *The
Black Anglo-Saxons*, and Price M. Cobb and William Greir's *Black
Rage* — are uniform in their denunciation of black middle-class life.
Though they describe different times and places, these authors all
conclude that the black middle class embodies the worst of white
America. Repeatedly they assert that the black middle class is concerned almost solely with emulating white society in its values, its
styles, and its focus on the material features of the "good life." Their
general conclusions are best summarized by the most influential of
their number, Frazier: "The black bourgeoisie has been uprooted
from its racial tradition and as a consequence it has no cultural roots
in either the Negro or the white world" [p. 113]. Frazier went on to
argue that the quest for a place in the American scene by the black
middle class resulted only in the creation of an extended fantasy
without substance: "a world of make believe into which the black
bourgeoisie can escape from its inferiority and inconsequence in
American society" [p. 174]. He argued that this condition produced,
in the final analysis, a way of life that was in its worst manifesta-
tions, pathological, and in its best, utter nothingness.

Two recent attempts to analyze the life-style of the black middle
class — *The Middle-Class Negro in the White Man's World* by Eli
Ginzberg et al. and *The Black Middle Class* by Sidney Kronus — are
more positive in their approach to the black middle class. These
authors argue that the changes brought about by the upsurge in
black consciousness in the 1960s have resulted in a more realistic life-
style. To them, the black middle class is an aware, competent set of
individuals whose outlook and aspirations are focused on real possibilities, real goals, and realizable achievements. Unlike some of the
earlier studies, the work of Ginzberg et al. and Kronus is competent

social scientific research, the conclusions of which reflect the facts as given and not as perceived or assumed. Since both studies are based on attitudinal research gathered in interviews, however, both suffer from problems of validation. Their data were gathered from individuals who were aware that they were being interviewed as "ideal" representatives of their race, and so there is the possibility that the information obtained describes not the life-style of the interviewees, but what the interviewees thought *ought* to be their life-style.

Nowhere, then, do we have a description of middle-class black behavior that derives from the observation of ordinary, day-to-day experiences of the people themselves. This study seeks to provide a partial contribution based on active participant observation. It outlines the manner in which the daily life and style of a black bar reflects the values of its neighborhood and its neighbors. It describes how the patrons of that bar build their everyday occurrences, molding them to conform to their desire to create and live within a world that allows them to be both black and middle class. And it demonstrates how this activity results in an ongoing cultural expression in which the larger demands of the community and the individual needs of the patrons are merged to satisfy collective desires. Moreover, it locates its description at the center of the "problem experiences" of the black middle class by observing their life-style and values in a context in which the extreme behaviors of which they are accused would most likely surface. By examining the routine experiences of Brown's patrons and by identifying what is meaningful to them from their perspective and within their norms as they stand apart from the concerns and the controls of the white middle-class world, their lives can be viewed, not in terms of how well or effectively they measure up to the standards others set for them but in terms of how well they measure up to the standards they set for themselves. The measures, then, on which this work is based are the very particular concerns of the men and women who frequent Brown's Lounge. It is their knowledge, the characteristic ways in which they categorize and define themselves, and their words that create the world described in this book.

The data were collected from the spring of 1972 through the fall of 1973. The observation periods in the bar were three hours and covered both the working day, 8 A.M. to 2 A.M., and the working week, Monday through Saturday. Initially I scheduled my time in the bar so that all the available blocks of times were covered periodically. From these preliminary observations I formulated a working typology of bar usage, which was then used to develop a more com-

plete map of the periods of the day and week in which significant activity went on in the bar. Though not absolute, significant activity
occurring when expected and when unexpected, this "use history"
allowed me to concentrate most of my time in Brown's during those
periods when the most action would be going on.

Throughout the process of observation, I acted (as best I could) as
a typical patron. This was, of course, a polite fiction. Nevertheless,
it permitted me to minimize, though never eliminate, the effect of
my presence. From the outset of my research, I was candid with
both the owners and patrons about what I was interested in: writing
a book about the happenings in Brown's. For those who inquired
further, I explained that I was working on my dissertation, though
not revealing specifically that it was in folklore and folklife. Based
on this general explanation, I was able to negotiate an initial,
unspoken contract with the regular patrons: I would be allowed to
participate and observe in Brown's, provided that I abided by the
explicit and implicit rules of the bar. As long as I demonstrated that
I was aware of these requirements, I was allowed to remain.

My effect on ongoing interaction was further reduced by my continual presence in the bar. By being there every day, and sometimes
more than once a day, I used the bar in the same manner as the regular patrons. At one level I became a regular because I acted like one
— driving people places when the need arose, helping to pick up bar
supplies when no one else could, tending bar when no one else was
in the room and the barmaid had an emergency, doing all the little
tasks that other patrons did and that cemented them into an institutional community. The result was that my presence in the bar was
much more obvious than my long-term project, and I became, at
least partially, part of the routine. My goals were out of the patrons'
sight, not out of their minds. Thus, on one occasion, in the midst of
an elegantly explicit harangue against an out-of-line patron, the
night barmaid Mary suddenly turned to me and asked: "Is this going
to be any good for that book you're writing?" She immediately got
back to the business at hand, while I pondered my dual status. Overall, however, I developed an insider's right to use Brown's for my
own reasons.

The data were gathered in three ways. The greater part of my
time in Brown's was spent watching and listening. Eventually, when
the patrons were comfortable with my presence, I brought in a tape
recorder to record conversations. My informants knew that they
were being recorded, and they did not object. Their only stipula-
tions were that the tape recorder remain invisible at all times and

that they could listen to any recorded conversation, though no one ever asked to do so. The conversations were taped on a cassette recorder with 180-minute tapes. These provided for uninterrupted recordings of 90 minutes per side and allowed me to capture extensive stretches of spoken interaction without interruption. These recorded conversations provided the raw data for the extended discussions of social interaction in the following chapters. Finally, I did several extended interviews with key informants to expand and supplement the information derived from observation and the taped interactions.

As I have stated, this work is concerned with establishing the relevant features of ordinary experience that constitute the middle-class Afro-American character of Brown's Lounge and the behaviors that occur there. Rather than take for granted the blackness of the bar or of its patrons, I aim to identify those features that are at the heart of its active creation. Instead of presuming that participants in bar life automatically know what is happening at any moment in time, I am concerned with discovering how these individuals come to know what is going on and what provides them with this information. My emphasis, then, is on the procedural basis of experience, on understanding how ordinary life grows specifically out of the practices that constitute it as meaningful for its participants. Throughout this work, I have sought to develop the everyday world of Brown's as it is experienced, interpreted, and understood by its patrons, and I have attempted to derive from these data an adequate model of what they perceive are the routine patterns of behavior subtending the practical organization of social interaction [Garfinkel, 1967]. These patterns—the ways of entering, using, and leaving the bar, the rules for engaging in conversation, the order of interaction, the organization of understanding—standardize and introduce sense in the world of the bar. Taken together, these activities are the means by which patrons and staff make and maintain contact with each other; they are the formal scaffolding that permits individuals using the bar to understand how they should behave and to interpret the behavior of others. My widest focus, therefore, is on the traditional, cultural features of a particular Afro-American identity; my intention, however, is to record this identity as it is represented epistemologically, that is, in terms of the formal knowledge necessary for its expression in the lives of people [Schutz, 1962, 1964, 1966, 1967]. Accordingly, institutional, social, and psychological structures are examined not in order to discover the origins of specific behaviors but in order to describe the end results of such behaviors. Instead of treating structure as the source of specificity, I have attempted to show that it is the activities of the patrons and staff that determine the meaning of the world from Brown's Lounge.

Such an approach to ordinary life presumes the need and the abilities of individuals to authenticate themselves and to convince others of their authenticity. It is based on the assumption that every interaction is a continuous exchange of images of self — of who and what one is — in order to convince the others present that all present are capable of acting coherently and correctly. This approach presumes, moreover, that such acts of authenticity are neither automatic nor entirely predictable. Social relations are open-ended and dependent upon the flow of interaction for a substantial part of their meaning. Accordingly, I have taken as the starting point for my analyses the belief that such manipulations of self — *impression management*, according to Erving Goffman [1959] — involve one in a continual process of convincing the world at large that one's actions are the proper way to act and that any interaction can be viewed as a dramatic interaction of managed selves whose goal is the organization of a convincing reality. Though dramatic, such presentations are not without consequences for those involved. The real world, after all, is one in which outcomes are relevant. Accordingly, individuals are expected to behave so as to discredit neither the world nor themselves. As Goffman has remarked, "There is no interaction in which the participants do not take an appreciable chance of being slightly embarrassed or a slight chance of being deeply humiliated" [1959, p. 156]. Thus, though it may be funny at times, the creation of any world is never wholly a laughing matter.

I shall also argue that certain of the interactions occurring in Brown's represent the creation and introduction of art into everyday life. One of the fundamental reasons why patrons returned regularly to Brown's was the possibility that certain individuals would attempt to transform the ordinariness of ordinary life into something extraordinary by the use of self-consciously artful creations — fictional plays and performances. Within such fictions the text, the stage, the audience, the response, and the evaluation are present all at once, and the limits of the fictions mark the limits of the world and what is not in these interactions does not, at one level, exist at all. Accordingly, the artistic experience generated at all levels — textural, stylistic, critical, and cultural — is for the duration of the patron's involvement the totality of the available social world and the only source of

the social world to follow. Within such interactions social experience and artistic experience are one; art is life and life is momentarily art, and the world hangs in the balance. This art is valuable
because it moves patrons from private subjectivity to public, objective expression and momentarily transforms the heterogeneous
desires of particular patrons into the more fundamental, more con-
crete desires and needs of the larger community. The presence of this
artful creativity within the world of Brown's is evidence of the kind
of place it is, of the kind of cultural values its performers and audiences wish to express, and the kind of problems that lie at the
center of their lives.

The defining mark of my analysis, then, is a focus on the aesthetics
of ordinary experience. It is not an attempt to fix or enshrine the
"creations" of the patrons as literary texts outside of time nor is it an
attempt to enhance the value of form and order. The dramas to be
discussed are cultural situations. They are scenes of experience that
arise out of the tension inherent in the interplay of the patrons and
the world around them. The artistry that develops in such a relationship cannot be separated from the general range of behavior in
the bar, and the participants, whether creator/performers or audiences, are not qualitatively different from others in the community.
The voice that speaks in these texts and fantasies is that of a vital
member of a community that uses art as a methodology for sustain-
ing a real and recognizable world.

Specifically, I believe the description of these aesthetics will show
that the world of Brown's, the environment and complex of human
activities that make it up, exists in order to permit the patrons to see
themselves and their actions while they are in the bar as consistent
with their own definitions of what it means to be black and middle
class. Within the complex world of its symbols and social communication, within its walls, its geography, its time, its ordinary occurrences, its dreams, and its harsher facts will be found images of
self and community that define those who use the bar as aware
members of the black community capable of dealing with the as-
sorted pressures of being black and successful. Moreover, these
images will not isolate the patrons of Brown's from the urban Afro-
American community but will connect the bar and its patrons to the
wider aesthetics that prevail in black America. Again, this does not
mean that performances of these fictions were valued by their participants or by me for their inherent perfection. Rather, they are a
part of the lives of those who frequent Brown's Lounge (and,

therefore, a part of this book) because they have the power to create, define, and even momentarily destroy the social reality, the language, and the patrons involved within a given interaction.

The phenomena under consideration in this study cannot adequately be described by referring directly to the shared cultural references that would ordinarily make them intelligible. Much the same can be said for my presentation of the data. The expectations I brought to the field were radically altered by my experiences, and this circumstance makes this work as fragile as the social world it is an attempt to describe. I must therefore explain how I came to see what I saw and how I came to write what I wrote.

About eight months after I began my research, I entered Brown's with the intention of observing the beginnings of the Christmas celebration. I had been told to expect some "heavy partying," and the bar was already on its way to being packed. About half an hour after I entered, someone tapped me on the shoulder, and I turned to see Rick standing behind me. Before I could say hello, he said: "You know, that was cool of you not to interrupt me while I was rapping with that woman. You're learning to party tough." I responded spontaneously: "Were you here? I didn't even see you," and he replied: "I was at the end of the bar talking with her when you came by. I thought you was being cool. You mean you were just blind?"

I wish I could say that I was anything but blind at that moment, but I cannot. The truth is that, though I had ample time, a fairly unobstructed view of my surroundings, and, as I later reflected, had surveyed the room several times, I literally failed to see Rick. This failure is all the more striking because Rick was my initial and most important contact in Brown's. Under normal circumstances my failure to notice him would have been a serious breach of our friendship. In this case, however, my "not seeing" him was not a violation but was judged by him as proof of my increased ability to behave appropriately in Brown's. By not seeing Rick, I had followed in an extreme fashion the bar's code of conduct, which excluded from view or public comment those male-female interactions in which a married man or woman was involved with someone other than his or her spouse. In the terms of the bar, I had, as Rick indicated, *partied tough*.

While I was pleased with Rick's praise for my increasing interactive skills, I was profoundly disturbed by the graphic demonstration of my failure as a fieldworker. My concern was supposed to be the description of a social life in which rapping with a woman was a normal behavior, and yet it was clear that I was systematically "not seeing" certain forms of that behavior. My "understanding" of what constituted relevant data reflected, in an extreme fashion, the situation supposedly under analysis. My limits of objectivity were no longer those I had brought to my fieldwork but were now those defined by the unfolding of daily life. In searching my field notes, it became apparent that this incident, though unusual, was not unique. There were other "lapses" and involvements that, when seen as a pattern, helped make some sense of my ability to "not see" Rick that afternoon. Together, they represented a systematic picture of my deepening involvement in the world of Brown's and of the process by which I came to be a partner in its creation. They were a measure of the ties of acceptance and of rejection that had moved me from fieldworker to "patron."

The ties of acceptance I experienced in Brown's dealt primarily with the possibility that I was "black." It was said jokingly that there was a "nigger in my woodpile" or that "you better watch your hanging around here or we're going to rub off on you so your wife won't recognize you no more." Likewise, my ability to hold my own in conversation was applauded: "Mike knows his way. He can talk shit with the best. You don't be defending him, Harriet. If he's gonna rap, he gonna have to stand on his rap." Finally, my success in involving myself in the affairs of the bar and the patrons was praised: "He don't talk trash," or "He's not lame. I'd trust him to take my back." In each case, my behavior was interpreted as evidence of my developing cultural skills and hence of my developing moral blackness. These compliments were not statements designed to deceive me but genuine attempts to explain my ability to behave appropriately, if not always adequately. I recorded them as serious statements and took pride in their indication that I was doing something right. More important, though, they served to place upon me a clear responsibility to continue to act as I had been. I was by no means an insider, but I had acquired the expectations of one. Thus, by building their idea of what was acceptable into my behavior, the regular patrons sought to reinforce those aspects of my participation and observation with which they felt most comfortable. Instead of reordering themselves or their world to my presence, they were placing the burden of change on me — as any good psychologist would — by positively reinforcing my actions. Within this redefined frame of reference, I increasingly experienced a full range of involvement. The simple acts of friendship and kindness, so much a part of everyday life, took on a special meaning as they cemented and secured my place in the world of the bar. They fed my ego and gave me, I thought, the freedom to observe interaction without arousing suspicion or causing harm. By being redefined, and gratefully accepting my redefinition, I was made *safe* to see my stated objective: "What went on in Brown's."

The first rejection noted in my field diary came as a result of one of those recurring explanations of why I was in the bar. The person involved listened to my explanation, sprinkled with my newly acquired knowledge of Brown's, and responded matter-of-factly when I concluded: "You know, when the Revolution finally comes, you'll have to be one of the first to die. You know too much." I might have laughed if I had been allowed to, but the person gave no indication that he was joking. The rejection that recurred most often was much simpler and usually came in the form of a message of trust. I was continually being told that I was trustworthy. "We know you Mike," the line would go, "and we know we can trust you," or "you don't have to worry about Mike, he's cool." Like the threat, these statements were delivered as serious statements intended to be taken at face value.

When, as best I could, I reviewed my responses to these events, I discovered that I was very angry, and yet in each instance I had not expressed my anger or frustration. In the first situation, I had been actively denied control over my own life. My increasing awareness of myself as an active participant in the social and moral order of Brown's, a result of my increased presence, was drawing me deeper into bar life while insuring my increased vulnerability. Trapped in a paradox, I was unable to act. I could not forget what I knew nor, if I was to continue research, stop learning. At best I could only find a way to use my knowledge immediately in the arena for which it had been intended. In the second situation, a similar relationship existed. Because I was white and a fieldworker, I had to demonstrate my self-worth. I needed to prove that I was trustworthy. Yet the bar was understood to be an environment in which such proofs were unnecessary and somewhat suspect. Also I had supposedly answered the question of my right to be in the bar and had even begun to acquire the knowledge essential to allow me to operate in there effectively. Yet, continually, I was put in the position of reaffirming my place. To be sure, this is neither unusual nor even unfair. After all, I had no right to be in Brown's, especially in the way I wanted to be, and no amount of time or talk could possibly make up for the years of knowledge the regulars shared. Still, such actions maintained the pattern of removing control over my experiences from my grasp. My attempts to act appropriately and my responses to signals that I was doing so were being checked against a consciousness that I was struggling to escape. The result was again a trap.

My most painful and, ironically, most informative rejection occurred almost at the end of fieldwork. One Saturday afternoon Rick and I were driving to pick up a third friend to begin our usual Saturday circuit of neighborhood bars. As I parked the car, Rick, who had been silent during most of the trip, turned on the seat and said, with his fist in my face: "I love you, you bastard. You and all those other whites always looking and checking to see how I run my program. Asking do I get my job done. I hate you and them because they've got no right to ask me such questions that they'll never ask you. Both of us are bright but you'll never have to prove to anybody but they'll check my credentials every time to see if my Ph.D. is real. I hate you because you're white and I hate all whites. And I still can't stop loving you and telling you things I don't say to anyone. Shit, why you? You don't know anything." In the face of this explosion, I said absolutely nothing. I sat facing him on the front seat of the car and hated him blindly for being my friend and for suddenly forcing me to feel things and know things I did not want in my life at that moment. It was Saturday, and I was supposed to be doing fieldwork. Instead, Rick was disrupting my safe, contrived, and shallow universe with the reality of our lives and the consequences of our feelings for each other. In less than a minute he had destroyed all pretense that we could be both friends and observer and observed; he had left me to choose one or the other, knowing full well that there was no choice I could make. Moreover, the nature of these demands was obscured. His words were belied by their tone and his clenched fist in my face; my feelings, by my silence. My right to be in the community was under attack, but I could not abandon the community. I was in the field to study social life, not to flee from it. So I sat in silence; I was not only bound—I was tied into knots.

My intent in presenting these incidents is not to suggest that one should neither study one's friends nor become friends with one's informants. It is an unavoidable part of the participatory-observational framework that such relations will occur. Rather my focus is on the effect that these relations had on what I came to see. The tension of belonging and being different I experienced eventually succeeded in drawing me into the world of Brown's in a way that went against every expectation I had had about myself and my ability to do fieldwork. I had come to the field prepared to be self-conscious

and aware; I had thought that such an attitude would make it possible for me to perceive those features of experience that underlie the
organization of daily living. I believed that I could control my observations of these processes, so that I would eventually be able to
report "how" my informants saw the world. I succeeded, but the
price was my research attitude. At the end of my fieldwork I could
describe what B. Malinowski so aptly challenged ethnographers to
capture, "the native's point of view, his relation to life . . . his vision of his world" [1921], because that vision was the only one available to me. I knew what I knew, and it was by no means all that
could be known; I saw what I saw, and it was by no means all that
could be seen because I had no other way to know and to see. I was
as fragmented in my perceptions of the world of Brown's as any regular. I had thought that I would be able to see everything and everyone impartially and that I would be able to maintain an appropriate
distance from the world at large. Instead I had slipped, almost
unnoticed, into the ways of the bar. I had been taught that "an individual does not communicate; he engages in or becomes part of communication" [Birdwhistell, 1970 p. 104], and yet I had acted as if
this idea were ancillary to the fieldwork process. Unlike me, my informants were guided by no such illusions about "I" and "them." I
had forgotten James Agee's injunction that "performance, wherein
all terror and dread reside, is another matter"; they had always
known its substance, if not its terms. Thus, though it is commonplace to state that distance is needed from an event under analysis
and to argue that such distance is achieved through the careful management of feelings, I no longer believe that such distance is possible. I am not arguing that fieldworkers should throw themselves
headlong into the personal lives and fortunes of the communities
they intend to study. Even if it were possible to be engaged in this
manner for a time, there would still come the time when it was necessary to leave the field and write. Neither am I arguing, as Gans
does [1962], that participation is an appropriate research strategy
under certain conditions. Even if I wished to stop there, my experiences would not allow me to do so. The point is not that we will affect what we study or that it will affect us; that is inevitable. The
point is that our involvement in the lives of others is a result of our
humanity. There are no informants, no contrived interviews, no
simple questions and answers, and no clear observations. There is
only interaction in which all participate, whether they wish to or
not, whether they speak or not [see also Cothran, 1973, 1974]. I
came to the field hoping to find a place for myself from which I

could record the patterns of daily life in Brown's. I left believing that not only will cultures find a place for those who attempt to study them but also that they will strive to make that place the only way of belonging. I never got into Brown's as a regular, never as a patron in the way that even the most casual neighborhood user was. But my performance was always that of an acceptable incompetent.

I believe that to fight against the process of natural inclusion, to exclude one's self from one's fieldwork or from reporting that field-work, is to confuse isolation with information and forced neutrality with social science. Ethnographers have acknowledged that the quality of their descriptions depends upon their ability to reach out with honesty and humanity while they have anguished over the sense of betrayal they feel with their methodological preoccupations with distance and objectivity. What is needed now is the recognition that participation is not seduction but rather a statement that even ethnographers are aggregates of parts of the human systems they study [Bateson, 1972, p. 446]. I do not mean that we should act to influence data, but we should not confuse this action with the ways in which our "data" mold and influence us and our informants when we are in the presence of each other. My experiences in the field caused me to see that the definitions I accepted and the blinders I adopted were public rather than private, and they made me feel that what they did not allow me to see should not, perhaps, be seen by anyone. Clifford Geertz has argued that culture is an ensemble of texts that an ethnographer interprets. The goal of such a process "is not to answer our deepest questions, but to make available answers that others have . . . given . . . and thus to include them in the consultable record of what man has said" [1974, p. 30]. For myself, what is contained here are such answers as complete, and only as complete, as the patrons of Brown's Lounge would wish them to be. It was, after all, their bar, their life, and their words. I was transi-tory to all.

1 Running Rabbits and Talking Shit

Early in my fieldwork, I was seated at the bar, explaining to one of the regular patrons whom I had never met why I was in Brown's. I explained that I had frequented the bar when it had been the Nassau Inn and that I was now interested in writing about what changes had occurred since Charlie Brown had bought the place. Another patron, seated a few stools away, turned in our direction as I finished and said: "*Hee, hee, hee,* why do you want to write about that? All we do is *run rabbits an' talk shit.*"

Running rabbits and talking shit is one way of speaking about the talk that occurs in Brown's. It is one of a multitude of Afro-American expressions that might have been used to describe what was happening. In particular, *running rabbits* referred to trying to pick up women and *talking shit* to ordinary talk, but the patron might as easily have said (as others did when I asked what went on in Brown's) that they were *telling lies,* or just *talking shit,* or *bullshitting,* or *woofing,* or *rapping.* In each case, the term would have been understood by the community and judged appropriate. This lack of consensus has been noted by other researchers of Afro-American social life, but it is not of great importance [Abrahams, 1973; Labov, 1972; Mitchell-Kernan, 1971]. It seems that everywhere in Afro-American communities the terms which describe speech are quite variable, while the activities involved are relatively consistent. As William Labov [1972] has noted: "People talk much more than they talk about talk, and as a result there is more agreement in the activity than in the ways of describing it" [p. 274]. A member of a community may be capable of a host of speaking activities and still be unable to define the precise nature of what he is doing when he speaks.

The most common term for speech occurring spontaneously in Brown's was *talking shit*. Patrons used the term generally to define the normal experience of being in the bar: "We sure have been talking *some shit!*"; or "Hee, hee, hee, listen to the *shit* he's talking"; or "I do like to come here to drink and talk shit with you, Harriet." It was used specifically to describe the nature of conversation: "We don't do much but sit around and talk. It's relaxing and it passes the time. We fun with Harriet and have a good time. It doesn't accomplish much but you need some time just to sit and shit without worrying about everything outside." To talk shit was to talk — to talk without pressure, without intention, without the need to determine the value of the words spoken and the gains that could be gathered from their use. To talk shit was to be released from the demands of the ordinary world outside the bar and to be concerned, instead, with the value of immediate experience. When patrons used "talk shit," either as an explanation of what they were doing or as a natural part of their conversation with others, they were not only providing an answer to the question "what happens here?" but also they were explaining the basic structure of interaction in Brown's. They came to Brown's to talk and that talk was valued for and defined by its playfulness, its intimacy, and its difference.

The playfulness of speech was understood in two ways. Talking shit was playful because one played with language and also because its *playing* was recognized as a specific style of interaction. Thus, a patron could remark: "I like to come here and talk with my friends. We get to talking and we really get into things. Like with Ricky — he really knows stuff and when you can get him to talk and stop profiling all over the place he has something to say. He knows what he's talking about and he isn't afraid to show it. And it don't matter what you're talking about — he treats you like you know something. He don't mess around neither. He lets you know where he's coming from and he expects you to come the same way." Talking shit grew out of the free play of participants. Such talk was not a product of shared knowledge, of everyone knowing the same things and having the same interests, but of the ability of the patrons to "really get into things." Who one was, what one did, and even what one knew were all submerged in the desire to allow each individual to demonstrate his verbal skills in conversation. Moreover, talking shit created a relationship in which each participant was expected and allowed to contribute to his full abilities. Participants operated from known motives, "let you know where he's coming from," and expected the same from the others involved. There was a shared understanding that the meaning of words, the success or failure of the words selected, resulted from their place in talk. What one might have meant elsewhere and what one meant here were not as important as how what was said fit into the action at hand. Sense, nonsense, drama, truth, all were relevant if they intensified and focused participants on the further exchange of talk.

The belief that talking shit was play was explicitly verbalized by the patrons in the difference between their uses of the terms *serious* and *playing*. In Brown's to be serious was to be concerned with responsibilities to home, job, and family—in essence, with the expectations and values of the "real world." Playing concerned itself with nonutilitarian goals. Its primary purpose was not the acquisition of goods and services but the maximization of self-expression and the creation of social equality. The two terms were used to indicate shifts in the kind or quality of conversation as well as to indicate arrival or exit from the bar. Thus, patrons would announce upon arrival: "I'm here today an' willing to play," or, as they were leaving, they said, "Well, Harriet, time to go and get serious." When something inappropriate occurred, patrons would be greeted with "Now, don't you go all serious on me now"; or "None of that serious shit, you hear. That ain't for here"; or "If you want to be serious, you come on up to the back booths." There was, then, a sense that the quality of talk desired in Brown's was best exemplified through a suspension of the serious and a focus on other goals.

The intimacy of talking shit referred particularly to the suppression of difference between people that occurred during its performance. The freedom to value speech for itself and speakers for their ability to talk allowed for a distinctively different arrangement of otherwise disparate individuals. Rick, for example, had a Ph.D. in education and was a director of an experimental psychiatric day-care program, and another patron was a retired city worker, but both could be involved with each other because the hierarchy of relations expected in the real world carried no weight in Brown's; this hierarchy was known and respected, but it could be overturned at any moment by the skillful use of speech. Everyone was equal because everyone could, in turn, interact appropriately. Leveled by the language system of the bar, the patrons were free to interact on the basis of skill in relating, instead of on the basis of the historical and social biographies they brought with them. Everybody knew something, and everybody expected to be treated with respect and "not be messed with."

The most clearly evident feature of talking shit was its rejection of

the constraints of the real world. "You can come here and just enjoy
yourself and the people. You don't have to worry about no one trying to hold you up or hassle you. . . . We just sit here and relax and
have a good time. Now I can't stand being home all day with the
wife. She's always after me to do this and pick up that til I'm out of
my mind. Here, I've got no responsibilities except to myself." Talking shit was a way to be released from reasons, intentions, and goals
of the world outside. No one was required to do anything, obtain
anything, give anything, or be anything in order to participate.
Talking shit offered a time to think of oneself and one's needs without feeling that one would be "hassled" or held accountable. The
patrons who frequented Brown's went there to escape the pressures
the world placed on them, and talking shit gave them that opportunity. They created a world in which the very forms of their interaction became self-sufficient and meaningful in their own right.
Patrons could have a good time because talking shit made them momentarily autonomous from the real-life consequences of their
words.

   In a fashion similar to that of play patrons recognized this sense of
autonomy. Being in the bar and talking shit and being outside were
associated with two kinds of business. *Business* meant the maintenance of self [see also Abrahams, 1972c]. If the term business was
used in the world outside the bar, it referred to whatever had to be
done to maintain self and family. "Take care of business — T.C.B."
meant work if that did the job, and something else if it did not. Being in Brown's was known as *nigger business*. Patrons used that term
to signify that what they were doing and saying in Brown's was the
opposite of what they did and said in the outside world. The term
was a parody of the concerns of real business. Nigger business had no
goals; in fact, much of the time the term was used to indicate open
hostility to goals. More than one informant echoed the sentiments of
the patron who said: "Thank God *nigger business* ain't good for
nothing." So intent were most patrons on maintaining this distance
between being in the bar and being outside that there was conscious
exaggeration in their pronunciation of the term. One informant,
observing a quiet moment in the social life of the bar, exclaimed:
"Let's get this nig*ga bid*ness on the road"; then, noticing my presence, he said to me: "That's [spelling loudly] N I G G A   B I D N E S S,
Mike. You be sure to get that "A" and "D" in there when you write
that book." Patrons knew that the outside world, black and white,
saw nigger business as the classic stereotype of the "lazy black," but
they believed that it was an affirmation of their right to take time

out from the gravities of the real world. The business of nigger business was time for self — not time stolen from the real world but time created in opposition to that world. By asserting that talking shit was nigger business, the patrons said that self-expression and self-caring were necessary to offset the responsibilities of their everyday lives. Talking shit became a way for the patrons to achieve verbal and social freedom; nigger business allowed individuals to separate themselves from all ties and to value the symbolic exchange of words and ideas for the fascination such activity possessed in and of itself.

This focus on the development of a world distinctly different from that outside the bar makes the usage of talking shit analogous to what Georg Simmel [1950] characterized as *sociability*, wherein the forms of experience "become autonomous . . . [and] come to play freely in themselves and for their own sake" [p. 42]. But this sense of distance does not mean that talking shit was empty of content or out of touch with the real world. In Brown's there was no restriction on the content of talking shit, as talk ranged from the mundane world of news and sports to the academic issue of the relevance of black English and Afro-American studies. In the second instance I was confronted with the task of defending the work of William Labov and other linguists to a group of high school English teachers and, in general, to the entire bar. This was a notable exception, and the usual topics of conversation were more mundane. The most common topics were drawn from the news, weather, sports, sex, and personal relations, but it was group interest rather than content that determined what was important. The ultimate requirement was that the topic be played to the maximum by all involved. The focus on a common sense of being together made any topic interesting if it was done appropriately and meaningfully. This focus on interest and not on content often seemed to signal to the outsider a superficial lack of intimacy and sharing [see, for example, Cavan, 1966]. In talking shit, highly personal information and powerfully intense feelings were indeed present, but the patrons did not react personally to their use. The freedom provided by the playfulness of talking shit meant that within limits facts had no moral consequence. As one patron said: "You know, it don't matter how off the wall you get. Long as you don't act all kinds of crazy doin' it Harriet don't mind." A patron could be crazy, or a patron could be intensely personal, but no patron should do either seriously or boringly.

Because the content of talking shit was defined by interest, there was a rapid movement from topic to topic, and no one topic dominated interaction. Talking shit was a tenuous process: the intensity of participation could often create a situation in which the talking could be overwhelmed by either seriousness or too much play. Accordingly, no single topic was allowed to retain attention for too long. Topics did recur over time, however. The general pattern of talking shit was that individual topics held attention for a short time, then disappeared, and then reappeared a short time later. For example, one afternoon Teddy, Rick, and Harriet and several other patrons were discussing money. Each in turn gave a description of how much money each would like to have. The focus of the interaction became a local Philadelphian who had become rich in the airplane manufacturing business. Rick and I left and returned two hours later to discover that, as I thought, they were still discussing this same man. I asked Harriet, who said: "No, matter of fact it just come back up again before you got here." One of the other patrons who had been there for the entire period then said: "Money been in an' out of here like Charlie Brown's o' lady. Don't say much, don't stay long, won't go away. Hee, hee, hee." The topics of talking shit owed as much to the world in which they occurred as they did to the individuals who brought them up. Here, in the multiple relations of patrons and staff, talking shit wove the individual fragments of experience and interest into a continuous pattern of talk.

. Talking shit not only defined how time in the bar was spent, but it also was a way of classifying more specialized interactions. In Brown's patrons not only talked shit; they could be *talking shit, telling lies, rapping,* or *cracking.* Each was a particular way of realizing talking, a potential script for the ordering of individual experiences. The use of talking shit as a generic term was not a breakdown of the taxonomic distinction between the definition of play and the system of genres. For some patrons the use of talking shit to identify a genre represented the introduction of a descriptive term used in the wider black community into the bar's taxonomy. Thus, these patrons identified both what was happening and one special example of behavior with the same term. Most patrons, however, avoided the problem by using the term *telling lies* to describe the specific behavior in question.

In particular, patrons used the terms talking shit/telling lies to characterize all situations in which stories were told or swapped. The most common form was the personal experience narrative [Abrahams, 1964; Hannerz, 1970; Labov and Weltselsky, 1967; Young, 1978]. In these stories the narrator transformed an individual experience into an exploit in which personal prowess or skill was demonstrated. The focus of these narrations, therefore, was on the development of a self/character capable of rhetorically conveying the necessary skill with words and actions needed to resolve the situation in question. The stories followed a fairly simple pattern: a situation would be described in which an actual or potential problem would be presented, its delicate balance would be defined, and then a solution that exemplified success would be provided. For example, a patron told me: "Shit man, you don't owe me nothing, Michael. Like I told you, I knew this guy from before. So I went this morning to see what I could do. See I told him 'I got this friend who needs a sticker for his car so what can you do.' And he said 'I ain't doing that. Shit, if it was you it'd be different.' So I worked on him a bit, you know, telling him how he owes me and he starts to come around and then he says 'You send him down an' I'll see what I can do.'" Though this is an extremely abbreviated example, it captures the essence of telling lies. The stories were usually longer, more fully developed, and, for the most part, dealt with social or sexual exploits, as the following dialogue illustrates.

No lie, Harriet, I see Ricky an' Wes an' Tookie down on the Avenue. An' they sure looked like they was after trouble to me. Lookin' for the baddest box in town. You better watch ol' Wes' company or you be losin' him.

I ain't gonna lose him. He had the chance. When I worked down at the Zodiac, Wes be sittin' up at the bar an' plenty of women be movin' on him. One time . . . one time, this bitch she be sittin' up next to him blowin' in his ear makin' a fool. An' Wes he start tellin' her all kinds of shit 'bout how beautiful she is an' how would she go with him. An' shit, she 'bout to wet her pants. So they get up an' he helps her on with her coat an' he takes her to the door an' opens it an' she turns back to me — lettin' me know she's takin' my man out the door — an' she steps out an' Wes he just closes the door on her ass. So if he wants to go he's had his shot.

Or the humor present in such events would be emphasized:

I knew one o' them bull daggers. She was always comin' in askin' me if she could do anything for me. She used to work at that car wash over on 59th. She'd sit up to the bar talkin' to me tellin' me how she liked my hair an' how nice I was an' could she buy me a drink. They not bad if they after you, you know. Only if they think they got you.

So it was Christmas an' I had my presents in lay away an' I couldn't get away to get them. She been askin' me if she could do

somethin' so I asked her if she'd get me them gifts. So she goes off
an' while she's gone Bobby comes in to pick me up. I was still with
Bobby then. An' she comes back just as I'm goin' off and gives me
my gifts. She's standin' there while I'm puttin' on my coat. An'
Bobby standin' there so I takes his arm an' I says to her "This here
is Bobby. He's my husband. Bobby this Mary. She went an' got my
presents." An' we just walk out with her slack-jawed standin'
there.

Such narratives were about everything. Their key was their presentation of a successful self through the development of a coherent narration.

Because these stories focused directly on the self as character,
there was always a tension in their texts. The character, no matter
how truthful the representation, always contained within him/her
elements of fictive display. To perform successfully, a narrator had
not only to complete his portrayal but also to satisfy the demand to
talk shit. Thus, built into telling lies was a tendency to exaggerate
for effect, to create larger-than-life self-images, accomplish larger-
than-life exploits. As would be expected, such characterizations
were ripe for attack, and telling lies often turned into verbal assaults
and character contests between patrons in which those involved
swapped personal experiences in order to "out class" each other [see
Abrahams, 1970b].

The second form of telling lies was gossip, defined as any narrative in which a moral characterization of an absent patron was
developed. Such narratives almost always contained negative information and usually were centered on situations in which known
patrons violated bar rules.

Your main man was in here last night makin' a fool out of himself.
Why does he have to act that way? He's got a good job; he don't
have to be showing off like he ain't got no common sense. It don't
make no sense.

He having trouble with his wife? I'm askin' 'cause he got that car
sittin' out front of his house but he never drives it.

Anyway, he was in here last night screaming and carrying on.
Telling Jimmy and Charlie how he's doing this and doing that.
And, how he's got so bad. He was drinking so hard Charlie had to
send him to the back booths til he quieted down.

Damn shame his acting crazy when he don't have to.

Here, the situation involved a loss of control and a removal from the setting. Moreover, this particular narrative exemplified several features of gossip/telling lies. The problematic event was followed by the presentation of the negative information and concluded with a moral. The key, of course, was the emphasis on the moral, so that the audience knew the crime [Yerkovitch, 1977]. Telling lies as gossip was by definition supposed to contain only information about bar activities, but, since the bar was almost exclusively a neighborhood preserve, information from outside the bar often entered into these narratives. Such inclusions represented a violation of talking shit, and so they were expressed obliquely, as in the statements about wife and car.

The second genre of interaction in Brown's was *rapping*, one of the most discussed Afro-American verbal behaviors [see Abrahams, 1970a, 1970b, 1971; Hannerz, 1969]. Rapping, according to Thomas Kochman [1970, p. 146] is "a fluent and lively way of talking characterized by a high degree of personal narration." In Brown's rapping described any conversation in which two or more participants engaged in an extended round of verbal dueling. It meant an exchange of self-image—"coolness," "hipness"—and of personalities, in which one participant attempted to persuade his opponent and the others present that he was the most skilled user of words. It differed from telling lies in that what was presented was not a story about self but a self in performance. Still, more often than not, this exchange of and commentary on self-images resulted in contests in which the presentation of self was designed "to get over and cap" an opponent. In these exchanges the demonstration of power demanded verbal skill — and the silence of the opponent.

In the bar there were three different ways to rap: man to man, man to woman, and man to barmaid. The first two corresponded to the encounters described earlier, although the man-to-woman rapping usually had obvious sexual overtones. Man to barmaid was a special case that grew out of the particular nature of interactions at bars. Implicit in both of the other forms was that the stated goal of "getting over" could be accomplished. In "sexual negotiations" with the barmaid the idea of "getting over" was consciously denied. Central to man-to-barmaid rapping was that the verbal relations established by the participants were not taken seriously. Were a patron to "get over" on the barmaid, then she would cease to be an employee and become instead another patron. She would then cease to function effectively in her expected role, and the result would be chaos. Rapping to a barmaid was, therefore, a play on social play or, more correctly, a social game in the literal sense — a highly structured form of talking in which an *as if* world is created. Within this discourse patrons rapped to the barmaid and she to them without neither expecting to gain anything "real" from the other. Accordingly, rapping with the barmaid was a specialized exchange, in which selves were developed and then maintained, modified, or abandoned for others, in order to affect the outcome of the conversation but not to affect the outcome away from the bar.

The final genre of talking shit was *cracking*, also called *signifying*, *woofing*, or *sounding*. In Brown's it was a ritualized form of insult similar to the *dozens*, but less formalized [Abrahams, 1962, 1964; Dollard, 1939; Kochman, 1970; Mitchell-Kernan, 1971; Labov, 1972]. There were formal cracks, but they were used by patrons to crack *on* one another rather than to crack *at* each other: for example, "You're so old that when you were born Fairmount Park was a flower pot"; or, "You, you're so old that when you were born Moby Dick was a sardine." Most often, however, cracking described uncomplimentary remarks delivered in a manner that could not be legitimately interpreted as insulting: for example, "Well I guess I know *who's* got somebody all strung out an' leading by the nose"; or, "If *you do* I wish you'd tell me unless you're just crackin' on me." This indirection attempted to convey for the most part an implicit message of play hostility and nonserious anger, but the effect was not guaranteed. As a result, cracking often treaded on the borderline between play and seriousness, and a central feature of its performance was that its location was under question. Several patrons were sitting at the bar making preparations to play tennis the next morning. One of them was distractedly cataloging aloud his clothing, making sure he had a proper outfit. "I could wear them, or the others but I really need to work up a sweat — shake some of this weight off — lose a few pounds. Means I'd hafta wash. . . ." At this point Teddy interrupted: "*Go naked*, Tookie, why don't you go naked?" Everybody laughed, including Tookie, who smiled and nodded acceptance of Teddy's crack: "You're popping today, Ted." Buoyed by his success, Teddy continued in this same vein for another two minutes until Tookie asked: "Are *you still* cracking on my head?" This response drew humorous comment from the onlookers: "Hey, Ted, you better watch it, Tookie get mad, he'll crush you." "Whoa, slow your roll Ted, Mr. Brooks is rising." Everybody laughed, and the scene came to an end.

Because cracking was a short form, it occurred most often at junctures in social interaction, particularly during entrances and exits.

As Sarah, one of the barmaids, said: "They crack like that when they're coming and going to let me know they're ready to party or they had a good time. It don't mean nothing. They don't mean nothing by it. Just funning, that's all." Cracking was thus a way of opening relations or of closing them off at the end of a stay in the bar. Cracking enabled the patron or staff member to set a tone for behavior in a short and concise manner. Though primarily a marker of passage, cracking also created a large amount of verbal interaction. In cracking patrons presented whole word pictures of each other and created an immediate verbal image capable of gaining group attention. Each crack could lead to a discussion and to more cracks until, as one informant described such sessions, "popcorn time" took over in the bar.

Associated with each of these performances was the idea of *going deep*. To go deep — or "get heavy" — was to become intensely involved in an interaction. Going deep was a risky, though potentially rewarding, act. The effort invested was of such an energy that it carried the potential to overwhelm and transform bar life. The act of going deep required that the participants involved recognize the potential danger in their encounter and take steps to insure that interactions did not get out of hand. The interactions were accompanied by statements like "getting into some heavy rapping," or "you're talking heavy shit now," which served to signal changes in intensity. Statements such as "don't get in too deep here," or "I don't go deep cause I don't swim" announced a desire not to shift the mood in the bar. Moreover, patrons who were unable to control successfully their actions were usually warned: "Look, you're getting too deep. Take it to the back booths." They were allowed to remain in the setting but relieved from maintaining the intention to play.

Thus far talking shit has been treated as if it were the only way patrons defined their time in the bar. Talking shit was not the only term used to define the world of Brown's, but it did represent the dominant way of making sense. For a few, however, the patrons were *talking trash*. Talking trash was not a different kind of behavior but a different system of values; it proceeded in the same fashion and was not obviously different from normal behavior. The difference lay in the values and perceptions that stood behind it. To talk shit was to interact in order to build an environment of self-creation and dramatization beneficial to all participants; it developed order. To talk trash was to treat interaction as a meaningless game in which nothing of value was found. Instead of building a world in which self-expression generated a stronger sense of personal

self-worth, talking trash built a world of "empty play." The themes
and events that were dramatized in order to create the source of a
beneficial self-image became meaningless. "All they do around here
all day is talk trash. Most of it is just a waste of time and half the
time it doesn't even make any sense. They could be making something of themselves instead of fooling around in here till all hours."
The definition of talking shit as talking trash reflected the values of
the world outside the bar. Since the outside world saw playing as a
source of disorder and as a threat to its own stability, it dismissed the
positive values of talking shit to the community and used trash to describe its function and purpose.

In Brown's the use of talking trash to define interaction came most
frequently from those who worked the bar. "Michael, did you ever
think how silly it is that I get paid for standing up here for eight
hours to talk trash?" This use was not altogether surprising. The staff
was required to talk to anyone in the bar, and their involvement was
often dictated not by personal interest but by the requirements of
their job. The value of the interaction for them was not measurable
in terms of personal development but in dollars and cents. It was no
wonder, then, that the process of talking shit could become trivi-
alized and sometimes meaningless. Their incentive for participating
was not always voluntary, and the effect was often to demean the
process until it was no longer pleasurable.

This same effect was seen, though not as readily or as often,
among patrons. They, too, could be "turned off" to the event and
disaffected from bar life. Under such conditions, talking shit became
for them talking trash. However, their freedom to withdraw from
the bar relieved them of the requirement to be present if their feelings shifted. Generally the use by patrons of the term talking trash
was the exception rather than the rule. Only one regular patron in
Brown's saw the defined social life as consistently talking trash, and
he remained aloof from the proceedings and consciously withdrew
himself from the ongoing events.

This withdrawal from the formulas of talking shit did not prevent
this patron from playing at talking trash. During most of his time in
the bar he stood apart, alone at the end of the bar nearest the entrance. To those who entered, he addressed the bare necessities of
civility, but his general demeanor and his replies to their responses
indicated, more often than not, that he wished to be left alone. Yet
he would continually involve himself in the proceedings, give his
opinions, argue his points, and strongly defend his positions.
Though it was "all trash" being talked and those talking were not

"worth any more than trash is," he still participated and demanded his right to do so on his own terms. "You don't have to like it, but I paid my 25 cents for this beer, and I can speak my piece just like any other person here," he said once when he was called on his style of interaction. The other patrons thought that he was "hard" and that his attitude was unfair, but they continued to include him in their conversations and even to bait him into intense involvement. "He needs to push. Can't play without pushing," one patron said; another added, "You just got to push back and not let him get to you. It's just his way. Can't change that." The difference was one of tone. It was not that he was dragged into speech; rather, he seemed to drag speech out of himself. He did not talk or let talk have its way. He attacked. His bite was angry, but there was no direction to his anger. Even at his most volatile, he seemed bored. Whatever he did, there was an absence, a performance not really lived or believed. "If he'd just lighten up, just lighten up," someone said once. But he did not; he continued to talk trash.

Accordingly, two understandings of time spent in Brown's were available, one applicable to a process of creative self-expression (talking shit), and the other applicable to a breakdown of such expression (talking trash). The use of either one depended upon the image of interaction the participants had of what was going on. The process did not change, but the value placed on carrying it out did.

The existence of this well-developed taxonomy had little to do with the practices that patrons used to define conversation. Patrons were in Brown's to talk, not talk about talk, and thus their focus during verbal interactions was on other matters. They did recognize a distinction between the "text" of an event and its "enactment." For the patrons there existed scripts that were available for performance and acting styles that differentiated one process of performance from another. The scripts defined the available, acceptable genres of behavior and the latter described the manner in which such behavior occurred, i.e., the style of the talk. As one informant stated, "Words don't mean shit. You can say all the words in creation an' it don't mean nothin' to a black man. You see, Michael, it ain't the words but the way you say 'em. Somebody can say the sweetest talk, you know, an' still be messin' with you." Most of the patrons agreed. In their talk they cared less for the products of talk itself and much more for the rewards of the skillful manipulation of the process of talking. "Doin', Michael. Doin' is where it is," the same informant said in another context; "you do it right an' they know you together. You go anywhere."

Accordingly, as a system of "doin'," rapping, cracking, and telling lies were evaluated not by the topic or by the form but by the accomplishment. The performer and script determined the particular form being enacted, but in Brown's it was the way of acting, not the text, that signaled the meaning of any interaction. In fact, in the course of fieldwork recognizable texts of any sort occurred only twice. In the first instance a joke was listened to without comment, but at its conclusion its teller was greeted with derisive statements. In the second instance, the same patron, again attempting to tell a joke, was interrupted with similar insults during the actual telling of the joke and at its conclusion he was characterized as "country."

Spraggins, that is the dumbest shit I have ever heard. Where do you come from with this country shit?

Now Harriet, I'm from Virginia an' I'm not ashamed of it.

You sure are 'cause it hangs all over you. Whoever brought you up North got you out of the country but not the country out of you.

Harriet when I go to the store I buys only 'leven eggs an' one orange 'cause I don't play no dozens.

Country was used in the urban black culture to signify that the individual was somehow "out of touch" with the appropriate way of behaving. To be defined as country was to be considered perilously close to violating the expected moral pattern. Though Spraggins took a certain amount of pleasure from the "pain and misery" his jokes caused, neither joke was intended to provoke such reactions. This was clear from Spraggins's response to his characterization. Had he truly felt his behavior to be appropriate, he would have been within his rights to question Harriet's use of the term and to have called upon the audience to adjudicate a moral dispute. On the other hand, had he intended his jokes to be ritualized ploys to draw Harriet out, then he would have followed her questioning of them with a remark designed to counter her assertion and begin an exchange. His ritualized refusal to discuss his actions — commonly associated with an attempt to defer from being drawn into "playing the dozens" — suggested that the response he received was unexpected. He sought to avoid the problem and disassociate himself from his words by indicating that he did not wish to rap. His unwillingness to rap on his actions or their value meant that he saw himself operating outside the normal expectations. One final element of proof occurred later, when in response to Harriet's raising his earlier behavior as a topic of conversation Spraggins defended himself: "Now you hold up on that Harriet, I'm as slick as *any dude* who comes 'roun' here. I know how to play. An' if *you don't watch your-self* I'll come back *there* an' *show you how.*" This overemphasis on his acceptability again suggested that such fixed forms as he had per-formed were not acceptable.

When in several conversations I raised questions concerning other known Afro-American performance types, toasts for example, the general response was to acknowledge their existence while indi-cating their unsuitability to Brown's. I was told by Uncle Nick, one of the most active performers in the setting:

N: No, you never hear anyone recitin' poems around here. I only know of one bar where that used to happen. There was a wine joint down by the river — over on Second by Bainbridge. We used to stop in when we got tired of cleanin' sewers. An' this ol' wine head used to come in there an' recite poetry for a drink, you know.

M: Oh, you mean things like "Signifying Monkey" and "Titanic"?

N: No, no street trash like that. That's for young boys on the corner. I mean real poetry — "Face on the Barroom Floor" an' all kinds of poems like that. He was real good at it too, you know.

Though the context dealt with was not specifically Brown's, Nick's understanding of what was appropriate is evident. Again the focus of Brown's life-style was away from the introduction of fixed texts or known routines. Such events were for "young boys on the corner." This distinction was significant. Brown's and its patrons were assert-ing that, though Brown's was a corner for its members, it was still a particular, distinctive kind of corner, where fixed texts were accept-able only if they had a higher status than the normal content of talk-ing shit. Hence, if a poem, it would have to be "real poetry — 'Face on the Barroom Floor' — an' poems like that."

This exclusion of all formal texts or routines except those classifi-able as "more moral" than the expected behaviors meant that such forms simply did not occur. The energy spent in accomplishing them would have destroyed for most patrons the pleasures of being at Brown's. They were there, after all, to meet the moral order, not to exceed its requirements. Thus, though "texts" were known to the patrons, they stood outside the community's perceptions of what ought to occur in Brown's. Such forms were "country," or "for young

boys," or were "too respectable" to be worth doing for fun. As Nick
said, the performance he remembered was clearly done not for pleasure but for gain.

For patrons there existed three distinct ways to talk shit. They recognized that any performer could be *playing*, *styling*, or *profiling*.
As discussed earlier, playing was the natural pattern of talking shit.
Casual, spontaneous, and matter of fact, it was what any patron
who entered Brown's expected to do. But it was not what they hoped
to do, and they would have been disappointed if it was all that happened. What they wanted to do was *styling*.

Styling in Brown's described a shift in conversation from the informality of playing to a more intense style of interaction. It was the
most prominent way of talking shit. Styling had several contradictory senses. For those patrons defined in the bar as people who
"brought noise with them" and "heated up the bar," styling had a
pejorative sense.

> I don't trust that sucker. He's always stylin' on me. Getting all up
> in my face an' talkin' trash 'bout how he could listen to my voice
> all day.

> You try talkin' to Jimmy! You can't have no conversation with him
> all the time stylin' on you.

> I had it with his stylin' so I told him to get himself together before
> he starts up talkin' like that again.

> *Stupid ass motherfucker*! So *fuckin'* dumb he can't tell when to
> keep his mouth shut. Stylin' on that woman when he sees me bring
> her. Where *is* his sense at? I jus' don't know.

For these patrons styling defined destructive performances. For
them, to style was to perform ineffectively. They did not deny that
styling was a different way of interacting but did emphasize that it
was poorly conceived. Styling was used by this small segment to dis-
tinguish their own abilities to create action from what they perceived to be less controlled attempts at creative action by other
patrons.

The second sense of the word styling came from the staff, for
whom any change in the tone or intent of conversation was likely to
be initially called styling. For example, two patrons were sitting at
the bar talking with Harriet. The conversation came around to another patron who seemed interested in Harriet, much to her obvious
distaste. The three talked for about five minutes with Harriet be-

coming more and more upset by this patron's loutishness. She wound up her rap by stating: "I wish to God he'd go find himself someone else to mess around with." One of the two patrons, smiling, mocked: "I know someone who's got his nose open." Harriet replied, seriously at first: "Well if you do I *wish* you'd send him over there"; and then, shifting into the same mocking tone as used by the patron, concluded: "Unless you just be stylin' on me." The three then broke into laughter. In this case, the patron's line of talk met Harriet's expectations. She was angered by what she believed to be inappropriate attention and was pleased that some other woman had the offending patron's "nose open," that is, had him so deeply interested in her that she could lead him around by the nose without his minding. Her initial response indicated the depth of her desire to be rid of the offender. Her question, however, signaled that she had caught up with the conversation and recognized the potential ambiguity of the patron's reference. Seeing that she could easily be the woman, she sought to discover if she had been successfully cracked on, and, if so, whether the cracking patron wanted to shift the intensity and flow of talk. Introduced as a question, her attempt to discover what had happened to her, to find out if they were suddenly styling, was an announcement of her need to know the nature of the change she was being put through.

The third understanding of the term was its common use by the rest of the patrons. For the most part patrons did not have to tell each other that they were styling. They expected the kind of flux styling represented to happen in conversation: they wanted it to happen; they sought it out whenever possible, and, thus, did not spend time telling each other that it was happening. They recognized that they were at the bar to play and were quick to see conscious stylized performance as profiling. There was, however, not the same need to recognize styling. Thus, when patrons used the term, it acknowledged a change in conversational tone that captured the essence of desired sharing and community. Styling described not the normal pattern but the hoped-for ideal level of involvement. The term was used in its rare appearances to identify the special moments when interaction turned in upon itself and all participants were able to draw upon the pleasure and creativity being generated.

Hey, Mike, haven't seen you for a while. How you been?

Working too hard, Ted.

Ain't we all, ain't we all. You should have seen them las' night.
Double flyin'. Right George?

What? Oh yeah. Hi, Mike, I didn't see you come in. Too busy
readin' this paper. Yeah, they did it to death las' night. Your boy
Ricky came in about eight and by nine everybody was *stylin'*.
They kept it up till pas' two. Hee, hee.

Thus, styling characterized how "right" the overall lively flow of the
previous evening's social life had been. "Everybody was *stylin'*" suggested that in this instance Rick had initiated an involved process of
individual participation in which the group as a whole adopted a
more intense, more pleasurable way of interacting. The use by
patrons of the word styling focused on the creations of group process
among patrons who acted both as actors and as audiences to each
other and who shared the responsibility for the joint accomplishment of the conversation.

Profiling described any interaction in which a central performer
attempted to construct skillfully a well-formed, integrated activity
for a recognizable audience. Unlike playing and styling, profiling
was self-conscious, and underlying all uses of the term by patrons
and staff was a clear perception that there was an aware actor manipulating the flow of social interaction. This awareness of self-consciousness as the defining characteristic of profiling expressed itself
in several usages of the term in Brown's. The first such usage was
that of "being in profile," which described an organization of dress
and manner designed to project an image of an ultimately "cool" individual inherently capable of manipulating the rules of Brown's
with ease and grace. To be in profile was to construct a front
[Goffman, 1959] that gave the audience an immediate picture of
personal power and coherence.

The particular articles of clothing used to compose this self-image
were a matter of individual taste. However, the exercise of this taste
was still restricted by certain group expectations. Thus, any shift in
dress from one's normal attire might draw a description of being in
profile; but more often than not the required shift would have had to
stand out not only from one's ordinary dress but also from what was
ordinary attire for the bar as a whole. Being in profile, therefore,
meant not simply creating a new look, but rather creating a new
look that caused the audience momentarily to change its whole orientation. It demanded, to use Shklovsky's term, the construction of
Ostranenie, of making strange the psychological effect on the audience [Shklovsky, 1965, p. 11]. For example, my clothes consisted

of faded jeans, a sport shirt, and sweater. No comment was made by anyone when I wore my best suit to Harriet's birthday party. When, however, one Friday afternoon after attending a conference with Rick and some of his co-workers at the hospital, I accepted a challenge from one of the women with us to wear Rick's Borsalino hat with my best suit into the bar, the reaction to this "short white gangster," as I was described, was general laughter from all the patrons. But my appearance also drew the description: "Shit, did you ever think you's see Michael all in profile in here. He's been with his road buddy too much." When Spraggins, whose normal work dress was an oil-covered pair of overalls on weekdays and sports clothes on weekends, arrived in an off-white suit and the requisite Borsalino hat one Tuesday morning, he, too, was greeted with: "Will you look at Spraggins all profiled up and ready for trouble. You gonna start some shit today. I can see that."

The second usage of profiling referred to a patron's treatment of the bar as a place in which to construct contained presentations of self. This idea of "come in here profiling" was used to characterize those patrons who stood out as constant performers in the setting. Rick and Uncle Nick were described as "always ready to profile every chance they get" or "them two, boy. They full-profilin'. They come in the door that way an' don't stop till they walk out 'o here." To enter the bar profiling meant to conceive of one's role in the setting as only that of performer, to treat any and all interactions as vehicles for conscious self-display, and to act toward bar life in the same way. Those performers who saw themselves in this role spoke of themselves and their actions as "heat" and "noise": "I'm gonna bring my noise and heat this bar." Moreover, it was this notion of profiling that was attached by patrons to the activities of bar personnel. From the perspective of the patron, profiling captured the essence of all employee performance. Since it was an assumed fact that personnel were paid to be in the bar and, therefore, paid to act the way they did, it was taken as a matter of fact that what they did was consciously undertaken. That this was not always the case, as shown elsewhere, was known within the bar. It reflected not a real perception of the ordering of reality but a statement of hoped-for expectations.

This third and final usage of profiling dealt with what Dell Hymes calls *breakthrough into performance* [1975], the assumption by a participant in an interaction of the cultural standards for known and accepted symbolic action: "There is performance, when one or more persons assumes responsibility for presentation. And within performance, as the double or repeatable, there is the role which can be termed full, authentic, or authorative performance, when the standards intrinsic to the tradition in which the performance occurs are accepted and realized" [p. 11]. In Brown's this last use of the term profiling focused on those moments when an individual transformed an ongoing segment of styling into full performance. To start profiling meant that an individual moved beyond simply being within the flow of interaction and began to control and turn it to his own ends. The key to this last concept of profiling, then, was its self-conscious demand that a patron act to keep his performance apart from the community and solely his own. Profiling was a type of consequential action because in its explicit assumption of dramatic responsibility it required that the creation and the performer would be judged. This opening of one's actions to judgment was made doubly dangerous because the decisions were both moral and aesthetic. Someone who profiled must not only do it correctly but also do it to please. Profiling was to be done with the wit of styling and the intention of playing if it was to be successful, and this demand of style and grace, consciously undertaken, placed upon the performer the burden of choice and the possibility of failure.

The language used in Brown's was organized, both in terms of distinctive genres and styles of interaction. Patrons could describe a system of scripts and styles that permitted them to play without having to "style" or "profile." The world of Brown's made sense because it was organized and defined by a coherent linguistic system, but it was, as well, a place, a time, a group of patrons, and a scripted world. Brown's responded to the larger constraints of culture and class and to the smaller claims of neighborhood and neighbors. It was, after all, not only a community of speakers, but it was also a bar.

2 Charlie Brown's Bar

Though a large part of our awareness of the world comes from the objects around us, that world is still kept very much outside of our consciousness. In fact, most individuals live out their lives without ever realizing that their actions are in part determined by the surroundings in which they occur. What is common for the majority of people is not, however, common for business. Businessmen, especially those involved in selling directly to the public, are acutely aware that the place from which they operate and the environment in which their businesses exist determine the products they can expect to sell, the kind of customers they can expect to serve, and, when the business is a bar, the kind of business they can expect to have [Hall, 1966; Sommer, 1969; Watson, 1970]. Indeed when the business is a bar, place is not simply an important index of use, but often a rhetoric of the world itself.

This was clearly the case with Brown's Lounge. Shortly after a new barmaid was hired to work the day shift, Charlie Brown threw a party to publicize her arrival and to attract her old customers to his place. Halfway through the party the phone rang, and Harriet, the new barmaid, answered it. She listened for a moment, then burst into laughter, and proceeded to give detailed directions to Brown's. A few minutes later, a group of her former customers entered and began to complain mockingly that it was impossible to find the bar. "Shit, we been driving around looking for a bar," one of them finally said, "and this party's in a basement." Brown's was, in fact, in a basement, and it was indeed hard to find. Charlie had purchased it precisely for those reasons.

I used to own a bar on "the strip" in Norristown. It was our first place. Man, they were crazy up there. Always fighting and messing around. It just wasn't safe. Now we were making money, but it wasn't worth the hassle of getting all shot up. I was afraid of Lorraine getting hurt by one of those crazy niggers. Now I had my eye on this place for a while. The guy who owned it was sick of the hassle with the kids and of being held up all the time, but it was just what we wanted. It's a nice quiet neighborhood, no problems like before. You don't make as much but ain't nobody crazy to kill you either.

Charlie knew the problems involved in owning a bar firsthand, and, though he wanted to own such a business, he did not want the trouble associated with ownership. Brown's represented the ideal compromise. It was quiet and safe, and it allowed him to buy a bar without buying trouble.

Charlie's assessment of his place was echoed by the majority of its regular users. Their consensus was that Brown's was a good place. "I like it here—it's quiet. I know everyone." "I come here 'cause I like to drink and be with my friends." "I can't take no place where I don't know anybody. Here I can come in and I'm pretty sure I'll meet somebody I'll know." "I don't know—I guess cause I know everybody. They all come from around here. It's like I see people in here I know. People I see every day. I can relax and not always be checking over my shoulder at who's coming in." Likewise, those who did not stay or who used the bar infrequently usually said that they found it dull. As one of the regular customers put it, "You don't see young boys like Steve or Chuck around here because this place isn't enough life for them. They go where they can party. Sitting and talking with the ol' heads is not their style." Brown's was thus characterized by its calmness. Its social life was not a constant round of charged activity, but a more orderly and relaxed time.

The maintenance of this sense of comfortableness was an ongoing concern and problem for Charlie. The law demanded that he be prepared to serve any and all customers who entered his establishment, whether or not they fit his notions of the patron he wanted. For Brown's to be the bar that Charlie wanted it to be and still remain within the bounds of the law, it had to present to those who had never seen it before and to those who used it regularly a specific, immediately readable message about how it should be used. To survive, Charlie had to show real and potential customers that it was a specific kind of bar located in a specific neighborhood serving specific people under specific conditions.

This image is dependent upon the existence within the bar of an orderliness that draws together the potentially random arrangement of the objects, shapes, and surfaces scattered about. If this ordering succeeds, sets of anticipations — sensory "chords" — are produced, and they, in turn, create a language whose individual elements convey attitudes, beliefs, and personal sentiments about what should and should not occur in the bar. The combination and recombination of these objects and shapes into patterns describe the multiple ways of being in Brown's [Ruesch and Kees, 1958].

The building that Brown's occupied was typical of the row houses in the neighborhood. A two-story house with a partially exposed basement, it was located on the corner of 95th Street and Nassau Avenue. Originally the owners of the bar had lived in the house and had built a red brick extension on to the back of the house across the alley to use for the bar. They eventually moved to the suburbs, and the bar was extended into the basement of the house with the back extension turned into a room for women customers and the upper floors rented as apartments. At the time Charlie bought the bar and the building, the first floor was kept empty for storage, and the second was rented, both practices that he continued. However, since he served women in the main bar, the women's section was unnecessary, and the entrance to it was kept permanently locked. The bar was entered through a guardhouse-like structure next to the front steps. This structure and a two-by-three-foot sign that said "Brown's Lounge" on both sides hanging off the front porch, an even smaller sign that said "Ladies Entrance," over the back door and two Schmidt beer signs in the windows of the back extension were the only announcements that the bar existed. This lack of advertisement was partially in keeping with Charlie's desire to regulate the use of his bar, and it also reflected the desires of the neighborhood. On several occasions Charlie discussed with me the possibility of using a larger sign, but these conversations usually ended with "My customers, you know, they'd kill me if I messed with a big sign lit all night 'cause if they didn't their wives would." Thus the bar remained unannounced to all except those who already knew it.

The front door opened onto a fifteen foot long by five foot wide by seven foot high hallway. Its walls were a deep brown knotty pine, its floor black linoleum, and its ceiling acoustic tile spotted in places by water. At the far end of the hall was another solid door, and while the effect was to close in anyone who entered it was not a narrow space. Halfway down on the right side was a doorway, with a door held on only by its bottom hinge. On it was a small sign that said "Men." Past it there were two more doors, one on each side of the room, and recessed into the ceiling above them, covered with a cracked piece of pink-tinted plastic, was the only light in the hallway.

The second door opened onto the main barroom. Thirty feet long, thirteen feet wide, and seven feet high, the room was divided down the center by the bar, which created a rectangular space on either side. The floor and ceiling were of similar construction as in the hallway—and in about the same condition.

Immediately to the left of the door, in the corner, was a cigarette machine. Above it on the wall were a heat duct partially covered by a plastic Seagram's Gin sign, a wooden coat rack, and another plastic sign that said "Cold Beer." This corner also had two cardboard advertisements promoting Watusi and Harvey Wallbanger cocktails. A pile of newspapers sat on the top of the machine. The back wall was covered from the floor to a height of three feet with the same type of knotty pine as the hallway and from there to the ceiling with a smoked glass mirror, on which were three torn pieces of masking tape that formed the corners of a forgotten square. At the ceiling, just below the molding, a string of Christmas lights ran the full length of the wall. Against this wall were three wooden tables, covered with green plastic cloths; each had two wooden chairs. Set between the first two and the last was a jukebox. The jukebox was a wide, squat, stainless steel and yellow-flecked plastic box, which extended halfway up the mirror behind it and dominated the back wall. On top of it were more advertisements for Watusi and Harvey Wallbanger cocktails. In the far wall of the rectangle was a closet for employees' coats and centered on the closet door was a sign proclaiming "We do not serve Minors."

To the right of the doorway, on the other side of the bar, covering the whole right wall, was the beer cooler, which held the bottled beer as well as the quarts and six-packs for take out. On the side flush to the bar were two plastic decals stating "Black Label Beer" and "Colt 45" and, on its top, angled to the room, a lighted "Miller's" sign. The back wall was occupied by identical whiskey hutches, which stood to either side of a smaller, lower cabinet on which sat the cash register. The hutches were divided into an open base and top; each base contained a single shelf on which were stored the empty whiskey bottles, the bottles of bitters, and the rarely used setups. The tops contained three shelves terraced from bottom to top with the least expensive whiskeys on the bottom, the wine cordials, rum, and vodka second, and the expensive whiskeys on top. In the space between the hutches were two shelves, running front to back on the hutches' sides containing the premier whiskeys and brandies.

Propped in front of the first bottle on the right was a Polaroid photo of Harriet, the day barmaid, and two smiling patrons. On top of the cash register itself was a white plastic clock advertising Seagram's and directly above it on the back wall was still another sign stating "We do not serve Minors."

On the far wall, opposite the beer cooler, rising up over the top of the bar and covering the wall was the ice machine. It had a square door in its lower left corner; in front of the cooler top was a plastic bucket that was covered by a plastic tablecloth. On top of the tablecloth were two metal clip racks for 10-cent bags of potato chips, an open box filled with bags of peanuts, and a round metal tray holding a coffee pot and some white cups. On the wall above hung another clock advertising Seagram's, a thermometer, and a large lighted rectangular picture of a black man and a woman seated at a piano in which the man was holding a saxophone while the woman looked on admiringly. The wall did not form a corner here, but bent from the other side of the bar at an obtuse angle to form a short wall just large enough to hold a doorway. It opened into a small unfinished room in which the garbage cans were next to one wall and on another hung the electric timer for the ice machine.

The bar radiated out from the beer taps at its center. The taps were set into a stainless steel cooler; on either side were black metal tubs divided into three sections, one for soapy water, one for clear, and one for ice cubes. Above the tubs attached to the bar, but lower, was a shelf that ran the full length of the bar. Here were piled the shot glasses, the beer shells, and the glasses for mixed drinks. To the right of the cooler, along this shelf, were three more spigots for Coca-Cola, ginger ale, and soda. The bar itself was made of wood, and the top was covered with white speckled Formica, worn in places so that the smooth gray wood shown through. There were ten stools. Eight of them were flat cushions on steel-leg frames; two had backs. On the small sections of wall above the bar to either side were two plastic "V.O." signs, and above these were two small wooden speakers for the jukebox.

At the very end of the barroom was a ramp leading to the back room. That room was almost as long and as wide as the main room. At the top of the ramp, to the left, was a stairway leading to the women's room and beyond that to the house above. At the foot of these stairs was a pay telephone, and next to it was a small shelf for the phone books. Along this same wall and the one to the back were six wooden booths. To the right of the ramp was a small bar, now only a shell, and piled behind it were empty beer cartons. The large space in the center of the room was kept empty, and the room was unlit except for what light came through its curtained windows and its now barred door.

The most obvious statement of organization in this catalog of objects was the separation of the hallway from the main barroom. The presence of the second door emphatically sealed off what occurred in this area from what occurred in the rest of the bar. Moreover, the general atmosphere of the hallway clearly indicated that it was a temporary and impersonal place. There was no decoration except the sign on the men's room door and, with all three doors closed, little to stimulate the eye. All the lighting was at the far end of the hall, and thus a patron's passage down the hallway moved from relative darkness to light. The hallway was a transition. It "felt" more inside than outside, yet it was not the main room, and this difference drew the patrons through it to the bar.

The break between the back booths and the barroom was less obvious. The short hallway that separated them acted as a barrier between the two, but the openness of the back room still indicated that this difference was not a finality. This separation was affirmed, however, by other means. The back area was not directly lit. What light it received came from the main room, from the stairway to the second floor, and from the windows to the street; the pattern of lighting was, therefore, diffuse. It was brightest near the ramp stairway, illuminating the pay telephone and the stairs to the women's room, next brightest at the far wall, and dusk-gray at the center of the room. The effect was to militate against passage into the room, an effect heightened by the upward slant of the back ramp. This slant was a frequent topic among those who had to go to the back room. Women, especially wearing heels, had to maintain a precarious balance to get up it, and their complaints were numerous. Harriet, the day barmaid, for example, refused to serve back there: "I ain't climbing up there and break my neck." Such complaints were not restricted to women; the men often bemoaned the arduous climb and rapid descent.

Since the back booths were simultaneously available and closed off from use, they served as a backstage area [Goffman, 1959, p. 112] where the demands of the main barroom were not enforced. The back booths were used as the place where customers who had drunk too much but were not drunk could go to regain control and as an arena for serious conversations. In fact, all serious business conducted in the bar was conducted in the back booths. Thus, in terms of use the back booths were part of the main barroom and yet

were distant from the predominant activities of it. They were needed
to insure that there existed a place where patrons could go to distance themselves momentarily without any loss of face.

In the space to the right of the bar the arrangement of objects was
in two lines, one against the wall and one at the bar itself. With the
exception of the jukebox the objects on the back wall were solely
decorative. The two tables closest to the entrance were bunched together so tightly that it was necessary to rearrange them to use them.
Moreover, the chairs at each table were pushed under and tight to
the table. The organization was made even more restrictive by the
angular placement of the cigarette machine into the nearest corner,
which further reduced the actual and psychological space in which
to move the tables and chairs. The table on the other side of the
jukebox was more usable — it occupied as much space as the other
two, but its use was equally limited. Most of the time something was
piled on it, either coats or newspapers or briefcases or boxes. However, during the barmaid's lunchtime this third table served as her
dining table. For the majority of patrons, though, the overall arrangement of the wall and corner precluded accessibility. It was to
be seen, not to be used.

The second line of objects was the stools. With the tables unusable,
the stools at the bar were the only available seats in the room, and
the result was that the bar became the focal point of Brown's. Moreover, the stools were so close together, six to twelve inches apart,
that patrons were literally shoulder to shoulder when they were
seated. Built into the seating pattern was an enormous potential for
unrestricted conversation. Because direct contact was lateral and
always open across the bar, it was difficult to maintain the consistency and stability of any group. In order to close out those
around, patrons would have had to shift either themselves or their
stools, neither of which was feasible. Accordingly, talk freely expanded and contracted, flowing throughout the entire room until
those who were not part of a group or an encounter inevitably found
themselves drawn into both. That the patrons could sit only at the
bar was reinforced by the placement of the jukebox, which was centered at the back wall in a direct line with the beer taps and the
center of the whiskey hutch. From the patron side of the bar, it
stood at the point of a triangle, and its music came from the wall
toward the stools and over the bar, reinforcing the impression that
attention was directed toward rather than away from the bar. Overall, then, the arrangement of the patron area was designed to make
the bar the center of all activity. With only seating at the bar, the

possibility that any patron might hide within the setting or absent himself from interaction or that any group might exclude itself from others present was greatly reduced; the result was a continually high degree of contact among those present, whether they wanted it or not.

The bar side was arranged to maximize the ability of the bar personnel to do their jobs. The area was arranged symmetrically from a central axis of the cash register and beer taps. On either side of this line the area was structurally the same, in construction, arrangement, and content. This built-in symmetry freed the barmaid from the need to fetch and carry any distance, and, accordingly, all "work" was done at the bar, which also increased contact between patrons and staff. This symmetry was designed for control. Because efficiency was built into the work area, the barmaid was free to move or to remain stationary without impairing the work routine. She could quickly respond to any potentially troublesome activity as well as immediately involve herself in any existing interaction by moving to it. On the whole, then, the barroom was organized so that the bar was the main stage for all interaction. Its features aimed at insuring that all present were available and accessible; it was a place in which there was no solitude, no room for patrons to withdraw. Brown's was an enforced collectivity, not an environment capable of supporting isolated users.

This collectivity was further enhanced by the ornamentation of the barroom. The majority of decorations were advertisements, announcing the availability of certain products. Yet there was a theme in their display and content. Since there were numerous potential advertisements from which any owner or barmaid (the latter most especially, as the posters were hung by salesmen only with the barmaid's permission) might choose, the specific selection projected the overall image of the bar. Such advertisements, whether functional like the stirrer holders or the rubber mats or symbolic like the lighted signs on the walls, described the kinds of drinks available and some of the appropriate choices for customers to make. In effect, they were a mini-course in how to belong.

The main advertisements in Brown's were for beer and whiskey. The walls were covered with the messages: "Cold Beer" from beneath the coat rack, "Schmidt's," "Schlitz," and "Colt 45" from the walls, "Seagram's 7" from everywhere, and "Seagram's Gin." They implied that the bar was for customers uninterested in either the extremes of fancy drinks or large glasses of cheap wine. Brown's was a "regular place," and the expectation was for simple, plain drinking.

Moreover, the images that altered this perception somewhat did so toward the mixed drink rather than toward wine. The two posters that were prominent — for "Harvey Wallbanger" and the "Watusi" — were advertising campaigns that did not affect actual choices. They were placed along the back wall, nearly out of the sight of the patrons. Added to these images were other views of Brown's. "We do not serve Minors" appeared in two highly visible places. Likewise, the notification "Barmaid on duty is . . . ," whether one was present or not, was a significant sign and placed Brown's in that class of establishment in which, because they held an institutional position, women were an active part of the milieu, instead of peripheral to it. Finally, the dollar bills and the snapshots were signs of small business, of closeness, and of "family group" — friendly faces and known people.

The decor in Brown's conveyed several ideas about the bar. Most visible was its physical smallness and closeness and its homeliness, but there was also a clear announcement of how the bar should be used. Brown's was not given over to serious business. With all of its seating at the bar, it was impossible to interact privately. Even if it were possible to exclude other patrons from a conversation, it would have been impossible to exercise similar control over those working the other side of the bar. Added to this was the openness of the pathway between the bar and the back wall, which gave freedom of movement up and down the bar but restricted the ability of those seated at the bar to *protect their back*; there was no guarantee that another patron would not come up from behind and enter the conversation. Patrons had no way to keep others out of their lives and their talk. People with serious purposes could, of course, enter the bar, but they were expected to conclude these activities or to transform them into acceptable behavior for the bar. Brown's was specifically arranged to maximize patron openness by reducing the possibility of privacy.

This organization of the main barroom was complemented by other messages of light, color, smell, and taste, which together created a special "feel" to the bar. For example, it was always dusk at Brown's. No natural light entered the room. Recessed into the ceiling over the bar were three light fixtures, each holding one sixty-watt bulb. The bulbs were not always replaced when they burned out, and most of the time they were not even turned on. In addition to these bulbs, there were behind the bar two neon lights, set into the top of the whiskey hutch to illuminate the whiskey shelves. Moreover, all of the direct light sources were covered by red- or green-colored glass shades, so that a "rosy glow" pervaded the room. The panel lights in the jukebox and the cigarette machine and the lighted beer advertisements on the walls provided indirect lighting. They, too, shone through colored shading and added to the glow. The mirrors on the back wall and behind the whiskey bottles also increased the glow, diffusing and redirecting the light and contributing to the overall effect of perpetual dusk. The absence of any natural light and the low level of artificial light deprived the patrons of the ability to gauge the passage of time by shifts in the light intensity; this artificially induced timelessness resulted in the perception of time as somehow suspended. Thus, patrons often commented on their arrival: "God, Charlie, don't you know it's daytime outside"; leaving, they often said: "You could stay in there a whole day and never know it had gone by" or "you never know that it's real out here." For Charlie, this control of light was conscious. He was aware that the lighting was comfortable and conducive to drinking, and he acknowledged that it was an attempt to cause people to lose track of time and thus stay longer than they might have intended. The whole point was summed up by one perceptive patron who said: "Charlie thinks he's so smart. Like people aren't going to notice what time it is and drink more of his whiskey."

Whereas light was used to induce a sense of special time, sound was used to create a stable level of noise for interaction. The sources of sound were largely internal at Brown's, since little street noise reached into the bar. Indeed, one afternoon a gang fight, complete with stabbing, police, and ambulances, occurred a block and a half away without anyone in the bar noticing. What noise there was came from the jukebox, which patrons and staff used in the creation of an appropriate sound milieu. The jukebox was known by the patrons and staff as the "Iron Pimp." The name was not casual, for in terms of the structure of the interaction in the bar, pimp was precisely what the jukebox did. It took the quarters and dollars of the patron and gave a limited amount of music in return — the return was limited, too, because from the patron's perspective there was never enough music to fill the need. Hence arose the continual outcries from patrons: "Who's got a quarter?"; "Gimme a quarter for the machine"; "Feed the pimp, need a quarter to feed the pimp." This categorization of the jukebox was a clear reflection of its status. Much has been written on the nature of the pimp in Afro-American culture [see Goines, 1972; Heard, 1968; Slim, 1968, for dramatic accounts; see also Milner and Milner, 1972], and it is sufficient to recognize here that the patrons' use of the term described a set of potential relations in which, because it was seen to interact like a pimp, the jukebox had a culturally defined, fully programmed role that it played. The result was a perpetual, ever-varying universe of sound in which there was a constant interaction between the jukebox and conversation.

The only constant feature of sound was the absence of silence. At all times there had to be some noise in Brown's. Thus, either the patrons or the jukebox constantly had to fill the available sound space. The bar did not have to be drowned in noise, however. Two patrons in the bar having a conversation filled the environment as effectively as a crowd, the jukebox, and a television set showing a sports event. What was important was that the structure of noise did not collapse. Because of this imperative, the jukebox was almost continually in operation, even when no one was present in the bar but employees. This was partially for their benefit, of course, so that they would not become bored during the slow periods. It was primarily for arriving customers, however, so that no one would enter a noiseless room. Consistently, fifteen to twenty minutes before the heavy influx of customers began, the barmaid would take a dollar and sometimes two (one from her tips and one from Charlie) and feed the jukebox, thus guaranteeing that patrons would arrive at a bar that was alive with "action."

A second dimension of sound was its quality, an aesthetic judgment by the patrons of the contents of the jukebox. This view was best expressed in what one patron described as "the search for the baddest box in town," that is, one with the best possible music and reflecting the widest range of interests. Such a jukebox was, of course, an ideal type. Jukeboxes were owned by music companies that were interested in making money. But the jukebox was also a business concern for Charlie, and he, too, recognized the necessity of having songs that made money—and that pleased his customers and employees. Thus, the contents of the jukebox represented a tension among multiple interests.

Statistically, the majority of play in Brown's were top-ten recordings, but this number did not reflect the qualitative sound environment and a distinction must be made between what was played and what was listened to. Play was anything on the jukebox; listening music for most patrons was jazz or big-band sounds. For example, during the revival of Billie Holliday, associated with the film *Lady Sings the Blues*, both Diana Ross's and Billie Holliday's recordings of "Good Morning, Heartache, What's New?" accounted for over half of the play. Ross's record, however, was merely played and elicited sporadic comment, consisting mostly of "nice sound" or "she's got a good voice." Holliday's original version, on the other hand, became a topic of conversation; it was discussed in terms of the situation explicit in the lyrics and in terms of Holliday's life.

Sound and light were the most obvious aspects of the mood in Brown's, but they did not overwhelm the more subtle and less manipulatable features of odor and taste. These, too, had their place in the texture of Brown's Lounge. There were no noticeable odors in Brown's, that is, none of which the patrons or staff was aware. There were, however, two odors that by their presence and absence said something about Brown's. The first odor was of tobacco. The main bar was not a smoke-filled room. The air within the barroom was well circulated throughout the day, and no clouds of smoke hung in the air. Moreover, the barmaids and patrons regularly emptied and cleaned the ashtrays on the bar, so that there was little burnt or smoldering tobacco in the room. These activities effectively insured that there was never a stale tobacco odor. The odor of tobacco was present — the predominant source being cigarettes — but it was never acrid. One regular patron smoked cigars, and another smoked a pipe; both were often accosted humorously by the barmaids with the fact that they "stink up the place," but even these smells were not especially offensive to the nose or the eyes.

The odor absent from the room was the smell of alcohol. Brown's employed a full-time porter, and Charlie was insistent about maintaining a clean place:

> You know I hate that. I can't stand to come into a place and see glasses and stuff sitting up on the bar half-full waiting to be cleaned. You know, when I had my other place I had this barmaid and no matter how many times I told her to clean up when a guy finishes she wouldn't listen. I'd come in and she'd have the bar full of empties. Now it don't take a second to clean them up. I came in one day and that bar was full. So I walked down the bar and I asked everyone to stand up, and then I walked back to the end I just knocked every damn glass and bottle off that bar. And when I finished, I told her to pack and go.

For Charlie, the smell of alcohol in a bar meant cheapness and that the bar was a "joint"; he did not choose to indicate to anyone that Brown's Lounge was either. Again, the atmosphere was consistent with the image I have described. The presence of the smell of tobacco fitted comfortably with a sense of homey collectivity, and the absence of the smell of alcohol clearly stated that Brown's was not a cheap joint.

Taste had a dual meaning in Brown's. It described the available food, and it was the bar's term for alcohol (as in "Gimme a taste, will ya Baby?"). The food consisted solely of bar snacks — potato chips (regular and barbecue), peanuts, Slim Jims, and, occasionally, hard-boiled eggs. All were salty and aimed at increasing consumption of liquids. On several occasions Charlie had attempted to expand the food service. There was an accessible kitchen in working order, and he had tried to institute a sandwich service. Each time, however, after only a few days, the service lapsed. Ostensibly, the reason was the unreliability of the kitchen help, or the amount of the barmaid's time the service took, or the messiness of the whole operation. But these problems were not insurmountable, and Charlie acknowledged that the more important concern was that his image of a bar did not include food service. "If I wanted to be in the food business, I would be. I like my bar to be a bar. I don't like the eating crowd you get anyway. They don't respect a place like regular customers do." Thus, when the demands of the customers for food seemed to be real, he started a food service. When the demands fell off, he discontinued the service. Since, in reality, there was little customer pressure for the food — the customers used the service but did not stop coming to the bar if it was not there — this cycle was intermittent. There was also little demand for a food service because Charlie allowed food to be brought in from the outside. Admittedly, by allowing people to bring food instead of selling it to them, Charlie lost a possible source of income, but this loss of income was more than compensated for by the increased control he exercised over who used his bar. By permitting food but not selling it, Charlie retained the option on food use rather than making that option available to all who entered his bar.

Taste was also the bar's term for what was available to drink. Beer or a shot-and-a-beer accounted for almost all of the drinking done in Brown's. Highly priced shots of wine took up most of the rest. Within this general framework there was a seemingly limitless vista of choices. Charlie stocked three distinct price levels of alcohol, described by patrons as "bottom shelf," the least expensive at $.65 a shot; "middle shelf" at $.75; and "top shelf" at $.95. There was, in addition, a "top of the top," ranging from $1.00 to $1.25, but this level was more a statement about Brown's conception of itself than a reflection of what the patrons bought regularly. Still, the patrons at

Brown's — and urban Afro-Americans in general — do not, when they have a choice, drink cheaply. Thus, the quality of alcohol consumed was quite high. For example, the highest quality of drink regularly purchased when the bar was still the Nassau Inn was medium-priced Canadian whiskeys, Irish whiskeys, scotches, Seagram's 7 (then the most expensive choice on the shelf). When Charlie took over, the Nassau Inn's top shelf was almost entirely moved down at least one notch and, for some whiskeys, two. Tanqueray, J and B, Johnny Walker Black, Dewars, and a top of the line Canadian whiskey became the regular drinks. The effect was to transform the place from a taproom to a bar.

Repeatedly, then, Brown's stated that it was the kind of bar in which action could be had but in which the basic mores of middle-class culture could not and would not be abrogated. The image of Brown's said that the quality of social life found there was neither out of control nor free to anyone for the asking. It was a meeting place for friends, a place to visit not a place to use, and a place to remain without loss of self. Brown's was a bar whose mechanisms of control were built into the image: "Brown's Lounge is a nice place, a comfortable place."

Accompanying the continual message that Brown's was a "comfortable place" were points of reference that demonstrated that Brown's was an Afro-American setting. Chief among these were the use of red and green to light the bar, the advertisements in the bar, and the contents of the jukebox. In the last few years red, black, and green have become the symbolic colors of the urban black experience. The combination of the three in flags, buttons, and stickers became the conscious choice for demonstrating group awareness within the black community. Red and green are also normal bar colors, so that their use in Brown's was not out of the ordinary. However, the combination of these two facts meant that the use of red and green could carry only one meaning — a bar — or another meaning — a black bar — or both meanings, or neither; the meaning rested with the patrons. The effectiveness of the colors was evident in two separate statements about the choice of lights in Brown's. The first was made by a former white patron whom I met in the bar that had replaced the Nassau Inn for the whites in the neighborhood. I asked him why he no longer came to Brown's. He did not answer for a moment — I believe because he knew I still went there and was friendly with the blacks who frequented it — and then he explained that he no longer felt comfortable there: "And besides, it's too dark in there. It's not anything like Jimmy's. It's full of colored lights."

The second statement was made by Charlie, when I asked him why he chose the shades for the lights. "When I chose [the colors] I didn't think any about them. They were just colors that I like. I had the same in the old place and I like the way they look, special, you know. . . . But after I put them in here some of these people asked me if I'd chosen cause of the black thing. Now you know I don't believe in any of that black thing-white thing shit but some people think there's something to it." For Charlie, the choice was one he felt comfortable with, a neutral act. But for some patrons, black and white, the choice was an act of identification that declared Brown's to be black. I do not think that the white patron's pun was intentional, but his choice of words was telling, nonetheless. Moreover, his negative perception of the lighting was a positive statement for some of the new black clientele at Brown's. The signal was ambiguous, however. It was an available but by no means mandatory interpretation and very much one in the eye of the beholder.

Another equally ambiguous signal that Brown's was a black environment was the contents of the advertisements displayed through the bar. On the far wall, opposite the entrance to the barroom, was the largest and most visible advertisement in the bar, a Schlitz beer sign showing a black man at a piano. Complementing this centrally placed poster were other advertisements that reinforced the identification of Brown's as a black bar, for example, the Seagram's campaign for the mixed drink the "Watusi." There were two signs for this drink, one was cardboard in the shape of a warrior and the other was a plastic statue of the same warrior. This was not an overt statement, but neither the choice of the name "Watusi" nor its placement in Brown's was likely to appeal to the average white drinker or to draw that drinker into the setting. Certainly neither of these images, in and of themselves, was the same as a sign reading "Whites Not Allowed." However, the absence of any characterizations of whites relaxing, though there were white-oriented drinks, such as a Harvey Wallbanger, available, said something about whom the owner was trying to convince to buy his products. Again, the signals were subtle. They were no flagrant announcements, only quiet inferences of the dominant identity of the bar.

The final signal was the jukebox. The records were exclusively black-oriented: soul, jazz, blues. Considering the status of the box and given its particular usage, the nonblack patron had better possess more than merely a "Top 40's" awareness of soul music. The average white patron who expected to listen to or play music in Brown's had to listen to and play black music. Since such exclusive taste was not likely to be acquired naturally in the everyday white world and since its acquisition required work not usually associated with participation in drinking contexts, the white customer was faced with the choice of remaining in the bar and being uncomfortable, or of learning to enjoy black music, or of not coming to Brown's. More than likely, the unacquainted white customer who found himself in a strange, loud, and unappealing soundscape, with no way to relieve his strangeness, would not stay long. A white customer whom I had never seen in the bar and who was unknown to the barmaid entered and ordered a drink. There were only five other customers present, so he began to talk to the barmaid, giving signs he intended to stay. He turned to the jukebox and asked her what she would like to hear, punched out the numbers, and stood for two minutes reading the songs. The barmaid called out two more songs, and he punched them out. The customer sat down and finished his drink in silence. When he finished the drink, he paid for it and left. After he left, one of the customers asked: "Think he didn't like the music?" Another responded: "Can't you see why?" Once more, nothing was overt; the signal was there only for those who wished to read it.

The features that suggested that Brown's was a black bar were few, and, in a sense, to discuss the blackness of Brown's is partially redundant. After all, any unsuspecting patron who walked in would be immediately aware that it was a black bar. Its blackness could be taken for granted. In part this is correct; Brown's was definitely black, and, accordingly, a great deal more effort was put into defining the kind of black bar Brown's was; however, it was still necessary that some signals exist. The historical definition of the bar as a white-owned establishment and the ambivalence surrounding its presence in a racially mixed neighborhood raised potential problems. Statements of identity, even ambiguous ones, solved this problem. They provided a ready-made set of interpretations that eliminated the possible question of who controlled the setting. In the case of Brown's blackness immediately placed the bar in an Afro-American frame of reference, and conclusions as to its proper use had to be drawn solely from that identity. In characterizing Brown's as black, Charlie insured that its use and misuse would be understood within the black cultural experience. Blackness defined the basis from which action in the bar grew and to which action was accountable.

This necessary indication of blackness could not be and was not a statement of exclusiveness. Charlie was not interested in having an

all-black clientele: "You know I won't exclude white or black long as
they don't cause no trouble. I don't want anyone to feel out of place.
This bar is for all people who want to come here. I don't have a
racial thing about my customers." Rather, blackness was a statement about what criteria would be used to order behavior. Despite
this, and much to Charlie's dislike, for he saw it as a personal rejection, only a handful of whites frequented the bar. But this was not
surprising. The identification of black values and rules of conduct as
the governing ethic within the bar placed any white who wished to
use the setting in a peculiar social position. To use the bar, the white
patron had to be willing to accept the black code of conduct. Unfortunately, few whites were even aware that such codes existed, and
fewer still were willing to abide by them. For most, such a violent
reconstruction of their social universe would be intolerable, and
whites stayed away.

Because of this desire on Charlie's part to allow anyone to use his
bar, provided they were willing to accede to the larger code governing conduct, expressions of blackness were at a minimum. Obviously, Charlie could not hand out a sign saying "No whites need enter"
even if he wanted to do so. Not only would it be a violation of the
Civil Rights Act, it would also have been an insult at the surrounding community. The communication of blackness, therefore, was
always ambivalently stated. The choice of images was in areas
which, while declaring the bar's identity, did not offend the sensibil-
ities of those who spent time there. Thus, though all of the effects
implied blackness, the acceptance of that implication was the customer's response, not the bar's requirement.

As a whole then, Brown's said of itself that it was comfortable,
orderly, and black. Teddy, the porter, summed it up neatly:

People come here cause they can see their friends, and talk, and
have a good time and not worry about who comes through the
door. I don't like to drink where I don't know the people, but
everyone knows everyone here. Now, over at P____, you go there
and shoot pool. Guys just go to use the pool table and drink. It's
like here only everyone is always shooting pool and drinking.
The only place I never go is L ____'s. They'll kill you down there.
All the time after you to buy them a drink. Looking at your
money. You go into L ____'s and you keep your back against the
wall all the time. You can't even get a trolley there on the Avenue.
They're all in front asking for nickels and dimes. Nickel and dime
you to death about whether they gonna get your money.

His images were clear, and their messages were well defined. There were joints where drinking was the aim, bars where games were played, and bars where conversation was the aim; and Brown's was definitely the latter. Though it consciously undersold its presence through the maintenance of a low profile, in conformance with its world and Charlie's desires, the bar as a whole said of itself that it was not of the ghetto, but of somewhere else.

3 "Up the Hill": The Patrons of Brown's Lounge

The neighborhood in which Brown's was located was generally known in the larger black community as "Up the Hill." The name had two sources. The first was physical — the area was situated on a small rise, literally a hill up from the rest of the black community; the second was social — the neighborhood and those who lived there were usually better off economically than the other residents of the black community. The name was, thus, an acknowledgment that getting "up the hill" was both a social and a physical climb.

Those who lived there neither liked nor used the name. It pointed to a specialness — within but apart from the black community — that they did not believe existed, and they resented its implications about their commitment to black identification — away from the ghetto, away from its problems. They saw themselves, their community, and their world in different terms. They believed themselves to be caught between contradictory demands and besieged by all those who felt let down when such demands could not be met. Where others saw in their lives and life-styles only the freedom provided by their economic security, they saw with equal clarity the tenuousness on which such freedom was based and the lightning quickness with which it could disappear.

It was from among those who lived "up the hill" that Brown's drew nearly all of its customers. And it was this community's sense of self-identity that set the tone for the talking of shit. What went on in the bar and what talking shit meant depended in large measure, therefore, on how those who used Brown's regularly saw themselves and their relation to the world at large. In this chapter I provide a portrait of this social group — the regulars of Brown's Lounge — in their own terms.

It is necessary to emphasize that this group portrait is developed from among only one group of participants in stable relationships and is only an index of the life-style of Brown's. This point deserves emphasis. There is a tendency in the literature on life-style in Afro-America and in minority ethnography in general to draw un-warranted conclusions on the basis of data that are obtained from a limited area or section of people. Local characteristics are gener-alized for an entire people. Thus, "the least 'respectable' people become the 'multiple-problem families' or the 'hard to reach' poor" [Hannerz, 1969, p. 36]. The result is that folk classifications are mistaken for analytic generalizations and naive beliefs for facts. A related problem is the tendency to be oblivious to the fact that a community's moral perceptions do not always reflect reality. Life-styles are potential ways of acting and are dependent upon social context for their meaning. There will always be places and times in which actions and life-styles differ. Thus, though a moral category by my definition, the life-style presented here is not a permanent definition of all the people who live "up the hill" but rather a description of patterns of behavior followed by one group of people who are similar to, but not identical to, all those who live there.

Accordingly, the life-style to be considered here is only one com-mon thread, one pathway in everyday experience, followed by cer-tain people in a specific bar. There are other ways to be "up the hill," and some people there would never go to Brown's. Still, much more than the bare facts of social class, income, education, and oc-cupation, the life and life-style of the "up the hill" people described here capture one sense of the existence of the black middle class in one Philadelphia neighborhood.

The first and most obvious measure of life-style was the "look and feel" of the neighborhood, and yet, despite its name, there were no firm boundaries separating "up the hill" from the surrounding com-munities. It was possible, however, to map the extent of the area. The borders were represented in residents' minds as the points where known subareas stopped and others began. Such horizons, however, were exceedingly fluid. Residents could not prevent anyone from en-tering and misusing the area; they could only dictate how one ought to behave and how one ought to be treated if one did not. It was this lack of finality, moreover, that caused residents the most worry and that they, ironically, pointed to as proof of their necessary connec-tion and commitment to the "outside world."

"Up the hill" was bounded to the north by "the Avenue." The Avenue was the major thoroughfare through West Philadelphia and at this end was populated by fast-food shops and car showrooms. The complex of Penn Central railroad tracks paralleled it, reinforcing its use as a boundary. Despite this, there was little or no distinction between the physical environments on either side. The southern boundary was Littlefield Avenue, a business street populated mostly by small stores and bars. It was recognized as a boundary because it has a trolley line, but, like the Avenue, it was a very fine distinction. The east and west borders were quite different. The eastern border was Heinz Street, and Heinz Street was considered the "bottom line." There were no through streets from it "up the hill," and it was further separated from "up the hill" by a line of factories, which very effectively closed off the communities to the east. This segmentation was further enhanced by the obvious physical distinctions between the two environments. To the east of Heinz Street, the homes were smaller and built to the sidewalk, and many were in need of repair. It was a ghetto by anyone's standard. The western boundary was Apple Street. It, too, was distinguished by its trolley tracks, but another fact made the difference. On the other side was one of the few white enclaves left in West Philadelphia, and it maintained its integrity with semireligious fervor. This side of Apple Street, according to several informants, was closed to blacks. While this was not strictly true, the perception that it was true was very much present.

Within these horizons, the area was residential. The surrounding neighborhood, some thirty-six blocks, was primarily single-family row homes, with a small number of detached twin and single homes. The businesses sprinkled throughout the neighborhood, such as Brown's, were located on the only north-south traffic way directly through the neighborhood. Most of these businesses operated out of houses, rather than using special structures. The definite impression conveyed was that the neighborhood was given over to living rather than working.

One indication of this impression was the treatment of the streets as pathways rather than places. For those living "up the hill" the streets within the community were ways of getting from place to place, not somewhere to be. Unlike the surrounding black communities, where the street outside the house was an integral part of the social life, the streets of "up the hill" were not centers of action. Life was individual and centered inside the house. Thus, "up the hill" was not an environment in which public and private display merged in a single whole but rather one in which the difference between inside and outside was maintained.

A second expression of this residential texture could be seen in the care of their property by residents. The streets and homes around Brown's were orderly. Most of the homes were row houses or duplexes, but all were set back from the street and had neat, well-kept front lawns, often landscaped with small bushes and hedges. The houses themselves were stone or brick, and they, too, were well kept and in good repair. Their orderliness was further complemented by the quiet security of the neighborhood. There were few people on the streets except for the children playing, and their freedom to play was seldom interrupted by passing cars. The impression was of a clean, neat, quiet, residential area whose families were particularly committed to the upkeep of their property. "Up the hill," as one informant put it, was "full of damned grass and hedges." His complaint was not over their presence but their need to be cared for, a chore he did not particularly relish. The more important point was that the area residents had enough land and enough time to create and keep their private green spaces maintained to an order of suburban respectability.

The people themselves were black working and middle class. They were, to borrow Hannerz's term, "mainstreamers," conformers to the middle-class American assumptions about the "normal" life [Hannerz, 1969, p. 38]. The men and women who came to the bar and formed its core population worked for a living, owned their own homes, sent their children to college, and were deeply concerned with "not losing ground" and "making it." Theirs was the "American dream," and they pursued it with dignity and vigor. There were about 150 neighborhood users of Brown's, of whom sixty to seventy were regulars, that is, patrons who were in the bar at least once a week. Of these, about thirty came every day. The figures are approximate because, though the numbers were stable, the individuals varied. Thus a patron could move in and out of regular attendance or everyday appearance over the course of time. Most lived in the immediate neighborhood within walking, or a short drive's, distance. Their ages, for the most part, were between thirty and sixty, and all were at least high school graduates. Occupations varied from city employees, to public school teachers, to salesmen, to independent businessmen, to the director of a community health program, to factory workers, to saleswomen. All were either employed or retired. Only two regulars, besides myself, were white. Mr. Hanson

was in his seventies, had lived most of his life just down the street
from the bar, and saw Brown's, as he had the Nassau Inn, as his bar.
"I been coming here ever since it opened back when it was Jimmy's
father's bar. Then, they lived upstairs and the bar was in the back
room. Everybody said it changed when Jimmy sold, and they stop't
comin' by. Anywhere else is too far and I haven't ever seen what the
fuss was. It's still the same to me." The respect accorded the bar by
Mr. Hanson was reciprocated in full. He was universally admired,
and no regular would pass him by without a comment. The other
white regular was Joe, the mailman, who arrived six days a week
around lunchtime. Joe saw the bar as a convenient stopping place on
his route. "It's the best place to stop. You go into a diner and you eat
and run. Here I can stop, talk to some people, and relax before I go
back to work. It gives me a break from the routine. You know?" The
patrons, even the whites, then, were in accord with the bar they
came to so regularly. They were its neighbors, and it was theirs.
Like the bar, they sought middle-American respectability.

The regulars' sense of themselves was particularly reflected in their
understanding of how far they had come, where they were at, and
where they were going. As one regular put it:

> Oh, we moved here—let me see—must be about ten to twelve
> years ago. We were the second black family on the block. The first
> was my next-door neighbor. It wasn't like it is now, he really had
> a whole lot of trouble. They threw garbage on his lawn and
> smashed his garage windows. But some of his white neighbors, the
> guy who lives to the other side of me was one, got involved in
> helping him. By the time we moved in, a few months later, every-
> thing had quieted down and we didn't have any trouble. My
> neighbor, the white guy, came over the day we moved in and said
> how he was happy we moved in. He invited us over and we've
> been friends ever since.

The regulars saw themselves caught in a unique and lonely position.
Because they had acquired status and many of the symbols of success, they were free to live (within limits) where they wanted, to
move into a nice neighborhood. Because they were, for the most
part, black, there was a gap between their dream and their reality, a
gap, moreover, that could not finally be bridged. Thus, though they
might move into a nice neighborhood, such a move had, in varying
degrees, a price. One reflection of the cost was how life used to be in
the bar:

I never had no complaint about Jimmy. I don't think he liked
havin' blacks in his place but he didn't let it get in the way of business. He kept his opinions to himself. Some of his steadies were
real S.O.B.'s—you know what I mean. They'd smile and joke
with you an' all the while they'd be pushin' at you. They'd kid
about the colored taking over and how you was different, you
know. To some of them, shit, you was a nigger when you weren't
here and your name when you was. What was worse was that half
of them couldn't do a damn thing, wasn't worth shit to speak of. It
used to burn me, them being so all fired sure they owned this
world and we's here on their say so.

Their sense of achievement and their awareness of how little it was
valued by all too many whites pointed out how tenuous was their
grip on a reality they had to work overly hard to maintain. "Michael,
you know, I worked all my life to get what I got now. No one, but no
one is gonna take it from me. Some of those people out there is just
waitin' for a chance, just waitin' for this nigger to slip or be pushed
aside. It ain't gonna happen! I paid what's due an' I'm gonna take
what's mine even if I gotta waste people who get in my way. I worked
hard, harder than most, an' nobody gonna say it ain't rightly mine."

Not surprisingly, their sense of their place in the real world
reflected a wider set of attitudes about the way life ought to be lived.
These attitudes portrayed themselves not as "black bourgeoisie . . .
uprooted from its 'racial' tradition and as a consequence [without]
. . . cultural roots in either the Negro or the white world" [Frazier,
1957, p. 112], but as a people conscious of their culture, the real
world, and the differences between the two. In particular, their attitudes dealt with blackness and with the good life. Blackness was a
sore point with the patrons of Brown's.

I told her if she was coming home this vacation I didn't want to
hear any more of that Black Power Bullshit. These kids—well,
Mike, you see them every day, you know—shit, they go away an'
all of a sudden they know everything about being black. Study it
up one ways and down the other. An' talkin' about their oppressed
Brothers an' Sisters. She didn't know one end of oppression from
another until she went away. She can stand there talking to me,
and I say somethin' back an' she says: "What do you know. You've
had it easy with going to college and becomin' a Public School
teacher"—like it was wrong to try to get ahead. You can't say a
thing about workin' your way to any kind of decent life. I just
won't take that talk no more, not in my house.

Those who came to Brown's knew that they were black and, more important, that they had experienced their blackness as an intense and not always pleasant part of their own lives. They were both angered and dismayed by their inability to convey to others, often their own children, that their individual struggles were positive accomplishments and not "selling out" for a better life. They had sought a world in which an individual was measured by his abilities and his accomplishments. As another patron said: "I want my degree because I'm good, not because I'm black." To be confronted with a new definition of self-worth was to lose the very foundation of reality. Hence the hostility of many of the teachers to black studies and to black English. "I don't believe any of it. I just don't. My job is to teach them to read and write so they can survive out in the world. This black English isn't worth a damn thing. Nobody out there is going to listen one minute. If you tried that in an office they'd have you out on your ass in five seconds, five seconds. You tell me what good it does me to have this, or my students. They learn this shit and end up in an unemployment line. They learn English and they might — *might* get a job. You think I'm gonna handicap them more and you'll be as off the wall as Labov." Blackness was real and relevant but not to be confused with the real world where real decisions were made.

Linked to blackness, but in a more private arena, was the question of respect. The successes and failures of Brown's patrons were theirs and not those of all blacks; therefore, they were not to be judged by comparison with others. Four men, including Rick and myself, were seated at the bar. Charlie entered wearing, unusually, a business suit and shirt and tie and carrying a briefcase. One of the patrons said, as he was greeted: "Charlie, you sure look good — not like your usual self. I do like to see a man dressed nice. It makes him look like somebody. Not like some bum on the street, you know." Rick spun on his bar stool and said: "Where you come off sayin' that. You never do that. You never judge no man, specially a black man, that way. You born with sense, or what. A man's not his clothes no way." The patron answered in a soft voice: "I only meant he looked good." "I know what you meant," Rick replied, "An' wrong is all you'll ever be. A man's a man no matter what he's wearin'. You got that?" A third patron said: "You got that right, Rick." Rick was expressing a generalized belief among the regulars. They knew, all too clearly, that respect based on externals was part of the cultural baggage that had permitted discrimination to flourish for three centuries. Rick's anger reflected his awareness that even the simple and harmless forms of such belief represented threats to hard won rights

and privileges. Respect, in Brown's, was for the "person," not for the
position he could achieve or the personality he could display. Aware
of how fragile and sometimes deceptive appearances were, they
tried to go deeper. Again:

Well, I jus' laid inta him. He come home from school yesterday,
and he starts talkin' that street trash. He be doin' this an' be doin'
that an' motherfuckin' teacher this and that. Talkin' that black
English he's supposed to speak. I told him "black English, shit."
That's jus' dumb nigger talk an' I wasn't havin' none of it in my
house. I wasn't sendin' him to school so's he'd end up with no head
full of trash. If he's goin' a' learn somethin' it'd better be right.
Them teachers know shit. Fill'n their heads with fuckin' nonsense
'bout black culture. It ain't no damn culture worth shit soundin'
like that. Black culture this and black English that. My black ass.
I knows better than that an' I never went to no college. What's he
think's gonna happen when he knows all that stuff — ain't gonna
make him no smarter. He wants to be somebody. He's gonna hafta
go a damn sight farther than that silly shit. You gotta bust ass in
this world, not be doin' this or motherfuckin' that. I can't respect
him or no teacher sound like some gutter trash. I askt' him how
you gonna know he's got any sense talkin' like that. Be black — he's
got to be somebody before he can be black. Noway bein' black is
ever gonna be enough in this world. You gotta work if you wants
anythin'. You ain't gonna get it by bein' *black.*

Blackness was, for the patrons at Brown's, a characteristic, not a
class. It told nothing of who one was. This was discoverable only in
the individual, in his or her words and his or her ability to back
them up with knowledge and follow through with skill. To be black
meant only to be like them, it could not guarantee that you were one
of them. They were individuals who knew that hard work achieved
ends and that such achievements were personal, not public. They
had succeeded in obtaining a part of the good life; others must do
likewise: "Life don't come on no silver platter. Them that wants has
got to bust ass to get. The only thing ever given free to us niggers is
sweat."

Within such a program of independence, it might be expected
that the good life would be measured in terms of material possessions. While these were certainly part of the good life, they were not
its sum and substance. As it was understood in Brown's the good life
was measured in time.

Teddy: You can have all of that Howard Hughes's money. I wouldn't want the worry. All them people followin' after you with their hands in your pockets tryin' to pick your loose change. I'd never be able to close my eyes at night. Now for me, I'd jus' want me enough so's I could lay back an' party the way I wants to. No foolin' now, Michael, you know bein' rich ain't all its supposed to be.

Mike: You don't think that's what the rich tell us so we won't go after their money?

Teddy: Course it is, but that ain't the point. The point is havin' as much fun as you can. You know we's only here for a short time so's there ain't no sense wastin' time doin' what don't mean shit in the long run.

Earl: You sound jus' like my ol' man up in his high pulpit with the two choirs singin' the changes, talkin' we here for only a short time — shit.

Teddy: Your daddy wants his partying up in heaven. I wants mine in the here an' now. Do you hear me talkin' 'bout the here an' now?

Earl: Amen, Brother. Michael ain't you learned yet, you say Amen to the truth.

Mike: Amen.

Life was exceedingly short, shorter yet under the threat of social repression — "Charlie, 'scuse me Mike, *Mista* Charles, gonna take it first chance he gets" — and, accordingly, good sense dictated that life be lived to its fullest at each moment. This belief was not evidence of "a world of make-believe," nor was it meant to "conceal the feelings of inferiority and of insecurity and the frustrations that haunt their inner lives" [Frazier, 1957, p. 213]. The patrons of Brown's were committed to the legitimacy of playing because they saw it as a type of fulfillment and meaningfulness not available in the white world. "Michael, you sit here every day tryin' to figure on what it is, bein' black. No way you gonna get there. You know that. Let me hip you to one fact you put in that book you' writin': Bein' black is the only way to be, you dig where I comin' from?"

The life-style of the men and women who frequented Brown's was concerned with creating a good life out of individual achievement and their own sense of what it was to be black. They were concerned with the better things in life, including the symbols of the wider American society, because such things permitted self-expression:

"Michael, havin's no good 'less you got time to party." Their sense of
their life-style, then, was of a tension between the goals of American
social order and those of blackness, and their resolution was a social
style in which individuality was championed, but only because it
freed one to be black.

In practice this self-identity affected the understanding of talking
shit in several ways. In particular, it made Brown's into a bar in
which everyone was known, in which everyone was safe, and in
which social relations and interactions were quiet. Knowing everyone and being known by everyone were fundamental. Brown's
Lounge was different for its patrons because the clientele who frequented it existed in intimate relations with each other. Under ideal
cultural conditions, it is necessary for participants in interactions to
develop identities before conversation can move from the superficial
to the serious. Such identities are seldom achievable in most bars because most bar relations have a tentative and superficial character
[Cavan, 1966, p. 67], and hence most bar encounters remain incon-
sequential. In Brown's, however, such identities already existed as a
result of mutual interactions, in and out of the bar, over time.
Patrons knew one another because they lived with each other. They
knew interests, feelings, histories — real or imagined — and this
knowledge permitted a more intense order of social life. Moreover,
this knowledge was known not only to friends; it was shared among
all patrons. With friends, any one individual's knowledge of another
can be selective and limited by social ties. This selective knowledge
permits classifications of friends (best friend, close friend, etc.) and
control over what each knows about the other. In Brown's the inability to achieve such selectivity made each person's activities the
property of everyone present and, by extension, the property of anyone who used the bar and heard about them. Knowledge about self
expressed in Brown's was thus passable from one patron to another
at will.

This intimacy was doubly dangerous. The world of the bar was
not selective about the information it saved. Incidents that were un-
favorable to a patron were given as equal weight as the favorable.
Patrons could find that the impression of them as participants in bar
life often placed them in an untenable position in the real world. For
example, a regular customer who was known and appreciated as a
caustic wit entered the bar. He sat down at the end of the bar and
drank in silence. Several patrons entered into conversations with
him that proceeded like others at the bar but with none of the expected verve. The patron remained for half an hour, quietly in-

teracting and then left. After his departure, a patron remarked: "Fred sure wasn't like he usually is. You think something's wrong?" He then began a discussion with his neighbor of this possibility. Thus such intimate knowledge, while responsible for an immediacy and depth unavailable in transient contexts, carried with it the possibility to box in a patron.

This intimacy extended beyond the bar as well. The patrons of Brown's were neighbors, and so what happened in the bar had the potential to become the property of the larger community outside the bar. True, the carrying of information from one world to another was a violation of the morality of the bar, but the possibility did exist. Husbands talked to wives and wives to husbands, and the results could cause problems. Since patrons were aware that whatever they did or said would be observed by people who lived in their community, their actions were not only the result of their own personal needs but also reflected the morality that they knew the community would find acceptable in any situation. Thus, patrons assessed their actions in terms of their effect at levels not generally associated with bar behavior.

It was in this sense that Brown's was truly a neighborhood bar. Because it was intimately connected to its larger world, what was acceptable in Brown's became a function of the way in which both the bar patrons and the neighborhood interacted. Each monitored the other, and each used the other to control and define what was morally possible. The result was a world in which behavior was judged both by its effectiveness in promoting talking shit and by the toleration that the residents outside the bar had for it. This effectively meant that all patrons must be able to return to the larger context without stigma. They could neither fail nor fall apart in the bar, and they could not appear to take such behavior into the community. Patrons could and did get drunk. But they did not, if they wished to be adjudged moral, appear this way on the street.

This aspect of neighborhood and neighboring was evidenced in several incidents that occurred during fieldwork. Once an unknown patron began to swear violently in front of a neighborhood lady, who had come into the bar to purchase a six-pack of beer. Another time a patron became drunk and, after leaving the bar, began to be loud and abusive to children playing on the street by the bar. On both occasions the staff took great pains to differentiate these acts from the normal course of events in the bar and from the expectations they had set. The control of the neighborhood was felt most strongly in an incident that did not occur in the bar or as a result of the use of Brown's but as a result of someone coming to use the bar. This fact made the incident all the more reprehensible because the actions could not be "legitimatized" by reference to excessive drinking in Brown's. It occurred on one Saturday afternoon, when I was seated on Rick's front steps, watching neighborhood children play street hockey. The children had set up two official goals and were skating madly in between them, much to the delight of onlookers up and down the street. A speeding car came down Nassau Street toward 95th and headed directly for the hockey game. The driver slammed on the brakes and squealed to a halt only a few feet from the goal. The driver began to sound his horn and yell loudly at the children to get out of his way. The children moved off the street, and the driver sped through their playing area, pulled alongside the bar, and noisily, with squealing brakes and slamming doors, got out of the car and entered the bar with his passengers. The whole incident caused comment among those who witnessed it, some of whom said that they were going to have to speak to Charlie about it. One woman who witnessed the incident spoke loudly: "Trouble starting up from that place. It's gonna run this neighborhood down if it isn't stopped." This incident was later taken up with Charlie by several patrons, who were insistent that such incidents must stop. "Charlie, you can't have them types around here. They're gonna bring trouble you don't want to see." Charlie's response was acknowledgment of his responsibility—but an awareness that he could do little. "How I'm supposed to know what goes on out there. These people want me to police everywhere. Well, I guess with a place like this it's part of the game." The irony of all this pressure on Brown's is that the public drinking establishment which in its most general form is characterized as a place where there is a sanctioned loosening of social and moral values should at the same time be required to uphold those same values.

The second aspect of neighboring was the desire to make Brown's a quiet place. In Brown's life was relaxed. There was no drive to do everything quickly, and there was none of the forced intensity characteristic of those bars designed for maximum interaction in minimum time. Patrons got deeply involved, but they were not expected to abandon themselves completely to the moment. Social life in Brown's was rather low key—more like a conversation than a party. As one patron said: "I like it here because I can come and be myself without having to party all the time. I can talk and have a good time without getting all messed up and losing control and all that." This atmosphere of restraint was in keeping with the desires of the neighborhood, but it reflected at a deeper level the desires of the patrons. Heavy partying was obtainable many places in the larger community, but for the patrons of Brown's there was no other location within their immediate community where they could be street-wise. The bar was, therefore, the most readily available context in which such behaviors could occur: "I guess you could say that this here's my corner, and them's [pointing around the room] my corner boys, hee hee hee." Brown's was thus the community's way of allowing necessary, if not always orderly, social interaction without the construction of an unneighborly example of its expression.

Brown's was also seen as a safe place. Like intimacy, safety was seen in two ways. The first was in the purely physical sense. Of course, no bar setting is completely safe. All are open to robbery, but Brown's was somewhat out of the way. Moreover, its reputation as a quiet place without continual action lessened the rationale for robbery. At Brown's the amount of money obtainable, when compared with other drinking establishments, was not worth the risk. The risk of robbing Brown's was increased further by the closeness of the patrons. While no patron was likely to oppose a robbery, the risk that one might was greater in such settings. The element of closeness increased the vulnerability of the thieves, for unless the thieves were regulars gone mad, they would be strangers to the environment and have a higher visibility than they would in a more transient setting. Hence, Brown's was seen by its patrons as safer than most other bars. "These days there ain't nowhere you can hide from those gorillas. They're gonna get your bread somehow. Here, at least somebody's got your back and you've got a little cover."

The second meaning of safety was more social. In Brown's patrons were protected from disorder. In its ordinary form the neighborliness of Brown's sought to protect patrons from unwarranted and unwanted intrusions. As a patron remarked: "You have to be careful about who you let come into your place. Some lowdown niggers — I'm not prejudiced against white or black but that's what they are — will mess you up bad if you let them. You have to watch and take care of the place." This does not mean that disruptions did not occur, but it was an explicit aspect of normal encounters that someone would control them and not allow them to overwhelm the conversation.

All of this would be fine and simple if Brown's were not a bar. But it is, and like all bars, it is in the business of selling alcohol. Accordingly, it is necessary to separate out from this portrait what part, if any, is alcohol talking and what part reflects the true sentiments of the patrons of Brown's. This is necessary for two reasons. First, there exists a general cultural understanding of the relationship between alcohol and human behavior. This conventional wisdom holds that alcohol not only causes changes in human behavior but also that the kind and nature of these changes can be directly traced to alcohol's toxic effects. It argues that we do things after drinking that we would not ordinarily do when we are sober and that it is the alcohol alone which determines the nature of those actions. "Just as changes in the efficiency with which we exercise our sensory motor capabilities are consequent upon the action of alcohol on our innards, so too are changes in the manner in which we comport ourselves with our fellows" [MacAndrew and Edgerton, 1972, p. 11; see also Heath, 1976, 1978; Strickler, Dobbs, and Maxwell, 1979; and Collins and Marlatt, 1981].

Second, this commonsense interpretation has been even more pronounced when applied to Afro-American drinking practices [see in particular Myrdal, 1964; Frazier, 1957; Maddox, 1968; Maddox and Williams, 1968; Robins, Murphy, and Breckenridge, 1968; and Vitols, 1968]. Afro-Americans are considered particularly susceptible to the effects of alcohol. Given the history of oppression to which they were subjected and the continuance of their marginal status in American life, some argue that blacks are not only subject to the normal problems inherent in drinking but also are driven by social and racial problems to constant excess [for a review and criticism of this point of view, see Harper, 1976, 1977, 1979; see also Rommel and Rommel, 1981]. Drinking by blacks has been seen solely as an escape from the burden and pain of the real world. Thus there has been almost no research into the social drinking practices of black Americans that has not assumed that the ordinary use of alcohol has as its aim the complete anesthetization of the black drinker [Rommel and Rommel, 1981, pp. 241–42; a powerful exception is Anderson, 1978]. Accordingly, alcohol use has been perceived as a pathologic feature of black life and as a destructive force in any social encounter.

In Brown's none of this was true, and accordingly it is necessary to formulate an alternative explanation of drunken comportment there [for a description of the model I used, see MacAndrew and Edgerton, 1972, especially chs. 5 and 7; Bateson, 1972b; and Heath, 1978]. The starting point of such an explanation is the patron's explicit justification of alcohol use in Brown's. Witness these comments:

I tell you one thing Charlie Brown, I sure as hell don't come here to drink, not at what you're charging.

You don't go to a bar, lessen it's a joint, to drink.

Shit, it's cheaper to drink at home. You look at that bottle of Seagram's Gin. Now a good barmaid can get twenty-four, twenty-five shots from a bottle, right Harriet?

Twenty-seven if they pourin' light.

Okay settle on twenty-six. Now at sixty cents a shot that bottle brings Charlie—les' see, six bucks every ten. That's double and half again—sixteen bucks. Now it can't cost him but five with his discount. He's making ten, maybe, eleven on each. Now if you want to drink, why do it in a bar. You throwing money away if you do. For five bucks you can drink the same at home.

Bars ain't for heavy drinkin'. You can't get enough to get drunk on. 'Fore you get that far you be push't out or to the back booths.

Those who came to Brown's did not come to drink, but rather they drank because they came to Brown's [see also Macrory, 1952, pp. 630–36; Mass Observation, 1938, pp. 82–83; Cavan, 1966]. Alcohol was a part of talking shit, but it was not an intrinsic part. From the perspective of the patrons, drinking was what was done in Brown's, not why one went there. "You can drink anywhere, man. Here you can bullshit first." This attitude was supported by Charlie Brown. His central and only desire was good drinking, and such behavior was obtainable only if alcohol was an adjunct to interaction: "They're no good to me if they get drunk. Drunks are more trouble than they're worth. They get mean an' start gorilla-in everybody."

This relegation of alcohol to a secondary status was reflected particularly in the patron rituals of treating. Treating in bar settings has been dealt with at length by Cavan [1966] and is characterized by what Mauss [1954] called an economic exchange in which the giving of the gift structures an obligatory contract between two parties. In a bar where the proffered gift is alcohol, such an obligatory relationship has the potential to create hazardous interactions. This is especially the case in neighborhood bars, where the network of obligations can be large and extensive. Thus, were a patron to *run the bar* and buy everyone a drink, he could expect to receive in return from each patron a similar gift. The potential effect on the treater is obvious, and, in Brown's, such hazardous situations were avoided.

Now, I don't hold with this buyin' for the sake o' buying. If I'm gonna spend my money I want to know who's drinkin' my whiskey.

Yeah, an' I don't like it when they send one back right away. I'm not lookin' for no handout. When I buy you a drink I'm treatin' you, not askin' you to take care of me. You want'ta buy me one, you do it when you're ready.

You right. You take care of someone, and they snap back like a fuckin' rubber ban' an' you know it don't mean shit. They obligated 'stead of givin' cause it means somethin'. Shit, what's the sense o' buyin' if you hafta. That don't make no sense.

You know what's jus' as bad, though. When you're a little light and someone buys you one an' then sits an' waits on you an' makes you speak a piece.

Shit, I don't care. I jus' tells em an' lets it go at that. If they're waitin' I couldn't care what the fuck they think.

The gift of a drink in Brown's was only an obligatory metaphor. The recipient was expected to acknowledge the gift and to respond when he felt he wanted to. For the gift to be meaningful, it had to appear to be unrelated to previously received favors. It must be something the giver wanted to do, rather than something he was forced to do; above all, it must make sense. A gift of a drink must not be unexpected, and it must never appear to be a bribe. The exceptions were the offer of a drink from a complete stranger, gift drinks from bar personnel acting officially, and free drinks from whiskey salesmen. In these cases the gift truly was a bribe, but it carried no implication of personal reciprocity, and it was accepted freely. On the whole, however, treating in Brown's aimed at larger concerns rather than at immediate individual relations. And the gift itself — except under special circumstances which were always announced beforehand, such as "my wife just had a baby" or "I got the job (or lost the job)" — could not be outrageous. As one patron said: "It don't make sense to give somebody what he wants if they only send down what you're drinkin'. Supposin' he's light. He's takin' care o' you anyway and you go an' make him out a fool. No, you do for them what they done for you an' you never be wrong." The gift must not exceed that which had been given. Were it to do so the relationship would be dominated by one of the parties when identity and order demanded equality.

Like so much else, then, the gift of a drink was caught up in the image the patrons had of who they were, why they came to the bar, and what they hoped to get out of being there. The patrons saw themselves as a community pressured from all sides to conform to standards that they were not allowed to choose and that they felt did not reflect their desires or their needs. Under these conditions, then, Brown's was for them a safe space, their corner, where they could be independent and black without having to pay, as they did not have to pay too excessively for a treat, a price for either.

4 Tending Bar at Brown's

When Charlie Brown bought the bar, the neighbors agreed that the shift to black ownership was good for the area. At the same time the women of the neighborhood were apprehensive over what changes the new management would institute in what had been a clearly defined part of their lives. For most people, the bar had been a place where they could know that their husband[s] "ain't about to get into nothing he don't belong in," so they waited, and, in the beginning, their worst fears were realized.

When the bar reopened, the women discovered two radical changes. The first was acceptable; they found that women would now be able to use the bar. This, they felt, corrected the discrimination of the previous owner and accorded them the same rights as their husbands and male neighbors. It also allowed them to frequent the bar without having a low status ascribed to them. Brown's became for them a legitimate arena of activity. This acceptance was prized because it restricted their husbands' ability to hide in the bar. The second was a barmaid. This change was potentially acceptable, except that Charlie erred in his choice of the first woman he hired. "I made a mistake. I could have had barmaids here sooner but the first one I had wasn't right for here. I pushed too hard too fast. She was good for a looser place but she made too many people 'round here up-tight. I finally had to let her go." This mistake was rectified when Charlie employed male bartenders, one of whom was from the neighborhood. They were the norm for almost a year while the bar integrated itself into the surroundings and established its identity. After indicating that the bar would conform to neighborhood norms, Charlie reintroduced barmaids.

Initially the day shift was worked by Lorraine, Charlie's wife, as a stop gap. "I'm only doing this until we find someone. I told Charlie that I don't mind the working back here, but I'm not interested in any full-time job. We went and had all those kids and I'd rather be at home with them." Because her working was temporary, Lorraine saw no need to act like a barmaid. "It can be fun for a little while, but, you know, Michael, I couldn't do it for long. It gets boring after a while listening to the same old stuff day after day. Now don't you go missing my meaning. I like most of the people who come around here. They're nice to be with, but it do get tiresome sometimes."

Lorraine saw bartending as a service occupation. Her approach to the job was concerned with supplying drinks. Her role, as she perceived it, was essentially passive. "I guess I want to give them what they want. They come in here to get a few drinks, and I'm here to serve them." Rather than create events, Lorraine was content to observe them. This passivity led her to act as if she were not a part of the event. One result was that she made no effort to act authentic. Thus, one patron asked her why she was dressed up like she was going to church and said: "Look, somebody who comes in here don't want to look at you like that. A man comes in here he's expecting to see something better than you all buttoned up and ready for winter." Lorraine was aware of her withdrawal, but she saw her actions in a positive light. "I never said I was a barmaid. Besides we don't want this place to go downhill. So I'm not about to be acting foolish for the customers." To Lorraine, the bar was a place to drink, and her responsibility was to insure that it fulfilled this function responsibly. She was not there to cause things to happen but to serve and to await interaction.

Lorraine's distance was understandable. Brown's belonged to her and her husband, and she was rightfully concerned with its survival. This concern expressed itself in a level of seriousness not in keeping with normal expectations. Lorraine treated interactions as purposeful and attempted to introduce orderliness into their unfolding. One patron commented: "Lorraine works too hard and fast. She doesn't relax and just let it flow. I think she's uptight about having to work here." The bar was too much her place to allow her to "act foolish." Instead of allowing herself and her patrons to open up, Lorraine sought to keep everything nice and quiet. She was not dull or boring nor did she consciously set about to disrupt or destroy the natural social life; on the contrary, she was very much a part of interaction. Her participation, however, was invariably dampening.

As a consequence, a shift with Lorraine was very subdued. Because she did not conceive of the bar as a forum for display and her role as that of actor, Lorraine did not interject herself into the inter-action process, except to serve drinks or as a participant in a short in-terchange of "serious talk." This effectively eliminated the bar from interaction and, in turn, reduced the flow of events between patrons. While she was working, patrons tended to cluster in small isolated groups or to talk only with their immediate neighbor. The result was that patrons spent less time in the bar than they had intended. Com-menting on the lack of "anything happening," one said: "I have to bring my noise with me 'cause there ain't much waiting here for me these days."

In contrast to Lorraine, Mary, the night barmaid, was over-involved in working the bar. "It's what I do best cause this is me you see here. What you see is what you get. I don't phony-up for anyone and I won't take no shit from anyone. Nobody gonna mess with me when I'm working. I'll let 'm know just where they get off." Mary treated the bar as an extension of her life, and bartending as an ex-pression of her personal life-style. Tending bar was, in her mind, not a job but "a way of getting paid to be me." This conception of her role as her own identity allowed Mary to be fully involved and to act no differently from any patron. Thus, while Mary recognized the nature of bar life, she did not see that she had any responsibilities in relation to it. Her performing was directed toward neither the patron's nor her employer's needs but to her own needs. She did not attempt to bring out patrons but to demonstrate her own compe-tence at talking shit. "I can talk it as good as any of them who comes in and better than most. Nobody mess with my shit less I lets them which I ain't about to do."

Mary's perception of her position as participant rather than as barmaid introduced a great deal of uncertainty into the ongoing pattern of interaction. Because she was the barmaid, the patrons ex-pected Mary to stand in a certain relation to their needs. In particu-lar, she was supposed to treat certain "raps" as acceptable but not meaningful. With Mary, however, this was not always the case. Some raps would be treated in the right way, while others would be taken seriously and followed up or dismissed as not worth her time. Thus, some patrons were "rapped to" in a way which indicated that their actions were of interest, and others were dismissed out of hand. Moreover, because it was her real self rather than Mary-as-barmaid to whom interactions were addressed, Mary treated overtures as real and not as a form of play. The result was the creation of cliques where none should have existed. Those she liked received her atten-tions and those she did not were ignored except as customers for a drink. A shift with Mary was unpredictably dangerous; because she acted with little regard for her job, her actions were chaotic. As Charlie said:

I fired her because she never tended to business. All the time fussing at the customers acting like she owned the place.

One time I came in about nine and she was down at the end of the bar rapping with her old man. And the place is full of people waiting to get served. George was calling to her "Mary give me a shot 'fore I go, will you," and she's ignoring him. So I walk down and I said: "*Don't you hear* that man talking to you. You deaf or something. I told you *I* don't want this shit going on. *You* take care of business first, not talking shit. Who do you think *you* are costing me." And that dumb bitch says: "I *heard* him. He can wait 'til I'm finished." Do you believe that? In *my* place, *she's* telling me a customer can wait. She didn't have *no* sense.

This chaos was recognized by the patrons. Mary was seen as "touchy," "hard to get along with," and as "not being able to take a joke." One patron, not a favorite of hers, said: "She's crazy. You can't talk to her without she don't jump down your throat. One time you'll be going along fine and you'll say something and she'll go off all over your head. No way you'll be talking about her and she'll take offense. You don't even need to be talking to her and she's right in there shootin' off about how this and how that. I don't need her to mind my business." And even those with whom she responded well felt ill at ease with her attention. "Sometimes you can't tell with that woman what she wants. You just talking shit and she want to heavy rap. I don't need hassle. I like Mary but she's a funny woman. You can't be playing with her cause she'll be all the time messing with your meaning."

Mary's performance of the bartending role, while self-satisfying, was detrimental to bar life. Patrons had no way of interpreting interaction. The element of security implicit in proper bartending was missing, and its lack effectively transformed the bar into a world of serious consequences. In promoting herself instead of tending bar, Mary disrupted the patrons' desires, and the expectations of having good times in Brown's were ultimately frustrated.

For the majority of the time that I was in the field, the regular barmaids were Harriet, on the day shift, and Sarah, or "Symphony Sid" as she was commonly called, on the night shift. Unlike Lorraine and Mary, both Harriet and Sarah were considered to be among the best at their work. Another barowner commented: "Charlie has got two of the best barmaids in West Philly. Both of them are just golden. Shit, he wasn't doing nothing compared to what he's been doing since he's got them to go behind this bar." This opinion was reflected both in Charlie's weekly receipts and the general contentment of his patrons. The customers saw both barmaids as actively making Brown's into a "lively place". One customer said: "You know, Mike, I really enjoy comin' here lately. Since Charlie hired Harriet, this bar's been poppin' full time." Another patron remarked: "Sarah works a nice bar. You come in an' sit an' she talk with you whether you drinkin' beer or you drinkin' top shelf. She's friendly even when she's ornery an' lookin' to mess."

The basis of the barmaids' success stemmed from their awareness that working the bar was a job. In one encounter with Charlie, Harriet expressed this understanding quite vehemently:

C: You do know where you're working and for who?
H: Do I know I'm workin'? Do I know this! Charles Ulysses Brown, with my feet hurtin' and my back talkin' to me and my ears bent out of shape by you and these suckers. You tell me how I could forget. You find one of these river rats who'd let me.

Though she exaggerated, Harriet's spontaneous description of the hazards present in bartending clearly indicated that she saw her job as just that—her work. This was substantiated in her description of how she became a barmaid:

It was right after they passed that law that said women could work behind the bar. It didn't used to be that you could have a woman behind the bar. I started with _____ over in North Philly and I worked for him for five years before I came over here to West Philly. You know, when you're a young girl sittin' on that side of the bar it looks easy. It don't look no different from sitting out on the stoop talking with people or hanging at the corner. But, Michael, you learn fast. Cause if you don't, those people will run you ragged till they kill you with their shit. You know I don't drink when I'm behind this bar. If a customer comes in and offers, I always tells him I don't drink on the job. Now that just makes good sense cause you can either be working or having a good time. And ain't nobody paying you to have a good time. They buying your work which you either do or get fired. You got to see that this is a job, nothing more, and then act like it all the time.

Though not as complete in her statement, Sarah voiced a similar understanding to a patron who was attempting to monopolize her

time. "You got to understand I ain't doing this for fun. I got more
customers than you to take care of. Who you to be wailing about
'talk with me' and 'forget them for a while.' I ain't playing. This is
my job which I am paid to do with everybody who sits up at this
bar. So you settle down and don't go messing with me." Both Harriet
and Sarah saw their activities not as examples of who they were as
persons but as reflections of the expectations implicit in their work
[see Goffman, 1959, pp. 30–34]. Both Harriet and Sarah recognized
a distance between themselves and their occupation. From their perspectives their time in the bar was wholly professional.

This professional awareness distinguished Harriet's and Sarah's
participation in Brown's from that of their patrons. One does not
usually think about how to act in a bar. Being a patron follows
naturally from being in the bar. Bartending, on the other hand, does
not just happen. It requires that someone make it happen. Harriet
and Sarah knew they were playing a part, and they sensed themselves as *dramatis personae* and their work as a form of acting. Sarah
said: "Michael, on this side of the bar I can be using all kinds of
language and be acting all kinds of crazy an' not one of them will
look up. All's I have to do is be sitting up next to you and they'll be
all over me like bees on honey. Here I work, an', hee hee hee, there I
party." The work of Harriet and Sarah was more classically theatrical than that of their patrons. Like actors on a stage, they possessed a
framework of knowledge that allowed them to tend bar while they
simultaneously asserted that they were only actors and therefore not
culpable for the actions the role caused them to perform [Burns,
1972]. Moreover, this perception of themselves as actors altered the
efforts they brought to bear on their tasks. Their self-consciousness
not only freed them from the moral responsibilities of genuineness
incumbent on patrons, but it also permitted them to improvise a
reality not wholly consistent with the actual world inside or outside
the bar. Both Harriet and Sarah were free to become different people in ways that their patrons were not; they could "act all kinds of
crazy" without the fear of actually being thought so. Their awareness of the limits of their role freed them from the need to be consistent. In knowing that they were actors, Harriet and Sarah knew
more than their patrons and could be "self-conscious while [the
patrons] remained only conscious" [Husserl, 1960, p. 104]. The result was that in knowing the part — and knowing it was only a part
— they also knew the probable outcome of the play. Their patrons
could only guess.

This advantage was reflected in the manner in which Harriet and

Sarah worked behind the bar. Harriet worked in a highly calculated fashion. She viewed the day shift as a naturally quiet time and saw her responsibility in terms of creating life and evoking energy: "The men who come here during the day are pretty quiet. They aren't all the time talking loud. Mostly, I like to get a little life in them. Get 'm doing something 'stead of just sitting. Now some of them'd be plain drunks if you let them be. Just sit and suck liquor all day. You give 'm someone to talk to an' talk about an' they'll have a good time and not cause trouble." For Harriet, the focus of her involvement in Brown's was on the construction of a world in which her patrons actively related to each other. Obviously, such an atmosphere was conducive to drinking and served the economic purpose of the bar. Equally as important, the creation of a "good time" served the interests of her patrons by expanding their pleasure through participating with each other. Freed from the necessity of just drinking by the existence of a real attempt to keep them involved, the patrons were presented with the potential to choose drinking as only one of many available alternative claims on their time. Harriet's focus on action brought patrons together and kept them involved with each other and with their situation rather than solely with the consumption of alcohol.

This system of action was dependent upon her ability to establish relationships with the regular patrons. Harriet was aware that the construction and maintenance of such a network among the regulars gave her a way of articulating the stability and continuity she felt they needed. As she remarked, "Most of the customers who come here during the day are looking to bullshit with someone. If I can get something happenin', they'll play with it an' keep it going. Now, with this group here, I've got a head start. Most of these people know each other so I can use them at each other to get some action." Harriet's activity involved a manipulation of the already existing potential relations to create a continuous discourse among those present.

Harriet created this action with two distinctive forms of role work. The first kind attempted to build an information frame [Bateson, 1972, pp. 184–93, 315–21; Goffman, 1974, pp. 21–40]. Such work was designed to create a firm base on which to accomplish the aims of social life. The second type sought to involve the patrons, to make them become performers in, rather than observers of, social life. This division of role work is not intended to indicate a causal chain. The image of a supportive frame should not be of a static scaffolding but of a system of social boundaries developing as

an integral part of the unfolding of everyday life. A social frame
reflects the larger intent of the social setting. It is fixed, however, not
by this system but rather by the acts that generate social life. The
distinction of two types of role work is not an indication that bartending is exclusively distributed to either category. It is possible for
an individual act to be frame and acting at the same time. The distinction is based not on what is done — the activity's manifest goal —
but on whether the dramatic use of self is the means by which the
goal is achieved. For example, when Harriet "feeds the jukebox"
herself, then her action is frame and is intended to establish an environment for communication. When she "feeds the jukebox" by
calling out to those in the bar, "All right, you River Rats, I serve you
all day, least you can do is keep the music going!" or when she hands
a patron a dollar, tells him to pick some music, and then argues with
him over his choice, then she achieves the same goal — communication — but does so by involving herself in ongoing talk and manipulating her image to achieve her end. The distinctions between frame
and acting represent methodologies of defining involvement in social
life, not different classes of acts; both reflect processes and not ends.

Harriet spent most of her time talking. She saw her responsibility
as generating action and thus actively sought to create relationships.
Frame for her was limited to those moments when the bar was empty. During such periods she always saw that the jukebox was playing
and that the barroom was "neat." She said of this activity: "Michael,
you have to give them noise. No one's gonna come into an empty,
silent bar. Hell, I'd sooner drink in a morgue than in a dead bar.
Same with the cleaning. A bar that's all full up with empty glasses
and beer bottles just isn't inviting. I bet you don't like sitting at a
dinner table with all them empty plates, now do you?" Once the bar
was full, however, she concentrated on acting to gain her ends.

Harriet was constantly involving herself with patrons, monitoring
their needs and conversations in order to draw them out or to draw
them into existing interactions. She opened all closed encounters
whenever possible. She used her freedom of movement behind the
bar to expand the boundaries of conversation by moving away from
a speaker or a group while maintaining a conversation. Thus, she
would move to the far end of the bar while still talking to a patron,
increasing the volume of talk as she moved. The effect was to open
the conversation to all other patrons. She would perch on a stool in
the corner farthest from the entrance, so that all attempts to talk
with her were carried on at maximum distance and volume. This
meant that all interaction with Harriet was public, regardless of its

form. From greeting to exit, what any patron said to her and she to any patron was the property of the community.

A central aspect of this interaction was her manipulation of her self-image through her raps. She was considered to be "a woman who raps like a man," and she took this description quite seriously. Several patrons commented on her argumentativeness and how it was hard to talk to her. One noted: "She'll fight about anything. You start to have a conversation with her and the next thing she's rapping at you. She's telling you, you don't know anything and you better listen to her. And she won't talk no shit if you tell her otherwise. She is a hard woman." Most recognized her words as just that and responded accordingly. They knew that she was "just messing," as one informant put it, and enjoyed the opportunity to rap back. With Harriet patrons always knew where they stood: "It's cool, you know? She'll put you through some changes but she won't fuck with your mind. When she rap, you rap, and when she won't you don't. It's as simple as that." Thus, a shift with Harriet was one in which she was both the center and source of much of social life; it was marked by a high degree of energy being directed from her to those present. "I guess I come cause I know something will always be happening. She'll be after Teddy or Charlie or someone, and it's fun to watch, you know. It's never dull with Harriet behind the bar. She keeps the place jumping with noise."

Sarah directed her performance more toward frame, seeing her responsibilities as polar opposites to Harriet's: "The people who come here at night don't need me to tell them to party. They wouldn't be here lessen that was a part of their program. Nah, my problem is slowing their roll." Sarah perceived the night shift as one in which the patrons were already committed to action and her job as requiring her to maintain that action and to see that it did not break through its naturally evolving boundaries. Her work as bartender was quiet and direct and subdued when compared with Harriet's. "Mostly I just talk to 'em when they come in until they get settled. Then I can leave 'em alone. They let me know when they want me. Until then I just let them be an' have a good time."

This low-keyed approach was reflected in her verbal interplay as well. Sarah's conversations were usually short and served to maintain contact and to mark tempo and tenor rather than to invite involvement. This is not to suggest that they were not meaningful to the maintenance of bar life or that they were superficial. They were extremely functional and allowed her to observe bar life without disrupting its natural flow. She acted to preserve the world that her patrons had come to create rather than to formulate one for them: "When they're having a good time, it don't make no sense for me to be sticking myself or my two cents in. They can take care of themselves just fine."

Her conscious acts to remain outside of social life did not reflect an attempt to withdraw from the event; she was not a mechanical doll dispensing drinks, but her involvement was less social than Harriet's. For example, Sarah was dancing quietly in the area near the beer cooler. Her movements were slow and languid and directed toward the far wall. Observing her, a patron said: "You're sure moving good. How about I come over and you and me drag." Sarah, still dancing, replied: "Be cool now an' enjoy your drink—I'd be too much for you." A ripple of laughter flowed down the bar, and another voice said: "Too much to handle, huh Sarah?" She answered: "I'd be too much for all of you. You have troubles just watching." She finished her dancing with the end of the song and moved off to serve a customer. Whereas Harriet would have used the playing to initiate a verbal contest, Sarah treated it as a closed exchange. Her responses framed the incident into a routine "cracking" relationship rather than a public rap. Such acts of closure were characteristic of her style of performance. Sarah was present to social life but not wholly within it. She acted to entertain by action, not to create by interaction.

Her overall detachment from interaction and involvement did not prevent Sarah from actively maintaining bar life. The bulk of her time was spent insuring an adequate level of noise in the bar. She "fed the jukebox" not only to keep the music flowing but also to create an appropriate mood in the setting. She juggled the sounds of the music so that it would balance good interactions or lead patrons into good interactions. A patron who had been sitting alone at the bar walked to the jukebox, selected about five songs, and went back to his seat. The first two were slow, mournful ballads of lost love. As the third song, another ballad, started, Sarah said: "Is that all you played? You must be out of it. Ricky, go play some music. We'll see if we can't get this man out of his mood. Cause if we don't he'll have us all crying in our beers, ain't that right?" She then pushed the reject button until all his songs were off the box and said, "Buy that man some happiness on me. I ain't workin' no sad-eyed shift tonight. Tonight we all party, hee hee hee." Such acts were not uncommon, but mood was usually maintained by asking someone to play a specific song while he was at the jukebox, e.g., "Punch out 3–9–7 will ya, baby." Sarah also monitored each patron's drinking and was always ready to refill their glasses when necessary. As one patron said:

> You gotta watch Sid, you know. She'll have you drinkin' all night if you'd let her. She's not all the time loud talkin' at you: "Do you want another or are you just takin' up space." She just gets the job done by fillin' your glass. You put it down an' turn your head an', wham bam, there's a full glass where your empty was. Hee hee hee. Or she's got your beer glass under that thing. . . ." Sarah broke in and, smiling, said: "Spigot. 'Thing,' you got less sense than this glass." ". . . an' she's saying: 'You did want another, right?' She's real pretty doing it, though, you know.

A shift with Sarah was one in which the flow of bar life was maintained by the regulation of social boundaries rather than by the forceful use of self. Sarah accomplished her ends through subtle direction; she did not verbally abuse, insult, or attack her patrons, that is, "loud talk" her way into conversations. Those actions she left to the patrons, remaining content to aim rather than initiate action.

The fulfillment of the bartending role by both Harriet and Sarah exemplifies the best in bartending. The activities of each are examples of thoughtful responses to the tensions inherent in their jobs. Their accomplishment of the role represented the kind of active work necessary to protect the social universe, and their actions exhibit a real sense of the possibilities for action with control. Both actively sought to keep the flow of conversation under their watchful eye. Although their individual styles were different, the results were the same. Both held tight rein on how life would proceed, yet neither did so as a policeman outside the ongoing event. Each in her own way acted as a central focal point for ordinary "good times."

Within this universe of theatricality, there existed a further technique for insuring social order: the patterned raps between the barmaids and the other bar personnel, Charlie, the owner, and Teddy, the porter. These raps on Teddy and Charlie were a regular part of the process of tending bar and served as a device to structure and organize social life. Recognizable, repeatable routines, they served as a ready-made and viable means for concentrating patron interest on the behavior of bar personnel. For instance, it was ten o'clock in the morning. There were five customers, all regulars, in the bar. They were seated at one end talking and drinking, with the jukebox playing softly as background. Teddy, who had just finished with the trash, sat down next to but not with the group, and waited. Harriet

looked up and said: "What do you want? You taking a coffee break?
Get off that stool, you ain't a customer." Teddy smiled at the five
heads turned in his direction and replied: "Woman, give me a drink.
I have worked an' now I will rest." "Worked?" Harriet replied, "You
haven't worked a day since you started suckin' up gin. An' who you
callin' woman? I ain't your woman. An' if I was, you'd be dead
cause I'd kill a sucker like you. Any woman'd kill you, you so full of
gin one good shot an' you'd be dead." Teddy answered: "No way,
woman, I got enough for any woman, 'specially you." This "argument" continued with varying intensity for about five minutes and
then died only to flare into action in about half an hour when social
life had begun to quiet down. In another incident, the bar was nearly full but the general atmosphere was subdued. Sarah looked at
Teddy, who was cleaning up behind the far end of the bar, and said:
"Do you believe Teddy? He's so skinny if he'd turn sideways he'd
disappear. You just look at him, skin and bones. If he ain't the
raggedy-ass man I ever seen. Shit, if he get you between them legs
he'd cut you in two." "Who you shootin' off at, woman? You want to
see som'thin' you jus' let me get you up to the back, back booth an'
I'll give you lovin' like you never got," Teddy replied. The argument
lasted most of the shift, with patrons regularly joining in to take
sides. These incidents exemplify the basic pattern of the barmaid-
porter interchanges. In each case their effect was to focus interactive
energy on a public performance, a performance, moreover, that was
bar- rather than patron-centered, and therefore "safe energy."

Similar in structure and function to the barmaid-porter interchanges were those between Harriet or Sarah and Charlie. These exchanges had the routine quality of those cited above. Their only
noticeable difference was content. These contests centered around
Charlie's alleged tightness or his basic failures as an employer. For
example, one day Charlie sat up at the bar and ordered a drink.
Harriet poured it and said: "That'll be ninety-five cents." Charlie
turned to Tookie Brooks, a regular, and said: "Took, did you hear
that? My bar, my whiskey, and she wants me to pay for my drink."
Harriet cut in: "Charlie, I don't wanna rap. Just pay me my money,
you sucker." "You watch your mouth, Harriet, or I'll hafta take you
to the back booths for a lesson," continued Charlie. Harriet said
again, "Just give me my money — you be here at the end of the day
wantin' to know how many free drinks of your whiskey did I give
away. Well you ain't gonna be one of them. Now pay up." They
continued for fifteen minutes during which the assembled patrons
followed the encounter closely. At its conclusion, one remarked:

"That Harriet. Watchin' her give it to Charlie's worth the price of
these drinks."

Both sets of routines point up the essential nature of social control
demanded of bar personnel. In the performance of their various
roles Harriet and Sarah actively worked to generate an orderly social
universe for patron interaction. They created a world in which
energy was free to express itself, and, because its boundaries were
continually being established and ordered, they built a world into
which chaos could not penetrate and overwhelm everyday life.

This chapter has described the role of the staff at Brown's in creating and organizing the social order of the bar. It has examined the
background knowledge and the work of the barmaids as reflected in
the activities of tending bar. The barmaids had a specific set of occupational expectations, and they aimed at the maintenance of a social
environment in which patrons could fully interact without fear.
This performance of bar work represented a transformation of occupation into theater; at the core of the "normal work" of tending bar
resided actors performing plays for audiences. And in these roles and
performances existed the formal proof that someone was taking care
of the social world of the bar, that fictional creation of another
world was possible, and that the order the patrons perceived arising
out of the interplay of imagination and the experience itself were as
real and as contrived as they needed them to be.

5 Hanging Out:
The Sociology of Use

It is possible to treat everything that happened in Brown's as if it were unique, to argue that the ideas, feelings, and impressions that occurred there were meaningful only because they made sense to the regular patrons. These patrons, after all, saw themselves as very special with even more special experiences, and it was a cornerstone of their self-image that they and their lives were more particular than anyone ever imagined. Still, for all of its subjectivity, what the patrons did while they were in the bar was inevitably public. Their actions were done in the presence of others and for some reason. They had to make sense, and they could only do this if the actions were recognizable and interpretable, if they communicated something. At all levels of experience there existed not only what a patron knew he was doing but also a system of commonsense, cultural attitudes that provided a pattern to which the activities of patrons could be compared and against which they could be measured. Such a calculus is not a denial of the intersubjectivity of everyday occurrences; the world is always a human self-creation. Rather, it is a recognition that events can be viewed both in terms of their immediate and their cultural contexts. Hence, the description of such patterning provides a way of getting at the shared features of experience that made it possible for patrons to interact with each other all the time without having to wonder too often or too loudly if they were acting correctly.

A patron's time at Brown's began with *approach* and *entrance*. Approach to the bar was always purposive. Patrons walked toward it with their eyes fixed on the front door, clearly demonstrating that it was their objective. Their pace was brisk but not hurried, and they walked with little or no scanning of the surroundings. Although they were entering a morally questionable setting, given the neighborhood, patrons made no attempt to convince people who might see them that they were heading anywhere but Brown's.

Once inside the front door, patrons noticeably relaxed. Ties were loosened, shirt collars were unbuttoned, and jackets were removed and slung over the shoulder. In the same fashion pace slackened, and the torso and shoulders that had been held erect during approach were brought forward, allowing the arms to swing freely. This reconstruction occurred regardless of the intentions of the patrons. Even those who entered only the hallway—for example, high school students who sometimes used the men's room—still went through some reordering and rearranging of their clothes. The notable exceptions were the black women from the neighborhood and the white former patrons who only used the bar to purchase take-out beer. These patrons maintained throughout their stay the same demeanor as during their approach.

While the incoming patron was in the hallway, for usually ten seconds, those already present in the bar were timing his arrival. As the front door was heard to open, all present in the barroom paused momentarily in what they were doing and shifted their gaze to have a clear view of the door. This watch was maintained until the person entering was either visible through the window of the second door, his voice was recognized, or he entered the room. If the person entering was recognized by anyone, then all returned their attention to their encounters. If the newcomer was a stranger or if the passage down the hall was too long, then the patrons engaged in a range of protective actions. Rings were removed, wallets were taken out of pockets, cash was picked up from the bar, and watches were slipped off the wrist. These were placed in the left hand—the door being to the patron's right—and this hand was often held over the bar to the work side. These behaviors were accompanied by statements like: "What the hell's going on out there?"; or "Watch it, something's up out there!" The holding out of valuables was a safety measure. If the newcomer was too suspicious, then it would be possible to drop the valuable object into either of the wash basins. As Earl explained the first time I saw him do this: "This ring is just too valuable to give to some gorilla. If they have enough sense to fish it out of the water, well, that I can't control, but I ain't just giving it up." Rick followed this comment with the statement, "Yeah, and I don't mind wet money but they do."

Once inside the main barroom, patrons could use the bar in three distinct ways: to order a drink, to take out some beer, or to make change. Regardless of what they did, all began with a greeting ritual — the immediate announcement of a patron's status. It acted as a signal of a patron's involvement in the social life of the bar as well as an initial definition of who one was and of what one would be expected to do.

Those at the bar or the staff might extend greetings. With regulars, greetings were often from both, though the central and most important greeting was from the staff. The form of the greeting was not rigid. Strangers were usually asked: "Hi, can I help you?"; but occasionally they were greeted with "Yeah?" There was no fixed phrase, though the personal appearance and sex of the patron had a great deal to do with the level of politeness employed. The lack of any personal statement, however, was a clear notification that the new arrival was a stranger. Regulars and familiar customers were greeted by staff in such a fashion as to announce both their right to be in Brown's and their status within the bar. Thus, a greeting extended to a regular patron was usually in two parts. The first was a statement of their name: "Hey Ricky," "Michael," "Tookie"; the second half of the greeting was a statement of their social role: "What's happening, you old river rat," or "Well, you planning to worry me to death today?"

The response to a regular's greeting was consistent. Minimally it involved the statement of the staff person's name, usually in the same fashion as one's own was spoken. Thus to Harriet's greeting I would answer: "Harriet." Regulars with high status often embellished their greeting: "Harriet, sweet Harriet," adding as many "sweets" as they felt necessary. A regular who was greeted had to respond immediately. To fail to do so was a violation of social order and forced the barmaid to "call out" the offending patron on his mistake. Immediately the barmaid would loudly repeat the patron's name in a mock hurt tone and quickly (often before the patron could respond) follow this with a second repeat, this time in a tone of mock anger. Usually by this time the patron had extracted himself from whatever had distracted his attention — a patron greeting, the cigarette machine — and responded appropriately. The response was always delivered in a caressing fashion: "Hi, Doll. I see you there. *You know* I see *you* there"; "Sid, you are looking *good* tonight."

During the greeting patrons indicated their intentions. A take-out patron (regular or stranger) would remain at the door near to the beer cooler, point to the cooler, and say: "You got a cold six pack of

_____?" Once the transaction was completed, the patron was free to leave. Often this purchase would be followed by the purchase of a draft of beer or a shot and a draft. This purchase was made with a minimum of interaction and was drunk quickly and in silence by the patron. After it was consumed, the patron left. If the patron was a known regular, there was often some subdued interaction with others present. This involved quiet "Hello's" and questions about health, the family, and the weather at the moment of entry. Such a patron never attempted any extended conversation and did not usually leave his station at the end of the bar.

Making change for cigarettes or the telephone or attempts to make change in general began with the customer moving, during the greeting, toward the center of the bar where the cash register was. When the exchange was completed, the customer made his request. The request was met or rejected solely on the basis of the availability of change in the register. Once the money was exchanged, the patron would often order a drink or a bag of chips, which he consumed quickly and quietly, and then leave. In these two uses, then, once the manifest goal was accomplished, patrons did something more typical. This was not obligatory, in the sense of completing a reciprocal event, and it was not casual, in the sense of "while here, why not have a drink." If anything, it was affirmatory. By ordering without being required to, the patron acknowledged the service done for him and the specialness of the bar.

The third possible move was to order a drink. Like the greeting in which it occurred, this action was an announcement of status as well as intention. For regulars ordering was not necessarily a process that they had to initiate. Regulars merely indicated, usually by either moving to a vacant seat or to an established gathering, that they intended to drink for a while. This motion was sufficient to inform the barmaid, who then obtained the patron's usual drink. This act was sometimes accompanied by the statement: "the usual." The barmaid's words were often matched by a request for confirmation from the patron: "Give me a little bang, will ya, Harriet." The drink was served, and the regular then moved further into the social action.

Strangers' needs had to be discovered. When a stranger ordered a drink, he learned about both Brown's and the world there. It was a point at which he discovered whether he was appropriate to the milieu and, if he was, what he would have to do in order to remain. It also afforded him the opportunity to acquire the associated rights and privileges of a regular through "properly situated" behavior. The first aspect of this process was based on the drink ordered. As

described previously, there was a structure to the kind and availability of alcohol in Brown's; moreover, this structure reflected the
distinctive atmosphere the bar wished to present. A stranger was initially unaware of the bar's internal structure, though he possessed
clues to it; his order was a signal of what his needs were. For example, a man dressed in work clothes entered the room, seated himself
at the bar, and ordered a glass of wine. Harriet picked up a sherry
glass and a shot glass, placed them in front of the man, and asked
him which brand. The man, obviously taken aback, asked if the bar
didn't sell wine in glasses, pointing at a highball glass. Harriet said
no glasses, only wine in shots. He asked how much, and she said
$.70. The man stood up, saying that was too much, and left the bar.
After he had gone through the door into the hallway, Teddy, who
had been watching, said: "I know him, he knows he can't get that
here. Why don't he go down to Long's if he wants that."

Once the order had been placed and accepted, the stranger invariably offered to buy the barmaid a drink. This offer was made
either before or during the serving of his drink and would also often
be extended to those who were seated immediately to his right and
left. The most common form of the offer was: "Pour yourself a
drink" and, if extended to other patrons, "Pour my friend (demonstrated either by pointing an index finger or by the nod of the head)
here one, too." The acceptance or rejection of this gesture was of little consequence. In fact, the majority of such offers were rejected;
the offer was the point. It acted as an icebreaker and an announcement of the newcomer's worthiness. In offering, the patron stated
that he was open to an encounter and willing to accept whatever
obligations Brown's placed on its patrons. Thus, though the drink
was often refused, the overture was not. Invariably, the new patron
was included in the conversations of those to whom he had offered a
drink. For example, a newcomer dressed like a businessman in coat
and tie came into the bar and took an empty stool next to George.
He ordered and offered Harriet and then George a drink. Both refused, but George, after thanking him, asked what the weather outside was like. They fell into conversation for a steady half-hour until
George left. The man sat alone, staring ahead for a minute, and
then turned and offered a drink to Ernie, who had come in while he
and George were talking. Ernie also refused, but they, too, fell into
conversation. Later that week the newcomer returned while George
was in the bar. George greeted him and told Harriet to "give the
man what he's drinking."

Once the initial order had been placed, the purchase and consumption of alcohol were relegated to what Erving Goffman [1963] calls side involvement, something that is noticed only at appropriate moments. The central concern shifted to socializing with those present.

For those known in the bar entrance into social life had its beginning in the greeting. Thus, while involved in the acts of greeting and then ordering, the regular patron actively scanned the barroom in order to see who was present and where he ought to go. This act accomplished, the patron either moved toward acquaintances present and joined their ongoing encounter, or, if there was no known friend (for example, if the bar was populated by the younger crowd and one of the older group came into the bar), then moved toward the area usually occupied by his peer group. Patrons who did not move to join a preexisting conversation would initially talk to the barmaid. This conversation would be long or short, depending upon the status of the patron. The better known and liked the patron, the longer it would be. Once this ended, the single patron would again scan the bar and would usually move to join one of the encounters around him, regardless of its composition. This was usually done by asking a question. This use of a question served several purposes. Initially, it was an act of deference. By using this form of address, the patron showed that he recognized that his interruption broke the boundaries of talk, even if only momentarily. It set up a relationship in which the patron attempting to join the relationship acknowledged the existence of a right to privacy that, by definition, did not exist. This deference signaled that the person entering was well intended. At the same time the question placed obligations on those to whom it was addressed. A question usually demands an answer, and thus asking a question insured that the questioner would be minimally involved in the encounter. Once into an encounter, the patrons were free to stay within it as long as it was maintainable. Since talk in Brown's was open and available, however, this maintenance was always problematic. At any time conversations were expandable or contractable, and the introduction and exit of patrons could shift the focus and make up of a group at any time. In Brown's there was little clear indication at any one moment of the persistence through time of closed off groups or individuals alone, and it was possible for an entire day's or evening's stay in the bar to be composed of momentary exchanges among patrons.

No matter who initiated an encounter, however, any participant might terminate his involvement in it without the consent of the other(s). There were no rules that granted any patron in an encounter control over the process of the event. However, in Brown's almost everyone knew everyone else, and this "limitation" introduced orders of deference and demeanor not normally associated with drinking establishments [Cavan, 1966, p. 334]. Central to this civility was the necessity that termination occur in such a way as to leave no patron alone. Thus, if there were only two patrons present, they would remain engaged for as long as they stayed in the bar. If a third entered, he or she would be included in the conversational interaction. This threesome would remain in conversation until more patrons either entered or left or until the barmaid or porter entered into the interaction. In such cases where the potentiality for multiples of at least two existed, then it was possible for twos to break away momentarily from the central topic. In this sense, conversations could be said to flow into one another, weaving a pattern of involvement that facilitated the potential for a greater interaction between all present.

Withdrawal from social life ranged from ceremonial to unobtrusive. It began with an act of distancing. This separation, when most obvious, involved standing up and gathering one's possessions. This activity was accompanied by statements like "Gotta go now" or "Well, time to head home." Initial separation might have involved an act as minimal as placing one's empty glassware on the shelf to the other side of the bar. Whatever mechanism was chosen (and usually it involved many activities), the patron physically distanced himself from the bar. This movement was distinctively different from those used to signal temporary absence from the barroom. In temporary absences the motion away from the bar was motion into the traffic pattern of the lane between the stools and the back wall. In leaving the movement was straight back, to a standing position usually arm's length from the bar. Thus standing, the patron called for his tab. This call—"Hey, baby, total me up, will ya?"; "How much I owe ya?"; or simply, "What's the tab?"—set the stage for settling accounts.

Settling accounts involved calling for the tab, taking care of those with whom one has been engaged, and paying the bill. Calling for the tab was fairly simple, though potentially dangerous. Drinks were not paid for when they were ordered, but a running count was kept by the barmaid and totaled only when a patron left or when it was known that a patron was short of cash. Thus, a patron had only a vague notion of how much he had spent in the setting. In order to reduce possible tension over incorrect accounts, the customer was given first a total and then a recitation of what was purchased. This last part of the tab sequence was obligatory on the barmaid's part, but there was no necessity for the patron to listen to it. Among regulars, particularly those with high status, this recitation was usually dismissed. "You don't have to read me, Harriet; I know you ain't doing anything funny." Once the tab had been agreed upon, the patron took care of those with whom he had been most involved, usually those closest physically to his seat. Taking care by treating to a drink was most common and was indicated with a hand motion to the barmaid. This use of a drink to settle accounts was not required, and they might be settled with appropriate good-byes. Such good-byes were said so that those who would remain were made to feel that the patron leaving was sorry to go. Settling seldom involved the purchase of a drink for the patron who was in the process of leaving, and this withdrawal was a further indication of a leaving in process. If treating was involved, then this last round was included in the bill (complete with recitation), and the bill was paid. After the cash was exchanged, the patron was in a position to withdraw from the bar. Withdrawal was not always immediate, however. Often the patron would be given, at this point, a drink for the road. This parting gift was not dispensed only to those who had spent a fair amount of money; it was also given to those who had been very much a part of what had been occurring in the bar. Thus a patron who had drunk little but who had really been verbally active would be rewarded. This drink would be consumed quickly and with a very businesslike attitude. The patron would remain standing and away from the bar. The completion of the drink marked the beginning of the last stage of exiting.

Exiting was done rapidly. The patron would make his way to the door casually, stopping momentarily to make a comment or to explain why he was leaving. This departure at the appropriate pace could sometimes be carried to extreme. For example, one crowded afternoon a patron went through the entire process of leaving and then spent a half-hour walking out the door. He was finally noticed at the end of the bar, and the barmaid commented: "You still here, I thought you'd left an hour ago." The comment was telling of the process but also of the status of the patron in the process of withdrawing. In most cases withdrawal was accomplished more quickly. When the door was reached, the final act of leaving was undertaken. The patron, as he passed through the door, announced his exit. "Later," "take care," or a similar remark was a common way of declaring final passage out of the barroom. When the door closed, leaving was complete. Once in the hallway the patron restructured his personal appearance and prepared to reenter the outside world. Often this restructuring was accomplished with a trip to the men's room, where the patron straightened his hair and clothes.

Ironically, even though Brown's was characterized and understood in terms of the manner in which it was used, it was valued in terms of the collectively perceived moral order that determined if such use "ought" to occur. Thus, the meaning of any action was not only its acceptability but also its accountability. Accordingly, the use to which the bar was put was itself based on an understanding of the morality of ordinary actions:

> Hey Rick. How ya feel? I hear you sure did it to death last night. Cubby said you were partying tough right from when you came until closing time. And if he hadn't hustled you out the door you'd still be going strong.
>
> Tookie Brooks, my man. Hey! I was all tore up this morning. Let me tell you, we did it to death until the wee hours.

Set forth in this short exchange is a concise, if elliptical, summary of the *program* of Brown's Lounge, that is, the code of conduct for the interpretation of behavior in the bar. Patrons were seen as "within the program" and their behavior as "fulfilling the program" or as "written into the program." The program itself consisted of the three terms *party tough*, *do it to death*, and *all tore up*. Each term was a statement of the attachment and commitment of patrons to what was happening and a statement of the expectations that were brought to bear on the patrons' participation in what was happening. The program served to buttress and validate ongoing social interaction as well as to explain specific interactions. Ultimately, then, because it was concerned with the ability of a patron to give or withhold his concerted attention, the program provided a framework for making moral judgments.

The first term of the program was *party tough*. To party tough a patron had to treat his specific encounters within the bar as if they were the most serious, meaningful, and important occurrences in his life. Partying tough placed patrons under the obligation to suspend any awareness of outside evaluation procedures for the interpretation of behavior and to act as if every encounter was totally self-contained. Thus, while a patron might have had strong feelings that a discussion of Adolf Hitler as a leader, a topic that occurred quite frequently, was a waste of time, immoral, or trivial, he was nonetheless expected to participate. This did not mean that a patron could not ardently disagree with any topic, including saying that it was a waste of time, immoral, or trivial. Rather, it meant that the participants could not reject the topic at hand by staying silent. To be in Brown's was an indication of one's willingness to be involved, and partying tough demanded that those present either be involved or leave. The assumption was that presence was an undeniable signal of one's availability for conversation. To party tough carried with it a commitment to create social life. For example, Rick came into the bar and stood in the doorway, calling out the names of those present and telling each how it was time to party. He walked down the bar, exchanging greetings, and stopped at the jukebox, which was not playing. He inserted a dollar, punched out some numbers, and then called out for more suggestions. Finished, he turned to Harriet who, before he could begin, said: "No, I don't want to rap! You can do it without my help." Of course, not everyone was engaged at this level of action at all times. This incident was, however, indicative of the idealized tenor of activity that patrons and staff would have liked to maintain. The obligation to party tough was an act of total commitment to be involved with others.

The second part of the program was *doing it to death*. Doing it to death described the way those in the bar sustained their involvement. It was the level of intensity expected of a patron's stay in the bar. To do it to death was to treat interactions as binding and to engage in the ensuing encounter as fully as possible. Doing it to death was thus an indicator of how well a patron partied tough. The first obligation of doing it to death was that patrons, having agreed to create action, now gave themselves over fully to its maintenance. Participants had to interact as if nothing outside the event held any real existence. They were expected to explore as fully as possible the topic of their interaction. No nuance was left uncovered; no statement was allowed to go unchallenged. In its essence, doing it to death was a commitment by those partying tough to continue to do so at all costs.

This obligation to be involved extended to all aspects of being in the bar. Patrons not only had to be in the conversation but also had to be part of the drinking. Again, intensity was not a measure of quantity. No one, for example, was forced to drink; several regulars could not drink, in fact. But even they were active in buying rounds and thus in demonstrating their commitment to that feature of talking shit at Brown's. Doing it to death demanded, therefore, commitment and involvement. A measure of involvement through time, it described an idealized sense of how well patrons ought to party tough with each other; as a measure of commitment in any single encounter, it measured how much a patron was willing to give, what price would he pay for being in Brown's.

The final term was *all tore up*, the logical consequence of doing it to death. Sooner or later, every patron, if he spent enough time in the setting, would exhaust himself, perhaps drink too much, and would be unable to function appropriately, that is, would be all tore up.

Nonetheless, being all tore up, though physically debilitating, was clear proof that the patron had been deeply involved. All tore up was, then, a vital signal of successful participation, and a mark of time well spent in Brown's. Even so, all tore up carried with it certain obligations. Though a legitimate result of being in the bar, it was not an acceptable way of being there. Those who became all tore up were expected to withdraw until such time as it was possible for them to party tough again. The patron was expected to recognize or to accept the judgment of others present that he was unable to continue and to leave the barroom. This withdrawal could occur in two ways. If he was very much out of control, a patron would withdraw entirely. If, however, the patron was only partially exhausted or if he wished only to distance himself momentarily, he would often withdraw to the back booths to recuperate. Patrons in either state could not remain in the barroom. They were not allowed to put their head down on the bar or to sit at the tables along the wall. Patrons were never objects within the setting. To be in Brown's was to be wholly involved or not to be there at all. Of course, not every patron who did it to death ended up all tore up. Some entered the bar, got heavily involved, and left before they were overwhelmed. Other patrons seemed unable to achieve such results. Still others were incapable of even doing it to death and were always all tore up without appropriate reason. All tore up became a description of involvement and an expression of status. If the words were applied to an individual who had arrived at that point and had conducted himself appropriately, it was an act of praise. When the description was applied to an inappropriate response, it meant failure. In either case all tore up remained the moral consequence of actively partying tough.

Accordingly, to party tough and to do so by doing it to death demonstrated respect for both the bar and those who used it. It was a way of showing one's personal worth within the bar and in the community. By correctly conforming to the norms of behavior, the individual patron said that he was able to meet the requirements, that he was a competent participant, that he was a moral person. Of course, not all those who used Brown's did so appropriately. Some patrons behaved inappropriately because of ignorance, and others, because they were unable or unwilling to act appropriately. There had to exist, therefore, procedures for dealing with violations of the code of conduct. These procedures were not the product of formal rules; they derived their meaning from their continuous interpretation in the context of commonsense decision-making, that is, whether a given act constituted a violation of appropriate behavior varied from situation to situation. Violations of partying tough were fluid occasions: What appeared on one occasion to be a violation would on another occasion be ignored or seen as a moral act. Patrons and staff characterized violations as "messing around too much" and saw them as "going too far" or "talking off the wall shit." Reacting to one situation, a patron remarked: "I ain't gonna take much more from him. Running off at the mouth, talking some kinda shit about how he do this an' that all the time. He's always pushing that shit too far about his cars and his Cadillac." Here the terms *pushing* and *messing* convey the sense of going to excess, of crossing boundaries, of moving outside experience, of breaking frame [Goffman 1974, pp. 274–341]. Violations, then, were actions inappropriate to the developing expectations that accompanied any ongoing conversation.

The violators were expected to correct their actions — except under certain conditions. Offenders and offended individuals took care of their own business unless the offense threatened to overwhelm the ongoing life of Brown's. The task then became one for the barmaid, who was supposed to guarantee that all those present could interact without the fear of being enveloped in chaos. When it was obvious that tough partying was in danger of being upset, she would intercede. The meaning attached to such transgressions was determined by whether the action was considered intentional. If the patron had transgressed unintentionally and might change his behavior if he was told of his offense, then he would be corrected by the barmaid or other patrons without his losing face. If, however, the act was seen as intentional, that is, if the patron knew or had been informed that he was being offensive, then the solution to the problem was a process of control. In either case, as Erving Goffman [1963, p. 216] states: "offenses . . . tell us about the price the offender must pay for his offensiveness, and the price he must pay for his price."

Patrons who erred because they did not know how to behave were

educated as to appropriate conduct. This process depended upon
whether the patron was new to Brown's. If he was, then he was corrected directly, but in a low-keyed way. For example, a new patron
who entered the bar with some regulars began to use obscene language angrily in a conversation. Immediately his friends told him to
cool off because "that kind of talk don't go around here." The offense
was not the words but their use in anger. His immediate response
was deferential: "Sorry 'bout that, didn't mean no offense."

Patrons who knew Brown's were expected to know more about
appropriate behavior and to know better. For them, ignorance or
accidental violation of a rule was no excuse. Thus, their violations
were always treated as intentional. Because these violations were
generally unintentional, redress was ritualized. For example, had a
regular patron been involved in the swearing incident cited above,
he would have been told: "Slow your roll, Brother." Or, if a regular
patron got too far out of hand in rapping with a barmaid, he would
be told: "I don't want to rap." In either case the offense would be announced and minimized at the same time. Thus the barmaid would
exaggeratedly respond too seriously while drawing back her body into a pose of mock anger, or she would speak comically while posing
in a similar manner. Always, however, there was an emphasized
movement away from the offender, as if to ritualize the relationship.
The response of the patron in such a position was always direct: he
apologized and started again. Most of the patrons understood that
the barmaid's actions were not designed to institute any other kind
of interaction; rather, they saw that they were being given a ritualized script through which to reinvest themselves appropriately.

Patrons who violated the moral order because they were all tore
up and unable to control themselves were also considered to be acting intentionally. Regardless of who they were, customers were expected to be capable of controlling themselves or to be cognizant of
their gradual loss of control and exit before problems occurred. This
expectation was in conflict, however, with the practical process of
partying tough by doing it to death. Accordingly, though his actions
were considered intentional, the patron was not initially considered
culpable. Instead, everyone acted as if the offense were unintentional and the patron was offered the ritual escape. If it was obvious
from the response that the patron was unable to "slow his roll," or,
as often occurred, was too "tore up" to recognize the attempted re-
orientation and, for example, treated the response as a challenge to
confrontation, the patron was flagged. *Flagging* was the refusal by
the barmaid to continue serving the patron and a request that the

offender withdraw. Applied to a patron who was all tore up, flagging was, at first, a mild form of refusal and rejection. It was usually
stated as a sincere question. "Don't you think you ought to cool it for
a bit? Why don't you go back to the booths and rest up?" The sincerity of the request did not belie its intent. Any regular patron addressed in this fashion understood what was occurring. Regular
patrons, unwilling to admit the need to withdraw, consistently responded, "You don't think I can hold my liquor," and explained
graphically that they did not allow any woman to talk to *them* that
way and often closed with the phrase "You ain't my mother." Under
such conditions of increasingly serious and hostile interaction, the
patron was flagged out of the bar: "You better get out. You're in too
bad shape to be in here. I'll see you tomorrow." At this point the barmaid closed off her end of the interaction and withdrew socially and
physically from the encounter. Patrons usually attempted to continue the altercation, but they were firmly cut off at every attempt:
"I am not going to rap with you. I asked you to leave, now please
leave."

At this point a third element entered into the proceedings. During
the entire process, the other patrons in the bar were conscious of
and, at times, had a part in the interaction. Their involvement had
been limited to reinforcement of the order implicit in the barmaid's
actions. Her initial attempts at ritualizing the offense and at flagging
the patron were often accompanied by support from the patrons.
This support was usually in the form of counsel to the offender. In
the beginning the advice was a humorously delivered, ritualized signal that an offense had been given, for example, "You better watch
yourself. Harriet's up on you." In the second stage those involved
also attempted to get the offender to withdraw. After the barmaid
had withdrawn from the interaction, the patrons were responsible
for ushering the offender from the bar. They were not expected, nor
would they, throw the offender out. Their consensus was simple:
"You got to be crazy to mess with someone liquored up." The emphasis was on helping the offender withdraw without severe loss of
face. For example, one Saturday a patron who had been flagged was
standing in the center of the patron area, berating the barmaid loudly
and offensively. "You ain't nobody. Telling me I can't drink, who
you think you are. Dumb barmaid telling me what I can and can't
do anyway. I don't need you, and I don't need none of your shit."
Another patron stood at his side, agreeing with him: "You're right.
You don't need this. Come on, we get out of here and go back to
your place, we don't need to drink here. We go anywhere." After

about three minutes of berating the barmaid and receiving support from the other patron, the two left. The second patron returned to the bar about fifteen minutes later, and said to the group as he entered: "I took _____ home, he'll be okay'. He's just celebrating too much." Besides supplying a successful withdrawal from the setting, the helpful patron also furnished a formulaic explanation of the causes for the disturbance — overcelebration. While this act was not required of any particular patron, it was necessary that something like it occur to end the incident. In this way the violator was relieved of responsibility for his actions and was viewed as not culpable. This release freed the bar and the patron from the necessity of reestablishing relations. The patron was assumed to be incapable and was absolved from the necessity of apologizing for his actions. Although apologies were usually tendered, they did not carry any of the loss of status and accompanying embarrassment associated with situations in which individuals were responsible for their acts.

Patrons who deliberately violated the moral order were dealt with more harshly. There was no excuse for their behavior, and therefore their actions were the most dangerous to the continuance of social reality. Their activity was a purposeful affront to order and a direct threat to interaction. Purposeful violators had to be handled quickly and effectively. The solution depended upon the ongoing involvement of the offender. In the previous examples, this fact was of little consequence, since solutions to violations were designed only for the incident at hand. The solution to purposeful offensiveness was banishment from the bar, ostensibly forever. However, if a patron truly did not care, then the threat of banishment and its application were of little consequence. Thus, purposeful transgressors were divided into those who were flagged out and those who were thrown out.

Patrons who were thrown out of Brown's were removed without ceremony. In the entire process of fieldwork, this event occurred only once, and none of the regulars remembered it happening before. Still none thought the act particularly unusual. "Charlie don't have to have people like that if he don't want to. It's his place." The process was relatively simple. A group of unknown patrons had entered the bar and were creating a disturbance. Charlie, who was working the bar that day, asked them to stop bothering people. When they refused, he said: "Okay that's it. You guys leave. I've had it. I don't need trouble and you're it." The men stopped and said: "Come on, man. We're only funning. What's with you. This is a bar, ain't it." Charlie responded: "Unuh, and it's mine and I don't want you in it." After a few angry words they left. Throughout the process, Charlie

was calm and direct. There was no attempt to restructure the men to
the bar's social world. Charlie closed off the bar world and removed
them from it. Moreover, this removal was semipermanent. The next
week two of the group returned, and Charlie refused to let the barmaid serve them. Nearly a month passed before one of those in the
group, who had been persistent about returning to Brown's, was
allowed into the bar.

Because patrons treated Brown's as "their" bar, those who were
flagged permanently were accorded no special privileges when they
were asked to leave. They were given an initial indication, and,
when they failed to respond, they were unceremoniously flagged.
The difference was in the manner in which the flagging was done.
Patrons who were aware that they were out of order and nonetheless
continued in their behavior were not treated politely, as the following incident demonstrates.

Two patrons entered and began to talk with Harriet. One of them
began rapping with her, and for about four minutes the interaction
was fine. Another patron following the proceedings joined the encounter. The first patron told the second: "Hey man, back off, can't
you see I'm talking to the lady." The second replied that he was doing the same and that "nobody had a lock on Harriet's time except
Charlie." The first patron got angry, and, before he could respond,
Harriet said, laughing: "Slow up, fella. Nobody owns me. I talks to
who I want just like I talks to you and him." The patron backed off
but was obviously upset by Harriet's remark. He began to banter
with her again, but there was an introduction of hostility into his
words — so much so that other patrons began to tell him to slow up
and to cool it. He refused to listen and began to step up his remarks.
After about three minutes, Harriet told him very sternly: "I don't
want to rap with you no more. Not till you get some manners." At
this remark, he became more angry, and finally Harriet said: "I ain't
serving you no more. You can just pack up and leave from here. I
had it with you running off at the mouth all the time picking at me. I
want you out. Charlie, get this man out of here. I ain't serving him
long as I'm working here. What I need his shit for. Charlie, you better get him out of here." The patron responded in kind but did not
leave the bar despite general urging. Instead he turned to Charlie
and appealed to him to make Harriet serve him. Charlie responded:
"Look I can't go against her. Why don't you just leave? She ain't
about to serve you, and you gonna look silly just sitting there. Come
on, she's too mad, so you just leave." Harriet added: "I ain't mad.
Dogs is mad. I ain't putting up with his ways no more that's all and

that's final." After receiving no support from the bar, the patron
left.

Though it was explicitly stated that flagging under such conditions was supposed to be final, in practice it was only conditionally
final, and there existed a process of reinstitution for flagged patrons.
The basis of this procedure was renegotiation of the tacit conditions
that permitted orderly interaction. The offending patron through
his actions had violated the moral expectations of the event and had
to demonstrate his willingness to accede to them again.

The process of this negotiation occurred gradually. In the beginning the offending patron attempted to reenter the bar as if nothing
had happened. Such a patron treated his offenses as if he had been
all tore up and therefore neither culpable for his acts nor liable for
loss of face. He entered the bar on his normal schedule and behaved
as if nothing out of the ordinary had happened. Such action served
two purposes. First, it reintroduced the patron into the bar and established the necessity for the patrons to deal with his presence. Second, it signaled the intent of the patron to be a normal participant in
the environment. By behaving as if the offense could be categorized
in an acceptable domain, i.e., being all tore up, the patron attempted
to show that he was aware of what would have been normal behavior
and that he needed to classify himself within that range.

Reclassification was attempted through verbal redefinition of the
offense. In the incident just discussed, for example, the patron returned to the bar the following Tuesday and announced to the bar in
general as he entered: "Well, I'm back. Man, was *I* all *tore up* on
Saturday. Ain't that right, Harriet?" Harriet's response countered
this attempt and placed the patron back on his mark: "You, I told
you I ain't gonna serve you no more so it ain't gonna do you no good
to come around here sucking around after me. *And it ain't* gonna
help you to go following after Charlie, *neither.*" The patron countered by attempting to *sweet talk* himself into Harriet's good graces
and throughout the process maintained his pose as a person who had
been all tore up. She, on the other hand, continued to act as if he
were not present. She stared directly into his face, maintaining eye
contact — an atypical Afro-American social interaction — while verbally announcing that he was not there. During this negotiation session the regulars attempted to aid the offender by acknowledging his
attempt at reclassification and agreeing with his description of what
had happened. This behavior did not reverse Harriet's stand, but it
did serve to tie the offender back in to the world of the bar.

No patron was ever, during my fieldwork, allowed to reenter the

bar on the first try. There was always a second attempt at negotiation. This second stage proceeded much as the first, with one exception. During the second phase the activity of sweet talking became
central. *Sweet talking* was a quasicourtship form of talk in which a
male attempted to dominate a woman through an effective presentation of his worth. Rick described it in these terms: "Well you see she's
got something you want to get. And in order to get her to give it up
you've got to do your thing for her until she's ready. She doesn't have
to do anything unless she wants to so it's up to you to make her want
you bad enough to give it up." In terms of its usage in negotiation,
sweet talking had as its desired end entry back into normal bar relations. In this particular interaction the offender, after being put in
his place for the second time, countered: "Aw, Harriet. You ain't
gonna keep a' going on like this now are you? You know I was being
evil but that ain't no reason to keep at me like this." She answered
him: "I know but you ain't got no cause to be acting all the time like
you do, running off at the mouth." Having succeeded in having his
presence legitimized in the bar, the patron would soon be fully back
in Brown's.

The completion of the final stage depended upon the patron's
ability with words — as did the whole process. The better a patron
was at sweet talking, the quicker he could negotiate. Above all,
however, the patron had to keep the barmaid dealing with him
within this framework. The usual conclusion to the process involved
the barmaid's acknowledgment of return: "God, you're just gonna
worry me to death aren't you, until I give in. What do you want to
drink? You're *worrying* to sweet talk me to death."

This negotiation was a tension between two needs. The bar needed
to have its orderly ways acknowledged and adhered to, and the
patron had to find a way to reenter the situation without a loss of
face. By shifting into sweet talking, the patron fulfilled the requirements of the bar. From his perspective his actions were directed
toward winning over Harriet and in not submitting to her. The bar
received its due in the process, and both needs were satisfied.

Allied to the program was a system of localized characters who
served to relate individuals to events in Brown's. These moral selves
[Goffman, 1959] were not roles in the institutional or social structural sense but rather were the possible ways of dramatizing personal
involvement. In Brown's such selves were the potential ways of fulfilling the slots of patrons and staff. Accordingly, they were not fixed
to any individual throughout his career in the event; they were not
"a set of norms and expectations applied to the incumbent of a par-

ticular position" [Banton, 1965, p. 29], but an identification that arose through interaction and that explained experience both for those who acted them out and for those for whom they were performed.

The first identity was *river rat*. The term was introduced to the setting by Harriet: "Well, you know them kinda women who work down by the riverfront waiting for them sailors who come off the ship after being out for six months. Well a river rat is those guys who can't get no other kind of women." Though its general meaning was pejorative, in Brown's it was inverted. In Brown's, river rat was the highest compliment one could receive. It referred to a patron who was extremely capable of following the program of the bar. A river rat was a patron who was willing to be at center stage and to make the world come alive; he was a total performer involved entirely in his presentation, and through the power of his words he was intent on drawing his audience into similar action. Thus the term was endearingly applied to those regulars who sought to enliven social life. Harriet continued: "You know who I mean. Like Ricky an' Uncle Nick an' them two drunks Jimmy an' his road buddy Walt. All the time comin' in here shoutin' and carryin' on like there weren't no other way to act. They is talkin' sweet one minute an' the next tellin' Charlie how I be talkin' back at them instead of servin' his whiskey. Always causing trouble. River rats. Hee hee hee. River rats. They sure do make a lot of noise though. Better than some of these suckers. Sit here all day an' don't say nothin'." To be a river rat was to be able to use words to dazzle. Such patrons were always talking, anywhere, anytime, affirming with their constant stream that they knew the magic power of words to override and overpower conversation and turn it from mere talk to wit and music and art. River rats were powerful speakers, capable of turning even the most mundane topic into an interesting exchange. They made noise and through their noise brought the best possible "trouble," not the kind that created chaos but the kind that created life. They were *men of words* whose currency was the best spent in the bar [see Abrahams, 1962, 1970a, 1970b, 1970c, 1972b, 1972c; and Firestone, 1964, for further discussions of such performers].

In addition to the river rat, there was the *worrier*. "That man comes in here and he just worries me to death. He's 'Harriet this' and 'Harriet that' and 'Aw come on Harriet' just every minute he's here till I'm about to go crazy." A worrier failed to meet the program, either partially or completely. A worrier's attempts to be a river rat were often unsuccessful. His investments of energy went astray. In-

stead of successful expression arrived at through the manipulation of
the flow of talk and action, he introduced an emotional pitch inappropriate to the event and crossed the border into chaos; he could
not use the potential of chaos as a tool for creativity. Thus, "_____
thinks he can be so *bad*. He'll get a few drinks an' start up and he'll
wanta rap. An' he starts to rappin' and it falls before he can even get
it up. Pretty soon it just turns to off the wall shit and I have to tell
him *I don't wanta rap!*" To call someone a worrier was a way of accounting for a failure to carry out the necessary requirements of
talking shit. To worry was to fail to party tough, to invert its goals,
to dispel the positive drive of talk, and to create in its place "bad
noise."

Though these two dramatic selves were not fixed to any one individual or group, they did tend to divide the patrons on the basis of
age. Those who were river rats tended to be young, between twenty-
five and fifty, and the worriers tended to be over fifty. This should
not be surprising. The involvement expected by the program was
great, and it was difficult for older patrons to give of themselves continuously without succumbing to its inevitable ends. "They don't
have to be acting all the time like Ricky or Uncle Nick. I'm just glad
to see them some mornings to fill up the time." Nonetheless, over the
long run, older patrons were more likely to worry than those more
physically able to cope with the intensity of talking and drinking.
Still, that these dramatic selves were tied more to the flow of interaction than to personalities was shown by their normal use during the
process of greeting. One of the most common greetings to regular
patrons was: "Hey al' you ol' river rat. You planning to worry me today?" Here the incoming patron was confronted with the preferred
style and a challenge to avoid its opposite and disreputable form.
Thereafter, identities were defined only in those situations in which
a patron was at a juncture from which he could move in either direction. At these points, identities were used to call attention to the
state of affairs at the moment. "One minute he's worrying on me and
the next minute he's as smooth and cool as ice. That Richard certainly does know what to say to a woman when he wants to, but if he's a
mind to, he can be as bad as the rest of the fools who come round
here." Thus, a patron was a river rat or a worrier as a result of the
nature of his actions from moment to moment. Though these terms
were often attached to a person on the basis of his past record, they
were used to characterize only present behavior. Every patron at
each moment in Brown's was potentially one or the other — and
might become both if he spent enough time in the bar.

The two dramatic selves discussed so far have been treated as an aspect of the social and moral framework at Brown's. They have been discussed in terms of their place in bar life and their availability for use by anyone present. There was a third social self available in Brown's whose origin and application was decidedly different. Its usage was restricted solely to those women who regularly frequented Brown's. Women who occupied Brown's as a natural environment, including those who worked the bar, were defined as *crazy*: "All the women who come in here are *crazy*. Let me tell you." This idea of *crazy woman* is best understood in terms of the larger areas of behavior defined within the community, house, and street. Each was, at one level, a context for learning to be either male or female and, more specifically, of learning to be male and not-female and female and not-male; each displayed a dominant way of behaving derived from the characteristic foci of its attention, an orientation toward respect or reputation; and, finally, each possessed a particular way of fulfilling its moral requirements. The female role aimed to present an image of personal respect and to create a world of order and control [Wilson, 1970]; the male role was concerned with the display of reputation and power in the street [Abrahams, 1976].

This particular framework provided a way of accounting for the presence of both sexes in the distinctive social worlds. Women in the house were accountable at two levels. They had to be respectable — to deserve respect — and then to act out this respectable self in all of their encounters. Men in the street world had to make and maintain their reputations and then demonstrate this power in the street. Either sex in the opposite world was required only to know how to act appropriately therein. Women did not become masculine or men feminine when they entered the other world. Neither did they act as men or women. Rather they engaged in each other's domain in such a way as to show that they knew the rules and that they would abide by them or not stay. In either world the focus of concern was not on what sex one was but on how one behaved. [See Wilson, 1970; Young, 1969.]

Inevitably there were tensions between the maintenance of one's basic sexual role and the expectations to display oneself appropriately in the house and street. Accordingly, individuals were more comfortable in situations where role and self were in harmony, and the expectations from both were consistent. The shift into a world in which the demands of role were different and, at times, in opposition to the requirements of self forced the individual into the service of two masters and increased the likelihood of failure. Active participation was generally restricted to contexts in which role and self coincided; other situations were treated on a day-to-day basis as areas for passive participation or avoidance.

Crazy women were different. By habitually coming to Brown's Lounge and by actively playing out its program, these women were risking the possibility that they might either fail in Brown's or that their success in Brown's might shame them in the house. Women who used Brown's walked a narrow line where failure *or* success could cause them to be judged negatively. This was even more clear when their participation was viewed in terms of the relations between Brown's and the neighborhood. As a neighborhood bar, acts that occurred inside were public knowledge. A woman acting morally in Brown's ran the risk of having that fact used as a weapon against her outside the bar. Moreover, since the neighborhood was middle class, leaving the bar all tore up placed a woman in the position of denying both her role and self.

As with river rat and worrier, the identity of crazy woman was social, not personal. It, too, was a way of accounting for the presence of women at Brown's. To identify a woman as crazy was to credit her behavior as being correct while acknowledging the vulnerability of her position. Her loss of face was greater if she failed — but final if she were too successful. It was also a form of praise. Those who risked all stood to gain much. To demonstrate competence in both worlds was to establish oneself as a person with power who had acquired much status. Thus, a crazy woman, as one informant said, "takes her chances in taking the weight. But she sure do win a lot if she wins."

Unlike the use of river rat or worrier, a woman who habituated Brown's was always a crazy woman. The term was used in much the same fashion as the other two with its particular inflection and body idiom as the deciding factor in its meaning. When the emphasis was on the first word as in "she's a *crazy* woman," the implications were equivalent to identifying a male patron as a river rat. If the emphasis was on the second, as in "she's a crazy *woman*," then the meaning was that of worrier. Moreover, women were categorized after the fact. The term crazy woman was used as a way of locating a past or upcoming interaction. The introduction of a regular who was a woman into any encounter was met with one of the two uses defined above: "Here comes that *crazy* _____ again," or "that crazy *woman* has got to stop coming in and making trouble." Thus, the use of the term was more fixed and acted as an expectation or a consequence for an entire course through Brown's, not as a characterization of the moment as the terms for male patrons did.

As well as having moral and social dimensions, the dramatic selves also had a spatial orientation. River rats and *crazy* women physically occupied the far end of the barroom nearest the back booths, and worriers and crazy *women* occupied the end nearest the front door. This placement was not absolute, but it was a tendency observed in patron behavior. Those who heated up the environment, who were responsive to and successful in their actions, congregated between the worriers and the back booths. This placement between the more serious patrons and the back allowed river rats and *crazy* women to perform without fearing that their energy might spill out into the street. It also left open the option for safe withdrawal into the back booths when their energy threatened to explode and overwhelm them.

The social selves of river rat, worrier, and crazy woman were adaptations to the ongoing interaction in Brown's. They provided patrons with a way of recognizing and categorizing each other and themselves in the bar. Moreover, they provided a mechanism for establishing appropriate responses. The social selves of river rat, worrier, and crazy woman presented patrons with a set of models for determining how to react to each other's actions and for creating one's own actions. They were ways to discover the central character types, the "moral" men and women, who stood behind expected activity.

This chapter has explored the varieties of potential selves, relations, and moral involvements available to those who frequented Brown's. It has demonstrated that there existed within the ebb and flow of bar life a system of fairly formal relations designed to let anyone using the bar know what should happen, what could happen, and what would happen. The description of this system makes it possible to return to the particular processes of talking shit and to examine how the complex world of Brown's came to be.

6 Styling

The previous chapters have been concerned with establishing the predictable consequences of being a patron of the bar. Being a patron, however, was more problematic than it might appear; in fact, the finality imputed to the world of the bar was much less real and much less available than in the ordinary way of spending ordinary time in the bar. Being in Brown's, after all, involved not only possessing the knowledge necessary to survive but also putting that knowledge into practice. It meant being a participant in an interactive process in which every separable element could be continuously tested, repaired, weakened, strengthened, and even destroyed. Accordingly, no matter what the underlying rules — known or unknown — were, they were relevant only as long as the patrons were prepared to accede to the demands they placed upon each other. When they ceased to support each other, to perform, then their knowledge was worthless. In no sense was their freedom absolute, for they could not wish the world away; but even their limited potential to change in a moment the meaning of the world made what happened in the bar an expression of culture in its most fragile form, its most public circumstances, and its most terrifying complexity.

The most common way of talking shit in Brown's was called *styling*. Styling or "playing with style" referred to any interaction in which those involved sought to "hit on" each other. It was a style of talk in which the participants were constantly searching out each other's utterances in the hopes of discovering some aspect that could be turned around, turned inside out, worked over, and thrown back into the collective flow of talk. In styling patrons talked to each other as if the surface of their exchanges was somehow only a permeable membrane through which any number of alternative, not always pleasant, meanings could be drawn. Styling attacked ordinary conversation at its most fundamental and vulnerable point — its intentionality. Instead of allowing patrons to communicate with each other mechanically and allowing them to believe that their words meant what they said, those involved in styling communicated as if the meaning of any utterance was the use that could be made of it. For those involved, interaction became a relationship in which nothing necessarily meant what it appeared and everything had the potential to acquire another meaning.

Because of this structure of ambiguity, a description of styling inevitably revolved around establishing how such a problematic arrangement was accomplished. What needs to be examined is the relevance of the practical actions of talk to the maintenance and movement of conversation from moment to moment. As such, the analysis makes sense of experience by focusing almost exclusively on the structural links that relate any utterance to those which preceded it and those which followed. In particular, individual strips of conversation will be examined in order to determine the work their components perform and the social meanings that they create. Thus, every interactive component will be initially viewed as doing something in order to convey some message and to create some meaning, that is, a statement or action performed to achieve some end. The meaning that arises as a result of its use constitutes the work it performs in creating and maintaining the pattern of continuous shape underlying social reality. The presence of such "work" in everyday life does not mean that the individual performers were conscious that they were using it to make their world. Usually, they remained, as Max Weber, among others, has noted, "in a state of inarticulate half-consciousness or actual unconsciousness of its subjective meaning" [1954, p. 126]. Still the examination of the work of styling offers a special way into the strategic possibilities that lie behind the surface of daily life. Its patterning, after all, was immediate and thus the only real expression of what talking shit meant most of the time to most of the patrons.

The particular sequence to be discussed is from an interaction of six patrons over forty-five minutes. It opened with Harriet, Gill, Spraggins, Teddy, and me in the bar. Harriet was seated on a stool to the left of the whiskey hutch, Gill was directly across from her, Spraggins immediately next to him, and Teddy and I were several stools to his right. The effect was to create a tight triangular grouping of the three of them, with Teddy and me as observers. This original nucleus was expanded by the arrival of Jimmy Sailor, who initially moved back and forth behind the seated patrons, then sat at the furthest point away from Harriet by the entrance, and, finally, at the end of the sequence, rose and moved slowly toward the back booths and up the back ramp. The result of this staging was to create two triangles. In the first three participants were grouped so that interactions were possible across the bar as well as side to side with no participant in a position to exclude any other. Harriet's individual location, within but set apart by the bar, allowed her to act as a main performer in any relationship, if she so chose. In the second triangle Jimmy placed himself outside the initial core of participants and established in the process both the possibility of wider involvement by all those present and a position in which he could match Harriet's ability to dominate the flow of talk. By being furthest out, he could draw attention to himself in a way that no other patron could. The result was that he and Harriet occupied positions that permitted them maximum possibilities for interaction. Spraggins, the third point in the triangle, occupied the next most effective position, and the rest of us were grouped between them.

The establishment of styling began in an interaction between Spraggins and Harriet, as seen in lines 1–17 below.

(1) H: Was a . . . was a . . . (four-second silence) Jimmy Sailor in here yesterday?

(2) G: I didn't see him.

(3) S: Was Harriet here yesterday?

(4) Huh? *Answer that!*

(5) I'm gonna . . . I'm gonna answer a question with a question. (General laughter)

(6) H: No, I wasn't here.

(7) S: All right then . . . Jimmy Sailor wasn't here either.

(8) G: Now you see . . .

(9) S: He didn't want . . . he didn't want . . .

(10) Gill was here yesterday. *You* think he wanted to see *Gill*.

(11) H: (Laughter)

(12) S: He didn't want to see Gill. *Huh?*

(13) G: He knew you wasn't here . . . why he didn't come.

(14) S: Lord *have mercy*. Unuh. Hee hee.

(15) He wasn't commin'.

(16) He did . . . he did some work *yesterday*. He di . . . he worked yesterday

(17) He took care of some of his area that he was supposed to do.

Preceding the opening line there had been a seven-second silence. Harriet broke in at this point to ask (line 1) if Jimmy Sailor had been in the previous day, Monday, her day off. Spoken in a normal interrogative manner with neither emphasis nor embellishment, she was asking for direct information. The response she drew from Gill (line 2) matched in intent and delivery her question, treating it as a request for information and nothing more. However, any request for personal information carries within it the implication that the questioner has a legitimate right to such information. In asking after Jimmy, Harriet made it clear that she believed that it was appropriate for her to know his whereabouts. Under such conditions, the audience either responds as Gill did or requests proof that the question is legitimate. Spraggins chose neither alternative. Instead of answering her question or challenging her right to the information demanded, he responded ironically (line 3), "Was Harriet here yesterday?" The effect of this unexpected utterance was to question the whole flow of talk. By choosing neither appropriate response, Spraggins asked, in effect, if there were an alternative way of structuring the conversation.

The particular nature of this alternative was indicated by his twist of Harriet's utterance. By answering her with her words, save for the substitution of her name for Jimmy's, Spraggins brought into the conversation a reading of the relationship that legitimized Harriet's question; by implying that his pairing was the cause of Harriet's interest, he effectively forced Harriet to explain her question by defending her right to ask it in the first place.

Spraggins's intention was reinforced by the delivery of the line itself and the rest of his turn at talk. Line 3 was delivered without emphasis and in an interrogatory tone. Stress was placed on "Harriet" and "here" and both received acoustic prominence with "yesterday," which was spoken softer and with less rise in pitch than either preceding term. This faint vocal quality of irony turned into open sarcasm in line 4. The beginning interjection "Huh?" rose very quickly in pitch and loudness ending in a falsetto squeak. This was followed by "answer that," which followed a falling contour of pitch back to Spraggins's natural tone. The ironic quality continued in line 4 but was now accompanied by a lilt of underlying laughter. Harriet acknowledged both features as she brought her torso back and her head up from her knitting and broke into a smile. Line 5, which completed Spraggins's turn at talk, reverted to normal conversational tone, but the undercurrent of laughter in his delivery surfaced. Thus, the second half "a question with a question" was

chuckled rather than spoken. Harriet's response to line 5 was to pass
from a smile to a grin as general laughter ensued and to answer softly and directly without losing the grin, "No, I wasn't here." Spraggins immediately answered in the same manner in line 7, with the
first half "all right then" pitched low with an affirmative tone which
rose over "right" and fell on "then," and this tone was continued in
the second half of the utterance as it affirmed the logic of his coupling
of Harriet and Jimmy.

At this point (line 8), Gill attempted to enter the conversation, but
he was interrupted by Spraggins, who started in directly on Harriet
in line 9: "He didn't want . . . he didn't want" but who shifted to
indirection in line 10 as he returned to irony to make his point: "Gill
was here yesterday. *You* think he wanted to see Gill?" Both lines 9
and 10 were pitched very high and spoken very loudly. Moreover,
stress and vocal prominance were placed on "you" and "Gill" in the
second half of line 10. The effect of this was to drive home the intention of Spraggins's remarks. By introducing "Gill" into the relationship and rhetorically asking Harriet if Jimmy would come to see
him, Spraggins further limited her freedom to respond and accordingly pushed into further prominence the uniqueness of the proffered
tie between Harriet and Jimmy. The effectiveness of this transaction
was indicated by Harriet's extensive laughter, which was redoubled
by Spraggins's repeat of his style in line 12 and redoubled again by
Gill's acknowledgment in line 13: "He knew you wasn't here . . .
why he didn't come."

This first segment was concluded by Spraggins in lines 14–17. Beginning loudly in line 14 with "Lord have mercy" in which the last
two words, even given the established ironic tone, were heavily emphasized, Spraggins declared that Jimmy had used Harriet's absence
to catch up on missed work. However, his presentation dropped off
rapidly in lines 15–17 until, at the end, he directly answered
Harriet's original question.

Spraggins's return to the original mode of interaction left the talk
in flux. Through his verbal posturing, Spraggins had presented the
possibility that the conversation might move beyond ordinary talk,
but all of the work up to this point had been performed by him
alone. Harriet's involvement and Gill's asides had been simply responses to his actions. As yet they had made no attempts to participate except as defendant and cheering section. What was absent in
the conversation, then, was the sense that each member of the group
was prepared to match his intensity, challenge his position, or even
join him in the developing stylization of language.

The movement to a shared system of styling was the central focus
of the second scene (lines 18–51).

(18) H: Wes told him . . . "Sales droppin' off other places . . ."
(19) S: (Laughter)
(20) H: 'Cept Brown's.
(21) G: Wes, hee hee, tol' him that?
(22) H: Wes said: "Man them sales ain't . . . *V. O. ain't doin' too
          hot* down on the other side of Lansdowne Avenue."
(23)   (Group laughter)
(24) S: You don't reckon . . .
(25) H: Say they raisin' hell up here on this side of the street.
(26)   (Group laughter)
(27) S: You don't reckon . . . you don't reckon . . . you don't
          reckon . . . you don't reckon . . . Wes is a little . . . jeal-
          ous, do you Harriet?
(28) H: *I don't know Spraggins* . . . He . . .
(29) S: You don't reckon . . .
(30) H: He sound like . . .
(31) S: I mean I could detect a . . .
(32) H: . . . sound like that.
(33) S: A bit of sarcasm there.
(34) H: I could, too.
(35) S: I believe that.
(36) G: *A whole lot* of it.
(37) H: He say . . . he say: "The sales ain't too hip on the other
          side of Lansdowne Avenue."
(38)   (Group laughter)
(39) H: He said: "But Charlie's spot is raisin' hell!"
(40) S: I swear to God though Jimmy . . . though . . .
(41)   Between Jimmy an' Walt, boy what . . . They, them
          cats . . .
(42)   I mean . . . any day, they might be in, spend two-thirds o'
          the day in here.
(43) H: Yeah.
(44) M: Unuh.
(45) G: *Won't* leave!
(46) S: Hee hee, that's right. (Laughter)
(47) G: Only time Jimmy leave
(48)   Have to pick the wife up . . . boy he hafta go.
(49)   He gotta go then.
(50) S: *Got* to go then

(51) G: Yeah . . . got to go.

(Three-second silence)

The first to announce acceptance of Spraggins's styling was Harriet. Picking up on his verbal initiative, Harriet entered the creative process by stating still another, self-protective characterization of Jimmy's behavior. She began by establishing her own place in the conversation through the introduction of Wes as a character. He was known to be her special friend and his presence in the conversation as a commentator on Jimmy's behavior — "Wes tol' him . . . 'sales droppin' off other places' " — allowed Harriet to indicate that she was already involved and that Jimmy's interest was one-sided and out of proportion. This identification of Jimmy's behavior was greeted by approving laughter from Spraggins, which interrupted Harriet, and she had to pause before finishing her statement. Gill's response (line 21) was still straightforward and direct and focused solely on the accuracy of her assertion: "Wes . . . tol' him that?" Having established her conversational direction, Harriet moved fully into styling by introducing vocal characterization. Throughout the interaction until this point both Harriet and Spraggins had been reporting their own words. In line 22 this pattern changed, as the previously introduced Wes began to report his own words in his own voice. This speech was, of course, not oracular. Rather, it was Harriet's embodiment of Wes as a present member of the conversation.

Having introduced the voice "Wes said," Harriet then deepened her pitch and spoke the rest of the utterance in a lower "masculine" tone, forcefully punctuating the phrase "V. O. ain't doin' too hot" with clipped assertiveness. To emphasize her words further she set her knitting needles down on her lap and marked each part of the phrase with a bobbing index finger, indicating that it was Wes and not she who was speaking. Once completed, this characterization was dropped, and in line 25 Harriet reverted back to her own speaking voice, only now marking her lines, as much of Spraggins's speech had been, by an underlying vocal quality of laughter that finally generalized to the whole group expression in line 26.

Having accepted the new order of interaction, Harriet, Gill, and Spraggins discussed the meaning of Wes's words in lines 27–36, focusing on the emotional quality of Wes's words. Thus, in line 27, Spraggins once again ironically colored his delivery of "You don' reckon Wes is a little . . . jealous do you Harriet?" by exaggerating more than necessary the pause between "little" and "jealous," by using a rise in pitch over "little" that forced attention on what fol-

lowed, and finally by stressing and drawing out "jealous," as if to
store all possible meaning in the word. Harriet matched this irony in
her "I don't know Spraggins" and reinforced its effect by laughing
through, "He sound like . . . he sound like that" (lines 30 and 32),
which was affirmed by all participants in lines 33–36. Line 36
marked the entrance of Gill into participation in the evolving styling, since he, too, exaggerated his speaking style to match that apparent in the verbal transactions of Harriet and Spraggins. The
beginning portion "A whole lot" was emphatically stressed. It was
spoken with "A" lengthened and rising in pitch and "whole" and
"lot" following the pattern. The "o" in "whole" and "lot" were
sounded so that they came across as the fullest and most prominent
sound in each. The segment concluded, as it had begun, with Harriet marking her full participation (lines 37 and 39) through repeated use of the characterization of Wes as speaker.

This focus on a humorously ironic structure of conversation carried over into the discussion between Gill and Spraggins in lines
40–61. In this sequence the two expanded the image of Jimmy being
created by describing his attachment to the bar and to his partner,
Walt (lines 40–51), and then by elaborating a capsule description of
Walt (lines 52–61), which by association also defined Jimmy. This
sequence balanced precariously between the established styling
mode and the less demanding directness, which had characterized
the beginning of the conversation. For example, line 40 was spoken
laughingly as were line 41 and the beginning of line 42. Thus the
phrase "I mean . . . any day" was constructed so as to focus on the
emphatic delivery of the final segment. This was signaled by a pause
after "I mean" and the final "any day." They were clearly laughed.
Yet, the last part of the same utterance—"two thirds o' the day in
here"—was a simple presentation of facts, which brought forth only
factual audience responses in lines 43 and 44.

The flux between two modes continued, and in line 45 Gill indicated again the mixed tone of the conversation as he began his turn
at talk. His "Won't leave!" with an emphatic stress on "Won't"
marked a transition of conversational control to him; like Spraggins,
he began with an exaggerated delivery of his idea, "He hafta go,"
which was then re-expressed in lines 47–49, affirmed by Spraggins
in line 50, and repeated once more by Gill in line 51. However, none
of these repetitions was intensified in any way. Each was spoken
matter-of-factly and with little emphasis.

At this point there was a three-second silence. The problem facing
the group was in part where to go with the conversation. Everyone

had acknowledged a desire to style, but none had supplied any new material with which to engage the process. Entropy was building in the flow of conversation, and all concerned were faced either with finding a new subject to style or with shifting back into ordinary talk. Initially, therefore, two operations had to be performed. First, the willingness of all to continue styling had to be established and, second, a topic had to be established that would permit it to continue. This process of determination was begun by Gill (line 52,) but was soon transformed into an entirely different situation by the arrival of Jimmy Sailor himself.

(52) G: See Walt talk mo::re *sh::it.*

(53) S: That Walt . . . that Walt, *boy!*

(54)   That Walt run his mouth.

(55) G: He *swear* he done had Harriet in the bed already.

(56)   Dreamin' about it.

(57) S: (Laughter)

(58) H: Unuh.

(59) S: Hee hee, he got, look it . . .

(60)   He ain't got his marbles.

(61)   That cat . . . that cat somethin else, boy.

(62) H: Wes say: "Man, I'm gonna send me a anonymous letter to the house of *Seagrams*."

(63) G: Here come Sailor *right now.* (Loud group laughter. Door opens, and Jimmy Sailor enters the main barroom.)

(64) H: (Very loudly and in falsetto) *They were talkin' 'bout you!*

(65)   *They were talkin' 'bout you!*

(66) S: He was standin' . . . he was standin' out there eavesdroppin' . . .

(67) J: Hey, Spraggins.

(68) S: Hey, how you doin'.

(69)   Standin' out there *eavesdroppin'!*

(70) J: I heard you . . . *I heard you!*

(71) H: I jus' *ask. Was* you in here?

(72) G: You jus' walk right in the door.

(73) J: I was listenin' at the window.

(74)   (Group laughter)

(75) H: *You wasn't* listenin' at *nothin'!!*

(76) J: An' I ain't had a thing to drink either.

(77)   So I *heard* you. Hee hee.

(78) G: You don't need nothin', *boy.*

(79) S: (Loud laughter — six seconds) A . . . A . . .

(80) H: I tol' "Wes say you . . ."

(81) J: What you people talkin' 'bout me?

(82) H: Say I tol' Wes bout . . . Wes say:

(83) "Your bidness was pickin' up down on . . . up here . . ."

(84) J: What he *say!*

(85) H: "Fallin' off on the other side o' Lansdowne Avenue."

(86) S: Som'body . . . som'body (three seconds) jus' say . . . say, say was Jimmy . . . Jimmy Sailor in here yesterday?

(87) I said: "Was *Harriet* on yesterday?"

(88) (Loud group laughter. Harriet, Jimmy, and Spraggins predominate.)

(89) J: *Boy*, don't start tha::t *shit?*

(90) Jes::us Chr::ist.

(91) G: Where's your Road Buddy?

(92) S: Hey, you among friends.

(93) J: Hunh?

(94) S: You among friends.

(95) G: Where's your road buddy?

(96) J: Unuh. The madman gets up late, man.

(97) I been up since . . . 8 o'clock . . .

(98) *Watusi Drink* . . . try a Watusi.

(99) S: (Laughter)

(100) G: Oh boy.

(101) J: It's a bad dri::nk.

(102) G: Yeah?

(103) M: They invented another one to kill us.

(104) J: Huhn. *Bad.*

(105) Hey, Gill. (Slaps Gill on the back three times)

(106) G: Now *don't* speak to me no more.

(107) Spoke twice already.

(108) J: (Facing Harriet) I see you without your head gas too, huh.

(109) H: Unuh. I was tired a be . . . tired a bein' . . . *Afro* . . . with that.

(110) G: That's a hurtin' thing you say.

(111) H: (Softly) You don't like it, I know somebody that like it.

(112) J: I know that. (Turning to Spraggins)

(113) I saw your truck there yesterday, *Nigger*, when I went to pass.

(114) S: Where? Where? Oh wow, look here. Now wait a minute . . . Now.

(115) J: You were pulled all the way up on the corner right here.

(116) T: *Right.*

(117) S: Oh, I was deliverin'.
(118) J: I saw you.
(119) S: An' what happen . . . Let me explain somethin . . .
(120) T: Turn it around right in the middle of the street.
(121) J: Damn motor runnin' . . . Damn motor runnin' . . . no-
           body in the truck.
(122) S: Wait a minute. Wait a minute, now . . .
(123)   I'll tell you what happened, see . . .
(124)   I ran out, see, that's why I had to make the second trip
           back.
(125)   Now, see, I came back to give my friend Gill a play also.
(126) G: *Bullshit!*
(127)   (Laughter, Jimmy prominent)
(128) S: Oh wow.

The search for a new topic was begun by Gill. The content of line
52 ("See Walt talk mo::re sh::it") made little sense given the flow of
talk up to that point. It was more sensible when one knew that Walt
was Jimmy's main friend but still it seemed only minimally related
to what had transpired thus far. Seen, however, as an attempt to
bridge the breakdown in conversation the utterance fits quite neatly.
Picking up on an adjunctive figure passingly mentioned by Spraggins in his description of Jimmy, Gill used that figure to express in
the styling mode a new potential direction for the conversation. This
desire was evidenced most directly in the delivery of the utterance.
Up to this point Gill had been relatively quiet as a performer. But in
this utterance he deliberately attempted to develop a vocal quality
of intense humor. Thus, in the phrase "more shit" both words were
drawn out and spoken loudly. The stress was on the first half of each
word, and this stress was transformed into a rise in pitch to a high
whine in the second half of each word. Following directly on Gill's
statement, Spraggins matched Gill's use of loudness and pitch to
flesh out ". . . that Walt, *boy*" and "That Walt run his mouth" (lines
53 and 54), and the two of them then began to style with this new
topic. Thus Spraggins began to work on Walt (line 59), laughing out
the initial phrase "he got, look it." The second "he got" continued as
an extended chuckle but "look it" was said directly. This tone of expression was repeated in line 60 with "he ain't got" receiving central
stress and similar acoustic prominence. Again, the second half was
spoken directly and without emphasis. This pattern held for "that
cat" in line 61. Like Gill, Spraggins signaled that it was the styling,
not the topic, that should be maintained.

This pattern was continued by Harriet in line 62 ("Wes said 'Man I'm gonna send me a anonymous letter to the house of Seagrams' "), who continued as she had before to speak in dialogue but with no humorous coloration to her utterance; she, too, delivered a dual message by speaking through a character. In her case she chose to signal acceptance of the topic with no unnecessary ties to speaking about Jimmy. I also speculate that without the arrival of Jimmy a shift in conversational focus would have followed. Each active participant had signaled allegiance to styling, but none had demonstrated overt concern with the particular content of performance.

The arrival of Jimmy (line 63) marked the transition into the second episode of the performance. His presence fueled the existing topic by providing a target for group focus. Before this could begin, however, it was necessary that Jimmy be informed of the level at which conversation was proceeding. This process of negotiating Jimmy into social life (lines 64–109) was done through a series of individual transactions with each announced performer. With each Jimmy needed to establish contact, discover the person's particular involvement, and define his appropriate response.

Jimmy was introduced to the mode of behavior by Harriet (lines 64 and 65). As he entered, Harriet, who had risen to her feet during line 63, in anticipation of serving a new patron, called out very loudly and in a sing-song taunt, as Jimmy came through the door, "*They were talkin' 'bout you.*" The stress in the utterance was on "they" and "talkin' 'bout." This prominence of the first and third terms was accentuated by the rhythmic delivery of the statement. "They" was pitched almost falsetto while "were" dropped below Harriet's normal conversational tone, creating an up-then-down roller coaster of words. This was almost exactly repeated in line 65, only louder and with more melodic contour. Jimmy's response to this opening announcement was to smile broadly and nod while removing his coat.

Harriet's announcement was immediately reinforced by Spraggins in line 66. His first "He was standin' " was spoken directly but rose in pitch and loudness at the end. This was repeated more affirmatively: "He was standin' out there eavesdroppin'." At this point, Jimmy, recognizing who was speaking, greeted Spraggins, who returned the greeting (lines 67 and 68). The obligatory greeting complete, Spraggins again repeated his idea by using the now standard humorous undertone and ironic emphasis on "eaves*drop*pin'."

Jimmy responded to this two-pronged assault by Harriet and Spraggins in line 70: "I heard you . . . *I heard you!*" The first segment of the utterance established contact with the flow of conversation. It was spoken matter-of-factly and with no emphasis. The second portion of the utterance acknowledged Jimmy's recognition of the tone of the talk. It began with "I" pitched high and then dropped off rapidly through "heard" and "you," so that the phrase was marked by a falling contour. This was accompanied by an increase in volume and a movement to laughter underlying the overall expression. The contrast between the two statements indicated Jimmy's acceptance of the need to style and, as well, allowed him to sidestep the disadvantage under which he was operating. Having been absent from the previous conversation, Jimmy had no knowledge of what had been said. By claiming the opposite, he neutralized the power of their words. Since he "knew" what had transpired, he could not be controlled by those with greater knowledge. By manipulating the tone of talk and meeting exaggerated speech with exaggerated speech, he shifted the burden of ignorance to Harriet and Spraggins. In claiming to know what they said and how they said it, Jimmy subordinated their ability to speak about him with his own ability to speak on them and on what they had said. Whereas Harriet and Spraggins could only discuss what had been said, Jimmy could question if it ought to have been said.

This attempt to establish conversational parity was continued in line 73. The laughter it generated was an acknowledgment of its aptness, but once again Jimmy's attempt was squelched first by Harriet's playfully scornful rebuke in line 75: "You wasn't listenin' at nothin'." Jimmy continued his line of attack in lines 76 and 77, but he was unable to keep from breaking up into laughter at his hopeless position. His increased vulnerability was particularly obvious in his statement "What you people talkin' 'bout me" in line 82. Despite its laughing delivery it was still a request for needed information. Having lost his gambit, Jimmy had then to seek other means to establish equality with the group.

This was accomplished through a recapitulation in lines 82–88, in which Harriet and Spraggins recreated and re-enacted their individual vignettes for Jimmy. Both acted as they had previously, indicating not only the content but also the stylistic features of their actions. Jimmy's response to this catalogue, once he had shown his appreciation for the wit in both (line 88), was to acknowledge the acceptability of both in lines 89 and 90. His "Boy, don't start that shit" and "Jesus Christ" were styled to convey not threats but a laughing involvement in what had happened.

Lines 91–104 marked a transition in the conversation. Their intent was to further establish Jimmy within the already developed flow of talk. The conversation began in line 91 with Gill's question on Walt's whereabouts and moved without any seeming continuity to Jimmy's commentary on the new drink he was advertising. These comments were transitional because they literally served to move Jimmy from one end of the barroom to the other, from where he entered to where the central performers were seated. What was spoken, therefore, was much less important than the fact that it was spoken. Addressed to the developing relationship rather than a particular individual, Gill's talk served to maintain contact until real conversation could resume.

Having reached the end of the bar where the others were seated, Jimmy now began actively to enter into the conversation. Until now he had simply responded to things said. Starting with line 105, he began to generate his own topics and involvement. His first target was Gill. Jimmy's "Hey Gill" (line 105) was accompanied by loudly slapping three times on Gill's back, and it was the slaps rather than the words that signaled Jimmy's attempt to initiate a styling transaction with Gill. They were exaggerated actions whose friendliness was so perfectly executed that they parodied all pretense of true meaning. Gill turned aside Jimmy's parry in lines 106 and 107 and rejected the gambit by allotting Jimmy a number of times to speak to him and by stating that Jimmy had exceeded his limit: "Don't speak to me no more. Spoke twice already." The delivery of the lines was direct and final and left Jimmy no opening to continue.

Turned aside by Gill, Jimmy cracked on Harriet next (line 108), "I see you without your head gas too, huh?" referring to the fact that she was wearing a different wig from her usual Afro style. Spoken directly and matter-of-factly until the final "huh," which was delivered much louder and with a rising ironic pitch, this questioning tone contrasted to the direct statement preceding it and reinforced the "fighting" content of the commentary on her appearance. Like Gill, Harriet turned aside Jimmy's attempt to rap by ignoring his challenge and answered very directly: "Unuh, I was tired a be . . . tired a bein' . . . *Afro* . . . with that." Her straightforward admission that she had tired of an Afro style silenced the bar for five seconds and the implication was sufficient to remove all possibility of Jimmy rapping with Harriet about her statement. Gill indirectly in line 110 pointed out sincerely the problems in what she said, but Harriet defended her actions, "You don't like it, I know somebody that like it," thus announcing also indirectly that she made the change because Wes wanted it. Jimmy concurs with the reasons and ends the exchange in line 112 by defending her: "I know that."

Jimmy now turned to Spraggins, his last hope, and cracked on him (line 113), "I saw your truck there yesterday, *Nigger*, when I went to pass." Again, the utterance was a spoken challenge. However, unlike the other two, Spraggins did not succeed in deferring the thrust of Jimmy's remark. His response (line 114) was momentary confusion, and Jimmy seized the conversational opening to establish himself in a rap. His attack continued in line 115 as he began to lay out the point he wished to make — "You were pulled all the way up on the corner right here." Spraggins continued to attempt to get a word in by way of explanation in line 117, but he was overridden by Jimmy's laughing accusation in line 118, "I saw you." Lines 119, 120, and 121 all occurred at nearly the same time. Teddy, who had acted as an affirmative chorus to Jimmy's initial statement in line 116, introduced his own description of Spraggins's parking habits in line 120. Spraggins, intent on explaining himself out of the trap he had been pushed into, was still requesting permission to talk: "An' what happen . . . let me explain somethin' " (line 119), when Jimmy, in the midst of this cacophony, finished his point of attack — "Damn motor runnin' . . . damn motor runnin' . . . nobody in the truck" — in a voice louder than the other two and using a laughing, accusatory quality to his speech.

Spraggins, who had been recycling his speech until a break in the rap occurred, now took center stage in an attempt to defend his actions. Justifying his leaving the truck empty with the motor running in order to come to the bar and "give my friend Gill a play also," that is, to buy Gill a drink, Spraggins sought to counter Jimmy's assertion with an appeal to Gill for help, but, even as he spoke, he denied his own statement by quietly laughing. His failure to counter was further amplified by Gill, who rejected his action with a deadpan "*Bullshit*" in which the "Bull" was clearly and stressfully emphasized and the "shit" clipped short. The result was a vocal quality of finality and absurdity, which brought everyone to laughter and left Spraggins only able to sum up his loss, "oh wow" (line 128). At this point, there was a six-second silence in which Jimmy moved past Spraggins toward the front door, stopping at the center of the bar. Here he turned his attention on Harriet, directly rapping with her.

Breaking with the flow of analysis for a moment, I would like to draw some initial general conclusions as to the nature of styling in the bar. Styling in Brown's was essentially a humorous system of social interaction in which the focus of conversation was on the development of the social ambiguities of ordinary talk into full-fledged attacks on the solid structure of meaning. For example, this episode began when Spraggins "opened up" Harriet's chance question on Jimmy's whereabouts the previous day and used several of its potential meanings to undercut the simplicity of her request. In so doing, he turned it into a multivocal statement which she had not intended and over which she had no control. Having thus freed her language, he was able to continue translating and transforming her speech until it was not only full of hidden meanings, unexpected meanings, and threatened meanings, but it was also able to deny her the right to speak. Thus she responded initially with laughter and later with another's words and voice. Likewise, when Gill entered into the styling or when Jimmy announced his intention to style by systematically engaging each participant in a similar exchange, each burlesqued the playability of conversation by rendering unordinary the serious intentions of their utterances.

This exaggeration and amplification of the ordinary was accomplished through the use of a laughing or chuckling style of delivery that acted to deny the consequential sense of any utterance and to display instead its emotive and playful qualities. Thus, at some point in nearly every turn at talk there was a breakthrough into laughter which belied the seriousness of the attacks and threats contained in individual utterances. All involved laughed their lines, even when they were attempting to speak seriously, and the result was a chain reaction in which the joking aspect of any message was the one most recognizable and most available to the next speaker. Overall, then, the style of delivery combined with the ever-building exaggeration of the interaction to produce a discourse in which the "true" meaning of any text was defined solely by the abilities of the various speakers to make it mean something in its particular context. No text held fast to its sense because any text could be rewritten, laughed away, exaggerated, overstated, understated, or played until it was countered with another equally free utterance.

This aspect of styling was particularly evident in the use of dramatization by participants to convey their stances and intentions. In the episodes examined, a concentration of real and imaginary characters and events and narratives was used to undercut the ordinary expectations of talk, particularly through the invention of alternative fictional relations in progress between patrons. By creating other equally valid realities, Harriet, Jimmy, Gill, and Spraggins

were all constructing loosely formed fictionalizations of their own
and everyone else's selves that challenged the singular identities each
desired to possess. Potentially unsure who was who, who said what,
who did what, and who held power, they parodied themselves and
each other in an attempt to prevent the ground of interaction from
sliding out from under them. The result was an ever-increasing
geometry of social relations echoing in the multivocality of its every
action the serious question "Is this play?"

These features can be seen more clearly still in the progress of this
interactive sequence through the next episode in lines 129–232.

(Six-second silence)

(129) J: That Wes done really put you through *a change.*
(130)   Got you knittin' . . . sh::it.
(131)   (Group laughter)
(132) H: Wes ain't put me through nothin'.
(133) J: Made you process your hair.
(134) G: No, somethin' else will put somethin' through somethin'.
(135) S: (Laughter)
(136) J: Buy a knittin' kit.
(137) S: (Louder laughter)
(138) J: Hey, was Clark in yet?
(139) G: Yeah. He gone.
(140) H: He meant that shit 'bout not feedin' me on Wednesday.
(141) J: Oh yeah, *oh yeah.*
(142)   Wes told me: "Don't bring my girl no more *God damn*
             platters."
(143)   (Group laughter)
(144) H: He ain't tell you no such *lie!*
(145) J: He said: "Cause she ain't got no teeth to eat 'm you keep
             bringin' 'm."
(146) H: (Loud, high laughter — eight seconds)
(147) H: Jimmy, you gonna stop *lyin'*, Jimmy.
(148) J: That's what Wes tol' me.
(149)   (Group laughter)
(150)   Wes stopped me outside, you know . . .
(151)   I said: "Long as you don't mean my motherfuckin' teeth."
(152)   (Group laughter)
(153) H: *He ain't told you nothin'.*
(154) J: He say: (one-second pause)
(155)   "Jimmy, I'm not lyin'

(156)   That's my woman an' I don't want you to be feedin' her.

(157)   If I want her to eat I'd bring *her* own motherfuckin' food."

(158)   He said: "Now you keep the shit up . . .

(159)   Next time you see her, you won't recognize her.

(160)   You have to bring her some *soup* (Laughter) an' some straws."

(161) S: She mean . . . she be drinkin' turkey an' . . .

(162) J: Right.

(163) S: . . . an' cake an' all that stuff through a straw.

(164) J: I said: "Right Wes," I said.

(165)   He said: "Understand?"

(166) H: He lyin' . . . Jimmy lyin' . . .

(167)   Wes don't even talk like that.

(168) G: She'll hafta sip her Campbell soup, huh.

(169) J: He said . . . he said: "You understand where I'm comin' from."

(170)   (Mock humble) "A yes sir, Mr. Wes." (four-second pause) "Very sorry I been feedin' your woman."

(171) G: Now Harriet gonna give *'m up, O.K.?*

(172) H: I wasn't gettin ready to.

(173) M: He'll be comin' through the door.

(174) J: Oh, he'll be in.

(175)   *He'll be in shortly.*

(176)   He gonna walk in here with a bowl of soup.

(177)   Bus' Harriet in the mouth (Hits palm with fist, loudly)

(178)   (Group laughter)

(179) M: I brought you lunch . . . here

(180) J: Yea::h, bus' her dea::d in the chops.

(181)   (Softly) Wouldn't that be dirty?

(182) S: (Laughter)

(183) J: (Turning to Teddy) Sittin' up in that chair grittin'

(184)   You scared to laugh.

(185)   Harriet's scared . . . scared your ass so bad last week . . . Shit . . .

(186)   Gorilla-in' people las' week.
         (Three-second silence)

(187) H: Evidently I didn't gorilla you enough.

(188)   Got . . . You got *a* lot of *loose* lip this morning.

(189) T: Give 'm some Kay*opect*ate!

(190) S: See . . .

(191)   See I'm tell you somethin'.
(192)   See Wes s . . .
(193) H: *I'm starvin'.*
(194) S: See Jimmy don't talk too plain.
(195)   He didn't mean gorilla, he mean guru.
(196)   (Group laughter)
(197) J: You know . . . you need to bring some ham an' eggs . . .
             an' put 'm in the box upstairs.
(198) H: I leave too late in the mornin'
(199) J: *Too late.*
(200)   *Damn* . . . you get here at 8 o'clock in the mornin'.
(201) H: I be tryin' to . . . I be rushin . . .
(202) J: *Bring a lunch pail.*
(203)   Like them people who work on the railroad . . . *Shit.*
(204)   Hee, hee, ha . . . Pick up a lunch pail with coffee in it
             . . . Baloney an' cheese an' an apple.
(205) H: (softly) I don't like baloney an' cheese.
(206) G: We got the coffee.
             (Four-second silence)
(207) J: Yeah, fix me a cup, Harriet.
(208) H: I *wish to hell* I would.
(209) S: Whole two pounds of Maxwell House.
(210) H: I wish to hell I would (softly) fix *you* some coffee.
(211) J: (Turning to Teddy). You gonna let her talk to me like that.
(212)   I'm talki::n to you, Nigger.
(213) T: Well (two-second pause) let me put it this way.
(214)   (Group laughter)
(215) M: Teddy learned his lesson a long time ago.
(216) J: *Yeah. No lie.*
(217)   Las' week, Harriet gorilla-ed that little . . .
(218)   Look, said "Look Motherfucker, when I tell you somethin'
             I means it."
(219) H: I didn't do that . . .
(220) J: Teddy said: "Now Harriet . . ."
(221) H: I did not do . . .
(222) J: He said . . . he said: "You dumb ass *barmaid.*"
(223)   (Group laughter)
(224)   An' *boy* when he say that, boy . . .
(225)   He said "dumb broad barmaid . . ."
(226)   An' she went of::f.
(227)   (Group laughter)
(228)   Boy, she sit over . . . an' she sat there . . .

(229)   . . . Hi Earl . . .
(230)   An' stared at Teddy so hard Teddy's eyes almost
                  started bleedin'.
(231)   Look like daggers was goin' in.
(232) T: Why you hafta lie?

The development of this scene began with Jimmy's refocusing of
the conversation in lines 129–39. Finished with Spraggins, but still
in control, Jimmy turned again to Harriet and began anew to rap on
her. In a mock accusatory manner, characteristic of rapping with
the barmaid, he started: "That Wes done really put you through a
change. Got you knittin' . . . Shit." The utterance was spoken without any noticeable stylistic indicators until "Shit" which was drawn
out such that the "sh" and the "it" were especially emphasized and
lengthened. The attack drew laughter from those others present, but
Harriet responded directly in line 132, "Wes ain't put me through
nothin'," stressing heavily "nothin' " in order to rebuke directly the
attack and scorn of Jimmy's "Shit." The conversational flow became
increasingly open as Gill rewrote Harriet's statement in line 134,
giving it a sexual tinge by trebling "somethin" against her emphatic
"nothin'." This drew Spraggins's laughter, and Jimmy, again with
mock scorn, repeated "Buy a knittin' kit." Since Harriet had said
nothing after her direct response, this attempted opening to a rap
failed, and four seconds of silence ensued, which Jimmy broke finally by asking a direct question concerning Rick Clark, which Gill answered.

Line 140 began a new focus of talk. Harriet, continuing seriously,
said to Jimmy: "He meant that shit 'bout not feedin' me on Wednesday." Jimmy responded in two parts. The first "Oh yeah" was
spoken directly and merely acknowledged Harriet's commentary.
The second *"oh yeah"* acted as an introduction to an extended rap.
Uttered loudly and with an exaggerated affirmative tone, the "oh"
was pitched high, and it rose further in "yeah." Moreover, the "ea"
was lengthened so that the rising contour created the image of increasing knowledge on Jimmy's part as he remembered.

Having established himself as the central speaker and indicated
that he still intended to style, Jimmy started to rap in line 142. His
approach was not to report but again to characterize Wes's words.
He began with "Wes told me" and then shifted to a different voice
for the utterance: "Don't bring my girl no more *God damn* platters."
In this segment the individual words were clipped short and pitched
well below Jimmy's normal voice. There was a brusqueness in their

delivery as if they were harshly spoken. This utterance was met by
general laughter, including from Harriet who, still laughing, responded, "He ain't tell you no such lie." Jimmy finished " 'cause she
ain't got no teeth to eat 'm you keep bringin' 'em" in the same voice,
and the group laughter continued with Harriet's overwhelming all
others. Her laughter rose rapidly until it was just an extremely high
whine. She then attacked (line 147), informing Jimmy that he had
better stop lying. He responded softly and with a mildly offended
but serious "truthfulness": "That's what Wes tol' me," which so contrasted with her laughing denial that once more there was general
laughter in support of his, rather than her, description.

Buoyed by this acceptance, Jimmy continued this line of talk in
lines 150 and 151: "Wes stopped me outside, you know. I said: 'Long
as you don't mean my motherfuckin' teeth.' " The expansion of his
description was once more done in character and drew the same results, group laughter and a loud accusatory denial from Harriet —
"He ain't told you nothin'." Harriet's statement was designed to deny
Jimmy's words, but it was too emotional and created instead the
idea that there must be some truth in his statements. Moreover, her
anger only served to increase Jimmy's control over the flow of conversation.

This control was evident in lines 154–70. Having briefly outlined
the basics of his conversation with Wes, Jimmy expanded this sim-
plified characterization into an actual dramatization. He set off his
first piece (line 154) by beginning "he say" and then pausing for one
second. When he began again in line 154, he was attempting to
replicate humorously "exactly" what Wes said. Lines 155–59 were
delivered as if he were playing. Jimmy used no emotive emphasis
whatsoever as he "conveyed" the threatening nature of Wes's supposed comment, beginning with an admonition to treat what followed as truth: "I'm not lyin"; it defined Harriet, "That's my
woman," and ended with a statement of who, and only who, can
feed her: "If I want her to eat I'd bring her own motherfuckin'
food." The second half of the turn at talk took the statement of line
145 and expanded this by detailing the only kind of food she would
be able to eat: "You have to bring her some soup . . . an' some
straws." The emphasis in this last line broke slightly his intent to
convey the seriousness of the words "spoken" by Wes. Both "soup"
and "straws" were spoken louder than the rest of the phrase, and
both slipped into laughter. The problem, of course, was that Jimmy's
dramatic intention was an attempt at straight reporting while his
goal was styling and, thus, the message of his style denied the mes-

sage of his text. The result was a constant tension between the two, which ended with him laughing at his own performance.

This tension between text and delivery appeared again in lines 161 and 163, when Spraggins questioned Jimmy on what Wes said. Attempting to validate Jimmy's words by surrounding them with a further aura of seriousness, he repeated Jimmy's assertions as rhetorical statements, which presumed Wes's involvement, and questioned only the manner in which he spoke. But, as with Jimmy, Spraggins was unable to contain his laughter, and his repetition of Jimmy's idea was underlaid with chuckling throughout.

Jimmy then (lines 164, 165, 169, and 170) explained his own participation in the interaction with Wes, but his "right Wes" (line 164) was a little too humble and his statement of Wes's "Understand?" (line 165) a little too serious. In line 166 Harriet again attempted to counter Jimmy's rap, but she was submerged by background laughter and Gill's "She'll hafta sip her Campbell soup, huh?" which freed Jimmy to conclude the drama in lines 169 and 170. Speaking his own words, he colored them in such a way as to signal distinctively his awareness of the manipulation inherent in his performance. In line 169 he repeated Wes's final injunction in more detail and then performed his "answer": "A yes sir, Mr. Wes . . . very sorry I been feedin' your woman." The delivery of this line was a parody of the shuffling stereotype of the black man. The "A yes sir, Mr. Wes" was slurred, and the "Mr." was heavily emphasized. This was followed by a humble and soft-spoken repentance for his misdeed. The effect of this pose was a great deal of laughter. This group laughter included Harriet, who was caught up in the folly of the performance.

Momentarily finished with his rap, Jimmy relinquished control of the conversation. In line 171 Gill, still pretending to treat Jimmy's words as serious, cautioned Harriet to give up Wes by implying that he was too dangerous. Her answer ("I wasn't getting ready to") was an attempt to regain control over this rap on her man by denying any validity to what had been said and, accordingly, any effect it might have on her. In line 173 I commented laughingly that Wes may soon enter, and Jimmy followed out its implications in lines 171–81. Again he began with a statement "Oh he'll be in" spoken directly and then followed with an exaggerated and humorously distorted repetition of the line: "He'll be in shortly." This focusing technique drew group attention to his next utterance. Jimmy then announced: "He gonna walk in here with a bowl of soup . . . bus' Harriet in the mouth!" He accompanied the statement by an exaggerated punch of his fist into his palm and a cackling laugh into which all but Harriet joined. I interjected, with half-humorous and half-serious intensity, my own rewrite of his original words, and he concluded in line 180: "Ye::ah bus' her dea::d in the chops." The entire line was spoken loudly and high pitched. The "Yeah" was extremely noticeable and was lengthened considerably as was "dead." Yet, even as he delivered his idea, he seemed to withdraw into his own thoughts to contemplate the image he had created, and, by line 181, when softly and almost to himself he said as he nodded his head, "Wouldn't that be dirty," Jimmy had fallen out of styling into a private world. This juncture was punctuated after four seconds of silence by a burst of laughter from Spraggins, which drew Jimmy back into the world where he turned his attention to Teddy.

Following the previous pattern, Jimmy's cracks on Teddy (lines 183–86) continued the mocking, assaultive tone he had used thus far. At the conclusion of his first crack, there was a three-second silence, which was interrupted by Harriet who attacked Jimmy: "Evidently I didn't gorilla you enough . . . got . . . you got a lot of loose lip this mornin'." This was followed by Teddy's crack (line 189): "Give 'm some Kay*opect*ate!" Teddy's line matched the accusatory model for cracking evidenced in Jimmy's and Harriet's styling in the previous lines and earlier, but its occurrence after both the silence and Harriet's response robbed it of much of its potential power as a response.

At this point, there was a momentary dissolution of the conversation (lines 190–96), in which an organizing topic was sought to reunite the participants on a single focus. This was provided by Harriet in line 193, when she loudly and exaggeratedly proclaimed "*I'm starvin'*." Her complaint, expressed with "*starvin'*" heavily stressed and lengthened, gave the impression that collapse from hunger was imminent. The line drew together the central thrust of the previous episode — her meals — and, accordingly, those present to supply her with food since she could not leave the bar. In particular, it connected back to the previous topic and challenged Jimmy, who had been called down for feeding her previously.

Her challenge was picked up by Jimmy in line 197 and rapped on between him and Harriet until line 210. The rap was built up out of his demand that she bring her own food and her responses as to why she did not. It was Jimmy again who took the accusatory tack and Harriet who defended. This interplay continued flittingly until line 206, when Gill interrupted this uncomfortable lull to explain: "We got the coffee." A four-second silence occurred that Jimmy, directly and with assaultive dominance in his voice, ended by saying (line

207), "Yeah, fix me a cup, Harriet." Up to this point, Harriet had
been content to let Jimmy have his way, bantering back only when
he stepped over the line, but this direct order was too much, and she
responded angrily (line 209): "I wish to hell I would," which she repeated immediately in a harsher tone (line 210), "I wish to hell I
would fix *you* some coffee." On the surface, Jimmy's statement was
no more dangerous than any other thus far delivered when it is considered by itself. Occurring as it did after a period of time in which
Harriet had been a direct target of Jimmy's wit, however, it increased
and made explicit a subordination that had thus far been only verbal. It also removed the indirection inherent in the previous rapping
and cracking and substituted a direct order. Faced with such a
threat, Harried informed Jimmy in no uncertain terms that he was
no longer free to say what he wanted.

Jimmy acknowledged the rebuke (lines 211–32) by turning on
Teddy and attacking him for letting Harriet talk that way: "You
gonna let her talk to me that way?" Teddy did not answer immediately, and Jimmy had a new and definitely safer target. In line 212
he began his full attack: "I'm talkin' to you, Nigger." The line was
exaggerated and laughed with "talkin'" extended so that Teddy was
presented as an individual who was unaware of what was said to
him. Teddy began to respond in line 213 but he did so so slowly that
I cut him off and characterized his slow speech as a hesitation based
on his fear of possible consequences: "Teddy learned his lesson a long
time ago." Jimmy picked up my theme and styled further on Teddy.

His "Yeah, no lie" was spoken very loudly and rose on both the
"yeah" and "no lie" from a low to a very high pitch. Underlying this
rise was a vocal quality of laughter suggesting not only styling but
the truthfulness of my remark. Jimmy then moved to explain why
Teddy was this way. In so doing, he was able to withdraw from a
direct attack on Teddy and indirectly continued his rap with Harriet. His opening in line 217 described Harriet as the cause and in
line 218 he dramatized the specific incident. "Look Motherfucker
when I tell you somethin' I means it" was spoken in a distinctively
different voice. "Look Motherfucker" was split rather than uttered.
The individual words were strangled in delivery, clipped short, and
angrily spoken. They created an impression of fury and the intense
speed in their articulation made it seem as if they had to be quickly
gotten out so that what followed could be spoken. This intensity was
continued through the rest of the statement. Harried denied Jimmy's
description in line 219, but Jimmy continued on in line 220 to be interrupted again with another denial by Harriet. In line 222 Jimmy

began to expand his description of the scene: "He said . . . he said: 'You dumb ass barmaid'." This idea was repeated in lines 224 and 225, and Harriet's response was recorded by Jimmy in line 226: "An' she went off." This line was the loudest of the four and the highest in pitch. The "off" was extended out and up until the final "f" was just a blur of sound. So exaggerated was this delivery that it even drew laughter from the offended Harriet. Having re-established a styling relationship with Harriet, as indicated by her response, Jimmy wound up as if to continue rapping with her, but the arrival of a new patron, Earl, interrupted his attack (line 228) and demanded that Jimmy stop momentarily and give the obligatory greeting, "Hi Earl" (line 229), before concluding his description. This disruption of conversation caused Jimmy to fall into a natural speaking voice as he finished his delivery. Teddy laughingly acknowledged this rescue by chance from a further onslaught as he laughingly but quietly said, "Why you hafta lie" (line 232), which brought the sequence to an end.

This second episode throws into clear relief the central performance features involved in successful styling. Here the features are near the foreground simply by their presence in what is essentially a continuous two-person relationship. The center of this episode was Jimmy, and he pulled out no stops in his attempt to duel with Harriet verbally. He began with a direct attack which indicated that he had chosen to style with Harriet and that his chosen topic was to be her relationship with Wes. Having placed himself in the performer's seat, he had to remain in control until an opportunity for performance presented itself. His initial "knitting shit" routine can be seen as an index of the sniping used in styling to keep opponents off balance and to generate the mistakes that would open up the conversation to extended turns at talk. Within the context of the first nine utterances Jimmy attacked on all of his lines. Each was delivered with a mock assaultive tone, and each was pointed directly to Harriet's dependent status. Her response was to deny his works — "Wes ain't put me through *nothin'* "— but to go no further. She forced him to continue to carry the burden of the conversation and allowed herself to stand back and parry his thrusts. Jimmy momentarily changed style to ask a question, which indicated that Harriet's strategy was working and that she was making him pay for his offer to rap. Harriet continued to challenge Jimmy to find a way of reaching her by reminding him and the audience that Wes had told Jimmy to back off Harriet: "He meant that shit 'bout not feedin' me on Wednesday." This intended put-down, however, gave Jimmy the opportunity he had been looking for, and he turned this negative characterization into an extended turn at talk (lines 131–89).

The focus of this rap was a presentation of self in which Jimmy took Harriet's negative image and transformed it into a weapon to be used against her. He undercut Harriet by accepting the self she gave him and left her without any method to continue. She could repeat, but the absence of a denial from Jimmy gave her no permission to do so. However, he could say anything he wanted about himself. Jimmy was in a position to style not by attacking another but by attacking himself. He became the context for his own performance; the world he created was valid because it was solely his, and whatever he dramatized, repeated, or reported was judged only in terms of the information he provided. Within this unassailable fortress Jimmy further assured his power to do or say whatever he wanted by actively dramatizing his new self. Having become a player performing all the parts, he used this position to reconstruct for the group the "actual" interaction in which he and Wes discussed feeding Harriet. He used all the available techniques of dramatic performance to bring his characters to life and to render his representation realistic. Doubly protected, he was able to play his "humble" self and Wes's "angry" lover with an extreme absurdity, one so extreme in fact that by the end of his performance even he was taken in by the perfection of the playlet he had created.

The uniqueness of Jimmy's position was the very feature that eventually undercut his ability to rap. Freed from the give and take of a normal rapping relation, he had worked himself into a virtually unchecked and ever increasing spiral of aggression. When he turned from his vignette to attack Teddy (line 183), he was no longer apart from the real world but was once again fully within its boundaries and bound by its constraints. Accordingly, what had been acceptable aggression when "turned against" himself was unacceptable when directed at Teddy and Harriet. Now instead of being in control of his rap, he was through his anger confronting the very basis of bar order. His aggression possessed none of the indicators of non-seriousness that had been provided by his dramatic presentation, and, hence, it was loose on the world with no defining features of style or signs of meaning. Having surrendered his dramatic place, Jimmy carried into the interaction an anger whose lack of disguise threatened to overwhelm the other performers by its very force. Harriet, who because of her responsibility to maintain order and because she was the explicit target of his anger, called Jimmy on his transgression in no uncertain terms, and the silence that followed her action effectively ended the styling.

Having, by necessity, ended the styling, it was also Harriet who indicated that it could continue again as long as every participant understood and remembered the rules of the performance. Her *"I'm starvin',"* with its exaggerated delivery, picked immediately up where the previous interaction left off and, in one sense, was an invitation to style that set her up for exactly the same kind of abuse which she had just undergone. The difference was, of course, that her call was an announcement that the appropriate way to style was through interplay rather than private play. In a sense her open challenge to the gathering was that they and particularly Jimmy should repair the breach created by re-doing the same topic only this time in the "right" way. Her offer to rap was again picked up by Jimmy, but in this attempt to rework the conversation both he and Harriet were smarting from the potentially dangerous breakdown of expectations, and both inevitably lost control of their words. Thus, Jimmy again exceeded the bounds of decorum by being too aggressive in his description of Harriet's lack of lunch and second by demanding that she pour him a cup of coffee. Harriet called him on his behavior, but she, too, was too aggressive and acted inappropriately to her given role responsibilities. Unlike the previous breakdown, then, this confrontation had an additional element, which threatened not only Jimmy's place in the bar but also the bar itself. His sniping had begun to get to Harriet, and, despite the fact that she was supposed to be self-consciously participating in the conversation, she was beginning to lose control of herself. In fact, her anger in line 208 — *"I wish to hell* I would" — exceeded even the acceptable bounds of normal anger in the bar. Jimmy's intense exaggeration in his attack on Teddy acted as a bypass for channeling the anger of the situation, and Harriet's participation in the laughter which followed meant that, at least momentarily, the group had been able to hold its fragile world together.

What is most significant in this sequence is the exemplification of the tenuousness underlying the construction of reality during styling. As this episode repeatedly points out, the free play of possibilities inherent in styling brought with them the reality that simple talk is always teetering too close to the edge. As styling progressed, those involved were increasingly drawn into the moment-by-moment creation of ambiguous experience that led finally to a situation in which no one participant knew where any other participant was or what he meant by what he said. The playability of interaction inevitably ended in producing relationships in which there were no common assumptions about the nature of action and the meaning of language. Hence, those who styled had to ask of themselves and of each other directions for interacting and direction for use. Any utterance and, in fact, every utterance made itself and its immediate world possible and brought as part of its use the possibility that the world would cease to mean.

As a general mode of performance, therefore, styling contrasted with the normal business of talking shit in that it had as its goal the intensification of talk through a manipulation of the ambiguity potentially beneath the surface of ordinary life. In the place of well-regulated understandings and minimal opportunities for mistaken choices, styling opted for the maximum interpretability of interaction. It thus called into question the normal grounds of inference and explanation by locating all action on the borders between those known expectations and the anarchy available in play. Here in this infinite space styling raised into the consciousness of patrons the scaffolding of rules that allowed them to interact and provided them with a method by which to question the basis for such interaction. Institutionalized in its performance was a way to get to the basis for communicating with each other in the bar without fearing that such a search would find nothing at the center of experience. When a performer fell out of styling, he merely fell back into the real world where ordinary solutions took over. Such breakdowns made everyone uncomfortable or embarrassed or angry, but in the end they did no more.

In sum, then, styling represented a method for fictionalizing reality without the possibility that such a transformation would change anything. In its ambiguity and its relativity, in its calling forth boundaries to test, break, and repair them, and in its focus on the need to work and rework all meanings, it allowed patrons to play with playing and to create in their exchanges a collective sense of how they made sense and what made sense for them. In its continual shift of understanding styling brought to those involved in it the realization that in their knowledge and skill and in their ability to remain interconnected rested the continued emergence of everyday life.

7   Profiling

The great bulk of time in Brown's was given over to the ordinary performance of ordinary life. There were moments, however, when the tentative fictional intensity of styling was manipulated by a patron into an extraordinary sequence. When such a powerful ordering occurred, profiling was "what was happening." As described earlier, profiling was any intensified organization of conversation in which a patron attempted to control and order interaction by transforming it into an obviously theatrical scene. It described behavior in which a central actor attempted to construct a recognizable artifact for an audience. Its analysis, therefore, is not based on the examination of the interconnectedness of long interactive sequences but rather on the description of short, well-defined acts. In profiling the organization of self was aimed directly at the conscious creation of distinctive texts, roles, and actors. Unlike styling, the concern was not only with establishing criteria for adequate performance but also with determining the features that separate good from bad performances. Accordingly, the discussion of profiling requires a focus on the structure and the skill involved in making it self-contained.

The following example of profiling occurred within the context of a discussion of Billie Holliday among Jimmy and Tookie, two bar regulars, Harriet, the day barmaid, and me. Our conversation had been generated by the revival of interest in Holliday's career as a result of the movie version of her life. To cash in on the renewed interest the jukebox distributors had placed an album of Holliday singing the songs used in the movie in all the jukeboxes, and it was receiving enormous play in Brown's. The album was playing in the background, and the conversation turned to the topic of the differences between Holliday's life and singing style and those of Diana Ross, who portrayed her in the movie. The song "Good Morning, Heartache, What's New?" started to play. After listening silently for a while, Jimmy began.

(1) J: You know . . .
(2) When you hear Diana sing that song . . . it's nice . . .
(3) But when Billie sings it . . .
(4) You see her standing in a doorway
(5) An' it's three A.M. in the morning
(6) An' she's wearing one o' them yellow kimono robes . . .
(7) You know . . .
(8) An' it's half open . . .
(9) An' she ain't wearin' her hair.
(10) Now she's lookin' up at this dude with sleepy eyes,
(11) An' you know . . .
(12) She ain't too sure she's too happy to see him.
(13) But . . . she don't want him to go away again . . .
(14) So she's sleepy-eyed lookin' at him,
(15) An' you know . . .
(16) She sorta smiles an' says

At this point in the rap Jimmy paused, and the voice of Billie Holliday sang:

(17) *"Good Morning, Heartache, sit down."*
(18) J: Sit down an' stay a while.
(19) T: (seriously) You got that right.
(20) Diana is a nice singer, but she doesn't understand what Billie does.
(21) You can hear what Billie knows.
(22) J: It's . . . it's just that Diana's too young to know the blues, that's all.
(23) Just too young.

This text exemplifies the essential features of profiling. First and most important, it shows the basic structure of the process. In this instance Jimmy wanted to bring to life Holliday's version of "Good Morning, Heartache." Her singing style and her approach to her material were extremely meaningful to him, and he wanted to demonstrate the totality and the depth of her presentation. He did this by creating a montage of images, three word pictures of the same scene. A woman in a doorway is confronting an unexpected welcome/unwelcome lover. It is very late, and she is half-asleep and half-dressed.

Unsure of her emotions, she stares, pauses, remembers, and then she speaks. Each word adds detail and clarifies the image, and each added detail intensifies the description until, at the end, the scene is frozen in stark brilliance. And then, having focused the audience's consciousness on Billie Holliday, the woman in the doorway, Jimmy ceased to speak, and Billie Holliday, the singer in the background, concluded the performance. Suddenly, two distinct discourses came together, and the two Billies became one. The final line of the song became the conclusion of the rap, and this connection of the two value systems proved the truthfulness of Jimmy's representation. The multiplicity of potential meanings available to both lines of discourse, while they were independent of each other, were reduced to one, and their separate rhetorical intentions were joined into a unified statement.

Second, this text exemplifies how a profiled rap was constructed. To succeed, Jimmy had to deliver his rap in such a way that his flow of talk and the final line of the record coincided. The dramatic effect of his performance depended upon his knowing where the song was going and when it would reach its destination. If he arrived too early or too late, the drama would be lost. He needed to develop each image in such a way as to maximize its use of time without necessarily increasing its length. He did this by manipulating his choice of words and his style of delivery. Each word picture had a frame, and within each frame specific words and phrases were repeatedly used to turn the performance into an extended turn at talk. Specifically, each image began and ended with the marker "you know," and each "you know" was followed by a pause in speech. This permitted him to check after each image the progress of the song and to locate himself in relation to that progress. Thus, after the final "you know" (line 15), he did not begin another image but paused and then introduced the song tag. Within each framed image "an'" was used frequently as an introductory marker, and its presence brought a rhythmical consistency to the speech flow. Neither of these devices occurred with either this frequency or this regularity in Jimmy's ordinary speech, and their uses reflected the necessities of this particular composition.

Added to these framing devices was the manner in which the lines were delivered. Jimmy spoke with sincerity and with seriousness in order to signal the meaningfulness of his montage. He delivered most lines softly in a hushed tone, and he extended individual lines to emphasize their details. His delivery was slow and precise — and again, unlike his normal pattern. The overall effect was an understated style of delivery in marked contrast to the expected speaking style of the bar.

Finally, this text demonstrates the nature of the creative process underlying profiling. In this instance there was a conscious development by Jimmy of a level of theatricality that formalized the scene and transformed the transaction into profiling. Simply put, he created a fiction. Not only was the story he told not true, but also it was not the story the song told. His fictive text was thus consciously false at two levels: false because he was creating a strip of behavior that he and his audience recognized as containing unverifiable information and false because his image imposed on the song text a frame of reference that was unrelated to the frame of reference it proposed. By fictionalizing his description, the relationship between him and his audience became one in which they were excluded from the process of creation. In creating a fictive text Jimmy claimed full and sole responsibility for uncovering the emerging story line. It was his image and only he knew what was coming next. In order to participate in the creation of the image, the others present had to move into the text. Even if they succeeded in this maneuver, their participation remained dependent on Jimmy's allowing them free access to his next moves. The effect of this fabrication was to place the evolution of talk beyond the reach of the others present. Jimmy's move into fiction negotiated a defined meaning in which the organization of action from moment to moment continually affirmed that what was occurring was not ordinary conversation but the self-conscious ordering of experience by a performer.

A second example of profiling can be seen in the following sequence. It occurred in a conversation between myself and Uncle Nick, a bar regular. We had just been "formally" introduced by the barmaid, having known each other but never having talked before. Nick began by asking me if I was married and more specifically if I had any children. I said that I was married but that my wife and I did not yet have children. Nick's response to my answer was an attempt to negotiate a rapping exchange with me.

(1) N: You got any kids, Mike?
(2) M: No, not yet. My wife and I are waiting until all this school stuff is over.
(3) N: Least ways, none he'd admit to.
(4)   Ain't that right, now!
(5)   (General laughter)
(6) N: Now, Michael don't you get to blushin'. Hee hee hee.
(7)   I'm only lyin' on you an' everybody knows it.

(8) E: You doin' the talkin' but I ain't heard you do any tellin'.

(9) N: Slow your roll, Earl buddy,

(10)   Now slow your roll.

(11)   Now you . . . now you know I got me two boys an' none in the woodpile.

(12)   Shit, them two . . . them two . . .

(13)   Listen here, you wanta hear some shit.

(14) (Nick stands up and walks from his stool to the jukebox, a distance of two paces. With his back to his participants he continues.)

(15) N: I'm gonna tell you how things are.

(16)   You listen to this, Mike.

(17)   Maybe you'll learn somethin'.

(18) (Having selected his song, Nick turns back to the group, and as the song starts he begins.)

(19) N: Now you see

(20)   Now you see, me an' my wife, we ain't been together for a while.

(21)   An' I know she been feedin' them two boys all kinds o' trash 'bout what kind o' man their ol' man is.

(22)   Cause you see it's been a bit since I been aroun'. You know.

(23)   So, you know, we been goin' out for holidays.

(24)   You know, Christmas, Easter . . .

(25)   An' we went out jus' this pas' Thanksgivin'.

(26)   We a . . . we a went to this restaurant downtown.

(27)   So you know I tol' my kids before we left the house . . .

(28)   My wife, see, she still has the house.

(29)   I tol' 'm . . . I said: "Now you know we ain't together but 'cept for holidays."

(30)   So I said: "You can order anythin' you want to eat when we at the restaurant."

(31)   Now you see my wife, she knows I mean what I say when I say it, but them boys . . .

(32)   So we went to the restaurant, you know . . .

(33)   An' we sat down to order . . .

(34)   So my wife . . . she, ya see,

(35)   she took me at my word an' ordered a lobster.

(36)   An' my one son, the eldest,

(37)   He be thirteen in a couple a months.

(38)   He steady readin' the menu . . .

(39)   An' finally, he orders, you know, one of them . . . a . . . a . . . chopped sirloins.

(40)   Now, shit, that's nothing but a hamburger.

(41)   So I says, "That's what you want? You sure?"

(42)   So he . . . he said: "Yeah . . . an' a baked potato."

(43)   Don't that beat all.

(44)   "An' a baked potato." Shit, so I says to the waitress, I said: "Give'm some onion rings to go with that."

(45)   Now I orders me a sirloin steak, rare, with french fries and onion rings.

(46)   Now my other boy . . .

(47)   He nine,

(48)   He says, "Did you mean what you said 'bout orderin' what we want."

(49)   "I said it didn't I?"

(50)   An' he nods, so I say:

(51)   "Okay then. Get what you want."

(52)   So he orders a steak jus' like mine.

(53)   Well, you know, the food, it comes, an' we start in to eatin'.

(54)   An' the oldest boy he is steady starin' at his brother eatin' steak.

(55)   So I said . . . I said: "If you wanted steak why didn't you order one.

(56)   "I tol' you before we left that you could order anythin' you wanted.

(57)   "So don't you be starin' down your brother for doin' what I told him.

(58)   It ain't his fault he knows who to believe an' you don't.

(59)   Shit. I says:

(60) (At this point, the song, "If You Don't Know Me by Now," which has been playing in the background, comes to its concluding chorus, and Nick stops speaking so that the rap is finished as the song concludes.)

(61)   *"If you don't know me by now, you'll never, never, never, never know me."*

(62)   If you don't know me by now, Boy, if you don't know my words is true.

(63)   You don't know nothin'.

(64)   You dig where I'm comin' from, Mike?

(65) (Nick sits down on his vacated stool)
(66)   Wasn't that pretty?
(67)   If you don't know me . . .
(68) (Singing) "If you don't know me by now . . ."
(69)   Harriet?
(70) H: Huh?
(71) N: Hey Baby, give me a little bang will ya?

As in the previous example, the feature that makes the segment distinctively different is not simply the organization of text and tune. This formal climactic relationship is important, but here the text being created by Nick was not fictional, and hence he needed another strategic way to develop his difference. This was accomplished through the conscious manipulation of our physical relationship into a recognizable stage. By merely moving from his bar stool to in front of the jukebox and remaining there until the completion of his narrative, Nick created a gap of about two feet between himself and the other patrons. Because of his placement of his body and their seating, this formed an intense angle of focus. The patrons, Nick among them, had all been seated at the end of the bar nearest the front door. In moving to the jukebox Nick created a triangle in which the others present had to turn partially, but not totally, around in order to listen to him. This arrangement focused the audience on Nick but did not force them to violate the unstated bar rule about not turning one's back to the bar. The effect of this staging was to generate a radically different relationship between Nick and the others present. In removing himself he introduced a distance, real and metaphoric, between his activity and that of those who observed him. From coparticipants in social interaction, his movement introduced an artificial barrier between him and the patrons creating two domains of action, actor and audience, bridged only by his organization of talk. Moreover, he maintained this distance by using his hands to push his audience back. His utterances from lines 19 to 59 were marked by a rhythmical gesturing of his hands out from his chest and then back in again. It can be argued that Nick's selection of this particular song for his rapping sequence constituted a conscious formulation and represented an additional or alternative source of transformation. However, had Nick returned to his stool and seated himself at the bar, there would have been no way to close off his performance. By remaining a member of the bar network, Nick would have been available to the others. His utterances and his narrative would have become the property of the group, and they, rather than he, would have been responsible for its performance. Under such conditions, he would have had no guarantee that his intended use of the important line would have been possible. Had he returned to the bar, any other patron could have participated in his rap. His narrative was straightforward and conversational, and there was nothing in its organization or its presentation to signal that the text under construction was anything other than ordinary talk. As such, his performance was open to involvement, and any other patron would have been able to contribute to or to comment on his rap, even using his climax line. By remaining stationed in front of the jukebox and staging his rap, Nick transformed the distance between himself and the other patrons from a physical space to a theater. The social arrangement of friends was replaced by an actor and his audience, and Nick changed from a patron to an entertainer.

A more complex example of profiling can be seen in the following sequence. This text offers a distinctively different manipulation of the relationship between performer and text. Here the organization of expressions is not between two lines of talk but between a text and a kinesic enactment of its meaning. The rap occurred on a Saturday morning as the bar was filling with customers. The jukebox was playing loudly in the background and an instrumental version of "I'm Walking" came on the box. Shortly after it began, Rick Clark entered the bar. He paused for a moment, and then, picking up the beat of the song, he began to walk in time to it while rapping.

(1) R: (Very loudly) Good morning, sweet Harriet.
(2)   Now . . . now you see . . . (Arrives at jukebox where he begins walking in place to the record. As he starts this motion, he turns to face the bar. The jukebox is now directly behind him, and he is the center of the bar.)
(3)   I'm movin' . . . *fast* movin' . . .
(4)   On Market
(5)   headin' down toward City Hall
(6)   hittin' my stride . . .
(7)   Lookin' fine, *real* fine
(8)   In my *best leather*
(9)   An' my two inch heels
(10)   Checkin' out the foxes
(11)   You know . . . a
(12)   Seein' what I like

(13)		An' likin' what I see
(14)		*Ooowee* yeah.
(15)		Comin' up on 19th Street.
(16)		Catch the light so's I'm waitin . . . you know. (Still walking in place, but now slower.)
(17)		I sees this fine . . . *supa fine* woman on the other side . . .
(18)		So at the change, I crosses over *doin'* my stuff.
(19)		Slows my walk an' she picks up on me . . .
(20)		An' starts to walkin' with me . . .
(21)		Still movin' down Market
(22)		Turnin' on 17th now
(23)		Doin' fine.
(24)		She's diggin' *my* line . . .
(25)		Turnin' into a doorway an' up the stairs.
(26)		Now I steady talkin' my talk . . .
(27)		Tellin' her how fine she is . . .
(28)		Sayin' what she wants to hear . . .
(29)		'Bout what I can do for her . . .
(30)		At the top she opens the door an' . . .
(31)		(The record ends, and Ricky moves to the bar.)
(32)		O::oowe::ee.
(33)		Watch me do my stuff
(34)	H:	Richard, you can take *your*self on out of here today.
(35)		I don't wanna rap.
(36)	R:	Sweet . . . sweet Harriet.
(37)		You lookin' fine . . . too fine to mess.

The surface difference between this text and the previous example is readily observable. In this example the text and tune are co-equal throughout the entire rap. Rick used the tune as a basis for constructing a new text, and the result was a relationship in which he and the jukebox sung together. Accordingly, his manipulation of the jukebox was much simpler than in the previous text and very similar to the normal usage of any background music by a performer in the bar context. The box was his back-up band, and he was using it in a straightforward fashion to improvise a new text to an old well-known tune. He used the speaking power of the jukebox but altered the impact of that voice. Instead of replacing one text with another, Rick merged two flows of sound into one. Again, as in the previous narrative, his text had no connection to the known text for the tune. What he developed was a personal narrative that used the beat of the music as a keying device to channel and control his audience's interpretation of his talk. The tune became the scaffolding on which his story hung.

This different use of the voice of the jukebox altered the nature of the creative process involved in transforming this rap. Here, the text was less important. As fictional as the previous example, its fiction was more open, and Rick's story was ongoing and from its initiation open to other patron involvement. They, too, knew the song, and without a competing formal text they could have easily walked with it as well as Rick. His text was not leading them into the song, nor was it about the song. Rather, it was the song; but the music was free, and anyone else could use it to make a competing song. Accordingly, Rick's declaration of this sequence as his own had to occur in another fashion.

This significant difference was observable in Rick's transformation of himself into a recognizable character. Not only did he manipulate the vocal quality and delivery of his lines, but also he literally "walked" them. From his entrance into the bar until the completion of his rap, Rick accompanied his steady verbal stream with a repeated pattern of body motion. Moreover, this pattern was not only an exaggeration of his own personal walking style, but it was also an exaggeration that displayed a culturally recognizable mode of walking. Rick's walking his rap involved a use of what is sometimes known in the bar and in the black community as "pimp walking," that is, "the basic soul walk (consisting) of placing one foot directly in front of the other, the heel hits first and the leg drops loosely which results in a bended leg effect. The shoulders sway very slightly and naturally, with a slight dropping of the shoulder which moves forward" [Cooke, 1972, p. 55].

The effect of this intensification of the rapping process was heightened by Rick's use of this walking pattern while remaining in the same area in front of the jukebox (lines 3-30). To have shifted into such a movement pattern was not in itself unusual, either for Rick or in the bar setting. Within the bar, Rick was known by most of the regulars to have the nickname of "Hippy-Dip" because of his occasional use of such a walking style. Maintaining this walk throughout his rap, however, added an additional signal to his activity. By walking his rap in place, Rick effectively cut off physical contact with those in the bar; he created a closed-off universe needed to complete his description. In order to enter the universe he was evolving, it would have been necessary to have or develop a character similar to the one he was enacting. It would have been necessary to formulate a fictive self, place that self in the action, and perform its part. But to accomplish such an act, the performer would have to develop as commanding an improvisation as Rick's, one especially suited to challenge his walking of "I'm Walking." Since Rick knew where he was going and could twist away from such a happening, any attempt to develop such a character would have been extremely dangerous and temporarily impossible. Such a character would have been extremely problematic, and its creator would have been open to acute social embarrassment. By walking his rap Rick transformed his potential interactors into an audience necessarily content to be entertained.

A second similar, but more completely orchestrated, example of the kinesic coding of profiling can be seen in the following scene, drawn from an extended conversation among Rick, Steve, Teddy, Mary (the barmaid on duty at the time), and me. The whole segment covered two hours on a Thursday afternoon and early evening just before Christmas. Rick and Steve had arrived sometime after work and were deeply involved in the ongoing social life when I arrived at 5:30. The bar was still crowded with before-dinner drinkers, and Rick stood out as the central performer among them. When I arrived, he was in full control of the flow of talk and was deftly orientating all present toward deep playing. He was not seated at the bar but was moving back and forth behind the bar stools spraying his conversation in all directions.

(1) R: Mary, how's you Christ::mas shop:: liftin' hold::in' up?
(2) Ma: Not too well, hee hee.
(3) R: Mmmm (spoken through a sip of beer)
(4) Ma: I haven't . . .
(5) R: You mean you don't have two busts already?
(6)   You fallin' *down* on the *J.O.B.ski*. (Laughs) (two-second silence)
(7) Mi: Hey!
(8)   Where were you on Tuesday?
(9)   I drove by to pick you up like we arranged
(10)   but I got no answer when I rang the bell,
(11)   so I just drove Kay in.
(12)   You get hung up?
(13) R: No, *Shit*
(14)   I tol' her to tell you I was down here.
(15)   She just went about her bidness.
(16)   Payin' nobody no min' but herself.
(17)   No. I was down here.

(18)   Eight o'clock in the morning.
(19)   I was here an' I was *dealin'*.
(20)   Somebody said:
(21)   "Oh Rick, come an' have a Bushmills, what the heck."
(22)   You know.
(23)   At . . . at eight-o-five
(24)   I had a Bushmills an' a shot a' beer.
(25)   An' then I had a couple more beers.
(26)   An' then I started lyin' to Teddy.
(27)   An' Teddy started lyin' to me. Hee hee.
(28)   Hee . . . An' then Spraggins came in an' we got to *lyin'*.
(29)   An' . . . an' *before* I knew . . .
(30)   An' the next thing I knew . . .
(31)   It was nine-thirty, an' I was flyin'. (Rick begins to laugh a soft, wheezing laugh as he begins to move toward Teddy who is seated near the entrance.)
(32)   I had a Air-Force breakfast.
(33)   *Four* Bushmills an' eight beers. (Laughter)
(34)   *Ooowee!*
(35)   *Flyin'*.
(36)   Wasn't that right, Ted?
(37)   *Thea::a::dore.*
(38)   Was that not a cor::rect description hee, hee of *our encounter* (Wheezing laughter.)
(39)   Ooowee! (arrives at Teddy's stool)
(40)   Oh child, *what you say*.
(41)   Teddy my *man*.
(42)   My man Theodore is a man among men.
(43)   Now he is a leisurely man.
(44)   An' he is like able to party tough *all* day.
(45)   Teddy, my man,
(46)   Will you indulge your*self*
(47)   an' have a Schmidts, *today*,
(48)   I am restricting your taste because of the *financial inequities* of m::y pocketbook.
(49) S: Speak on that.
(50) T: Ricky you crazy, hee, hee.
(51) R: It is *the day before* the day of pay, an' I am played out down to *the* end.
(52) Ma: In that case, you best show me my money before I serves you up any more drinks.

(53)   (Group laughter)
(54) Ma: Get it up.
(55)   It'd be my head Charlie'd be after.
(56)   Give me my money.
(57)   (Group laughter during which Rickey walks up to the
                center of the bar and gives Mary a twenty-dollar bill.)
(58) R: All at once.
(59)   A taste for their face,
(60)   goin' out in style is the only way.
(61)   Ooowee! (Sits down as Mary fills his beer glass)
(62)   Might as well give'm all a bang on me.
(63)   So's I can ride their tab later.

Logistically, this performance can be broken down into several
distinctive segments. Lines 1–6 reflected the general tone of the
overall interaction thus far. Ricky was standing between and behind
Steve and me, who were seated at the end of the bar near the back
room. During these utterances he was reaching between us for his
beer, then sipping, and finally returning it to the bar. Ricky's lines 1,
3, 5, and 6 placed Mary in a defensive position by accusing her of being a shoplifter in such a way as to make any denial an admission of
guilt. This rhetorical bind was reinforced through the organization
of the delivery of the line. Line 1 was articulated with extreme clarity. There was no emotive intensity in its delivery, but each syllable
was pronounced slowly and distinctively with extreme crispness.
Thus, the "t" in Christmas, the "p" in shopliftin', and the "d" in
holdin' were all clear and noticeable. Moreover, though the final "g"
on the latter two words was dropped, the "in" was very clearly articulated. This feature of sounding out formally what was normally
an informal, unmarked speech segment served to emphasize the effect
and to convey a sense of the verbal play being stored in the utterance. Furthermore, this intensification was not increased by the use
of the laughing mocking tone associated with styling. Thus, in line
6, "You fallin' down on the *J.O.B.ski*," the second half of the utterance was laughed rather than spoken.

This initial segment was followed by two seconds of silence,
which I interrupted with a question. This began the second portion
of the performance, lines 7–35, an extended rap by Rick on why he
was not where I expected him to be when I came by his house to pick
him up. He began his explanation (lines 13–16) by informing me
that he had been down at the bar and that his wife, who was supposed to tell me where he was, had left: "Payin' nobody no mind but

herself" (line 16). This introduction completed, he then launched into an extensive explanation of why and how he had lost track of time in the bar and thus failed to meet me on time. This embedded narrative covered lines 17 through 35 and, like the previous lines, it was text and texturally organized within the framework of styling. The flow of his speaking was exaggerated, and his delivery again was characterized by its underlying laughter. His intonation of certain words as well as his repetition of key rhetorical figures served to tie his message together. Thus, the story was framed by the idea of "Have a Bushmills" (line 21) and "Four Bushmills an' eight beers" (line 33), and was ordered by the contrast of the figure "lying" (lines 26–30) with that of "flying" (lines 31–35).

At the beginning of this segment (line 13), Rick moved directly backward from where he had been standing and throughout the segment remained a foot or so away from the bar. He was not stationary during this time but was moving left to right from behind where Steve and I sat to almost in front of the jukebox, which was in the center of the back wall. This movement caused Steve and me to swing sideways on our stools to maintain eye contact with Rick. We turned in parallel so that Steve's back was to me as we faced Rick. Our motion also caused several patrons to turn in order to focus on Rick.

This sequence ended at line 35 and lines 36–40 were a transition to a new focus of Rick's performance. Stylistically, these lines were the most exaggerated and intensified so far. They were marked by a sudden increase in volume and emphasis as well as a return to hypercorrected speech, which had characterized the opening of his rap (lines 1 and 6). Again, the formality of his utterances was belied by the vocal quality of the delivery. This increased emphasis of verbal dexterity continued until Rick reached Teddy who was seated at the other end of the bar. Upon arrival Rick maintained his station back away from the bar. By continuing his increased visibility, he remained the center of attention and thus continued to dominate the group's attention at a point of conversational juncture until he found a new topic.

This final segment (lines 42–63) began by focusing on Teddy but was quickly expanded to include Rick's financial state; it continued the stylistic intensification in use. For example, line 48 ("I am restricting your taste because of the *financial inequities* of m::y pocketbook") was built up out of a tension between its formal vocabulary and the informality and laughter underlying their delivery. Thus, *"financial inequities"* seemed to twist out rather than to be spoken. During this segment, Rick remained back from the bar and did not move forward until line 52 when, in confrontation with Mary, he was called on to settle his tab since his previous statements had been admissions of a "poverty" that would prevent him from paying a large bill. By line 57 he was at the center of the bar to pay Mary for his tab, and by line 63 he was again seated next to Steve.

As before, the organization of this sequence came from Rick's definition of himself as a character engaged in playing a specific role and again this fact was located not only in what was said, in how it was said, or even in where it was said, but rather in the manner in which it was enacted.

The *terminus a quo* of the profiling portion of this presentation occurred in lines 13–17. The change in the organization of the sequence was demonstrated initially by Rick's movement backward from the bar. This movement back from Steve and me opened a space for action, but this in itself was not the signal of profiling. Since the move was straight back, it did not allow for any real distance from us or the bar. As I followed his movement by turning on my stool to maintain contact with him, I could still have touched him without leaning forward from my seat. However, this distance allowed Rick to make his move by providing him with room to act. The assumption of profiling occurred in line 17, when Rick shifted his visual presentation into rapping, or player, stance. This initial position had five formal kinesic features: (1) The legs were spread apart with one forward of the other. (2) One arm was held close to the body in a straight line from shoulder to fingers with the fingers pointing straight back. (3) The other arm was held close and in toward the body from shoulder to elbow. The lower arm was held stiff to the wrist but flexed freely there and at the elbow. Finally, the fingers of the hand were cupped in toward the upper arm to preclude palm display. The pattern of movement of the lower arm was toward the center of the body, and its chief function was to emphasize Rick as actor. (4) The torso was stiff and moved as a single unit from the waist. And, finally (5) the head and shoulders were down and forward, "dipped" in informants' terms, to one side or the other. Their movements were angular, so that a motion of the head, which would normally proceed on a curve flowing from center erect to the right or left and thence down to center forward, became a sharp jerky bounding of the head on the same line. In this case the actual shift occurred in two quick phases. The first half of the utterance — "No I was" — was accompanied kinesically by the setting of the legs and the torso, and the second half — "down here" — by the organization of the arms and hands. In particular, "down" was matched by the thrusting of the left arm straight down by the body, and "here" was matched by a drawing of the right forearm into the chest. Beginning with line 18 and throughout the presentation, this new stance became the base pattern from which all of Rick's body messages flowed.

As well as marking the shift to profiling, this new stance was the first position of the performance to be accomplished. This position was held from line 18 through line 35 and marked the embedded narrative performance including coda. The unfolding of the individual points in this segment derived from this kinesic organization. Initially, this overall organization was tight and highly visible. Rick's movements in lines 18 and 19 were extremely angular in their flow and were performed briskly, if exaggeratedly. Line 18 was expressed by a sharp forward motion of the torso and a forward extension of the right forearm down and away from the body and a bobbing of the head and shoulders in the direction of the right hand. Line 19 reversed this forward motion. The first half — "I was here" — was signaled by a drawing back of the torso to a straight upright position, the upper arm back and into the body, the forearm into the stomach, and head down toward the hand. The initial movement was the back motion of the forearm, marking the spoken "I". The second half — "an' I was *dealin'* " — was accompanied by similar arm and head motions and a flexing at the knees, hence the description of "dipping" given by informants.

This tight holding of stance and resulting angular patterning of movement was relaxed in lines 20 through 28. In these lines the primary signal of the player pattern was in the use of the arms and head. At line 20 the left arm, which had been held stiffly at his side, was bent at the elbow and the forearm was brought up in front of his chest so that it now paralleled his right arm. Both were then used to mark the progression of narrative information. Their motion was straight out from the chest, alternating left and right. Each outward movement was accompanied by a dipping of the same shoulder giving the upper torso a rocking effect.

Rick tightened up the body flow again in lines 29–31. Here the angularity and sharpness of the arm and shoulder movements increased as the intention of the story was emphatically expressed. This tightness was loosened in lines 32 and 33, the coda to the story, and hyperexaggerated again in lines 34 and 35. Thus, "ooowee" and "flyin'" were highly exaggerated exemplifications of the base set. They were delivered with a slow motion, an unwinding of the rap stance for "ooowee" and a quick snap back over "flying'."

At line 36 Rick turned toward Teddy, who was seated at the other end of the bar and began moving toward him. This shift marked the end of the first position in the sequence. It did not, however, mark the end of profiling. On the audio-aural channel, Rick signaled that he intended to continue to perform by intensification of his verbal patter in lines 36 to 40. This was accompanied by an extreme exaggeration of his walk. As he walked toward Teddy, Rick "bopped," that is, transformed his stance into "pimp walking." Moreover, Rick's manipulation of this exaggerated walking style was in itself exaggerated. His overall movement was slower than one expects in this style, and each individual motion was more controlled than it ought to have been. Reaching Teddy (line 39), Rick stationed himself near the jukebox, still away from the bar, and resumed his tight player stance. Line 40 began kinesically in an explosive fashion with "Oh child" being spit out by a sharp forward motion of the torso, a snapping downward of the left arm, and a quick curling of the right arm toward the body; it ended slowly with "what you say" being delivered with an emotive winding-in of the arms to the body.

Lines 41–48 were delivered within the rapping stance already described. Line 48 was the most significant because, verbally, its delivery matched that described for line 1 with the addition of a clear kinesic signal. In this case the crisp exaggerated articulation of the utterance was matched by stylized and extremely angular movements of the arms, torso, and head. This delivery was, in fact, so exaggerated that Rick's performance drew stylized audience response (lines 49 and 50). Rick continued this exaggeration of the rapping stance in line 51, and Mary responded to his remarks by offering to rap with him (lines 52–57). These statements matched Rick's paralinguistic stylization and served to draw him out of self-conscious theater and treat Mary's declared performative frame as an obligatory challenge to allow another to join in the performance as an equal or to cease distancing himself from the group. When Mary began, Rick relaxed his stance and stood naturally, listening to her, marking the *terminus ad quem* of his rap. He then moved to the bar (line 57), again shifted position, and in lines 58 through 64 moved both verbally and kinesically back into a "normal" play stance.

Overall, Rick's performance can be seen as one in which again an unmarked rap was transformed into intense acting through the conscious addition of his fictive self, "Hippy-Dip." By "dipping" and "bopping" his rap, Rick used his alternative persona, already defined in the setting, to insure that he could not be drawn into the web of bar life unless by another character so defined. Thus, neither Steve nor Teddy who maintained "normal" selves in response to Rick drew him back into conversation, but Mary, a professional character in her own right, was able to challenge his constructed self and draw him into the world at hand.

This examination of four examples of profiling makes it possible to draw some general conclusions on the process as it occurred in the bar. As was the case with styling, profiling in Brown's was built up as a humorous system of social interaction. It, too, aimed at the development of the play aspects of an ongoing scene. In this case, however, the development was not concerned with the tension between the orderly and the playful but with the creation of wholly defined fictional performances. Profiling was obviously theatrical. It was intended by its performers to signal that a self-conscious presentation was occurring. Thus, in the creation and accomplishment of the profiling performances just analyzed, there was the addition of significant stylistic information in order to create a clear difference between their actions and those of the others present.

In the examples presented, this significance was displayed at the levels of text, stage, and performance. Jimmy created a fiction, Uncle Nick created a stage, and Rick created a characterization. Each added to a process of styling additional information that restrained the possible interpretations that could be made about the nature of the created image. This self-consciousness theatricality resulted in an organization of experience into multiple repeating messages. In this sense profiling focused attention completely on the fictionality of a presentation by eliminating from consideration any other possible interpretation of action.

Profiling, accordingly, required an actor, and this necessity reduced the availability of this style to patrons. Though theoretically any patron might profile, the skill necessary to do it well, and hence to party tough, was not possessed by everyone. Moreover, though profiling contributed to bar life by being the deepest form of play available to patrons, it was an individual action that excluded most patrons from participation except in the guise of an audience. Thus, it was at one and the same time the most intense process of interaction and the most destructive process of interaction. To profile was to draw apart from the group and to build an individual world in which the group may enjoy, observe, and even help create only by following the rules for audience response. Such situations, however, were not the normal manner of being in Brown's as it was conceived of by most patrons. Their perception of the orderly use of Brown's was less intense and more oriented toward a community of insiders building an order out of the needs, wants, and interests of the group as a whole. From their perspective, to perform best in Brown's was to follow the flow of life and act spontaneously in accord with its unfolding rather than to attempt to lead it wherever one wanted it to go. Those who profiled did so at their own risk, and the risk was truly great.

8 The Aesthetics of Talking Shit

Much of the effort of this book has been directed toward modeling the behavior out of which the world of Brown's was created by its patrons. The description has concentrated on explaining how a portion of experience — spatial, cultural, and conversational — was constructed and on determining why particular choices were made. The result has been that, while the process of experience has been documented in detail, there has been little concern with its meaning. People, however, do not usually operate in such a fashion. Rather than see themselves as interwoven with each other, most see themselves as individuals acting with a goal in mind and for a reason. Even when they only dimly know what they are doing or why, people act to interpret themselves and the others around them. Understanding what happened at Brown's, then, is not only a matter of knowing the codes, contexts, and rules or of reading the performances, but it is also a matter of capturing the interpretations made available by such knowledge; of discovering, as nearly as possible, what the desires of the community are in so far as they are discernable in what has been created; and of examining precisely what it is that real people in real situations attempt to locate in the space between the syntax of their relations and the intentions they bring to them. It is, then, a matter of describing what Kafka perceived as "the perpetually shifting frontier that lies between ordinary life and the terror that would seem more real."

What follows, then, is an interpretation of the cultural criteria that allowed participants in the world of Brown's to understand and evaluate their actions. It begins in the practice of talking shit.

Harriet and Teddy had been fighting all morning about the maintenance of the bar. She had declared herself disgusted with the condition of the place, and she was busily and loudly ordering Teddy to clean and sweep it from top to bottom. Teddy had been doggedly fighting back for almost an hour, stubbornly resisting every attempt to make him change his normal routine. Each had become increasingly angry, and the tension between them was growing minute by minute.

H: An' when you get done cleaning up back here, sucker . . . You can do them mirrors. That tape been on them since las' . . . a . . . April.

T: You ain't my boss. Don't you be givin' me orders. When you buy this place then you can be givin' me orders. You jus' . . . you jus' leave me to my job an' get about your own business.

H: Oh why don't you jus' shut up yappin' an' do your job.

Teddy went back to sweeping under the bar. He was using a short broom, so that he was bent over in a crouch with his head down and his eyes focused on his task. He was on the far side of the beer taps facing the main entrance of the bar. When he reached the taps, he swept the dust pile out from under the bar and toward him as he backed away. Harriet, who had been standing on the other side of the taps wiping glasses and audibly slamming them down on the bar during this time, turned, and, seeing Teddy thus bent over, walked on tip toes to where he was working and stood in front of his bent-over body so that her genitalia were directly above his face. Annoyed with her interference with his work, Teddy raised his head to complain and found his face between Harriet's thighs.

T: (angrily) What the . . . WHAT (stands up and moves back four steps) THE FUCK DO YOU THINK YOU'RE DOIN' BITCH? (Loud group laughter with Harriet's voice predominating over all others)

R: OOOWEE! Teddy gettin' lunch a little early. (More group laughter, including Teddy, who smiles and chuckles for the first time)

T: You keep that shit up an' I'm gonna hafta bring MY WIFE down here to take care o' you. Shit, she'll come in here and wipe your ass wit' this bar. Shit, you bein' all big an' bad now . . . but when she through messin' with you . . . You . . . You be NOTHIN'!

E: Harriet's a tough lookin' woman.
    You think your ol' lady handle her?
T: Hee, hee, hee, Ain't nothin' bad 'bout Harriet my wife couldn't
    handle.
            See so all big an' shit . . . hee, hee, hee.
            She dwarf that woman.
            Ol' big legged woman fix her but good.
            Gettin' all up in my face.
            Hafta bring my wife show you who the boss.
            Take you to the LAS' booth.
J: LAS' BOOTH. Watch yourself Harriet.
    She ain't be messin' with you in the las' booth.
H: Don't you worry 'bout nothin'. I can handle . . . I can . . .
    SHIT . . .
            Look at that sucker.
            Sittin' here all day suckin' up that liquor.
            What kind o' woman you think he'd get?
            Talkin' 'bout some ol' big legged woman . . .
            Shit, he get up there 'tween them big legs an' . . . HA, HA,
            HA, HA. . . .
            She'd kill that boy.
            If she didn't crunch the dude . . .
            I mean DAMN he can't weigh but a hundred pounds . . .
J: Soakin' wet.
R: SEAGRAM'S WET!
H: Yeah, full o' gin.
            She'd . . . she'd suck the life out of him on one shot.
            ONE SHOT AN' HE GONE!
            This worryin' dude GOT to have one of them skinny ass
            OLD women.
        I can take that kind fine.
    (Laughter)
T: You be waitin' I'll be bringin' her 'round this afternoon an' we'll
    see.
    She'll do you one better.
    YES SIR!
    You won't be messin' wit' me after this afternoon.
H: BRING HER AROUND!
    BRING HER AROUND!
    I'll be waitin' on you dude.
T: After this afternoon . . . Boy, after this afternoon.

No more Harriet.

Ol' Earl be measurin' you up for one of them hundred dollar coffins . . .

G: Lay her out, Huh Ted?

Charlie be weepin' and orderin' flowers.

Wes an' Bobby be fightin' for firs' car.

All them cars takin' you up to the cemetery.

H: Don't you be orderin' no coffins unless it be for yourself, sucker.

'Cause when I finish with your wife . . .

I'm gonna turn on you.

T: Don't worry me none.

NONE AT ALL!

You talkin' some fancy shit ain't gonna be nothin' when my wife finishes with you.

L: (a patron who had just arrived) You married, Ted?

I didn't know you got married.

(Loud group laughter)

T: No. No. We jus' talkin' shit an' lyin'.

H: NO WE AIN'T. Hee, hee . . .

You married all right.

You married to that Seagram's Gin.

An' you ain't never gonna give HER up 'till death do you part.

(Harriet breaks up into complete laughter.)

(Loud laughter from the full bar for 25 seconds)

(Seven-second silence)

In this particular example of profiling, Teddy is the subject of a series of rapid and unpleasant transformations. At the beginning of the exchange he is made out to be one kind of person and at the end quite another. In between he is the butt of numerous jokes, each more revealing and seemingly more painful than the last. His world is in chaos; he is not himself, and nothing is obvious anymore. His problem is literally one of self-control. Normally the relationship between Harriet and him was orderly and regulated. Each knew and acted out a set of well-defined responsibilities. They were at pains to insure that neither interfered with the work of the other and that neither challenged the social and moral status of the other. They were not perfect, but usually they succeeded in balancing the antagonisms of their relationship so that they could work together smoothly and efficiently. This was not the case here. Harriet had overstepped her authority in telling Teddy to clean the bar. She was right that the bar needed to be cleaned, but telling Teddy was Charlie's responsibility, and Teddy was perfectly right in refusing to do her bidding. At the same time he was expected to keep the bar clean and to follow Harriet's directions when Charlie was not there. The source of the conflict was, then, one of those petty quarrels over prerogative that continually occur in bureaucratic situations. What compounded it here was its public nature. Harriet and Teddy acted out their case before the patrons in the bar, and neither could afford the loss of face that would have resulted in a settlement in the favor of the one or the other. Each was in search, therefore, of a way of justifying his own stances, and each would settle only for absolute vindication. Silent except to hurl accusations, their anger had reached crisis proportions, and it threatened to overwhelm the social world.

Harriet's behavior signaled the depth of the crisis. Seizing an opportunity, she positioned herself over Teddy's face so that it appeared that he was "going down" on her. According to the patrons, in Afro-American culture "going down on a woman" (that is, performing oral sex) is the most despised of sexual acts. For the male it is a complete subjugation to the female and an absolute loss of power within a sexual relation. For the female any man who would willingly engage in such behavior is impotent and not worth having. In demonstrating that Teddy was potentially such a man, Harriet was challenging Teddy's manhood fundamentally. She knew that she was doing this in a safe way—her approach on tiptoes for the benefit of the patrons signaled that her comment on Teddy was to be understood as not serious—but there was no way for Teddy to know this.

From the moment Teddy raised his head, he knew he was in trouble. It was obvious what had happened, and he knew what his choices were. If Harriet was serious in her assertion, then to remain a man he must kill her either literally—by ending her life right there—or metaphorically—by banishing her from the bar. Teddy reflected this knowledge in his first action. His "WHAT THE FUCK DO YOU THINK YOU'RE DOIN' BITCH" was not just simple anger but also a response aimed at establishing a distinctive social tone for what was to follow. Profane language was not acceptable in the bar, and it was never tolerated if directed at the barmaid. For Teddy to direct it at Harriet and for it to occur within their professional relationship signaled that a new order and logic governed his behavior. On the other hand, if Harriet was not serious, then her action was the initial step in the negotiation of another kind of behavior, and Teddy must discover, without loss of face, her intentions and then formulate an appropriate response.

Rick's laughing description of the event provided this information. His comments called public attention to what had happened,
and his manner of delivery defined the nature of the transaction. By
publicly commenting on the relationship presented by Harriet and
Teddy and not on what was implicit in that relationship, Rick signaled that the text proposed was a contest, not a conflict, of wit.
This information was further indicated by the vocal quality of the
utterance: the "oooweee" was loud and extended; the rest of the line
was marked by an underlying chuckling and his use of kinesic marking — a rise up and back from his bar stool accompanied by a spread-
ing of the hands, fingers extended, and a movement of the arms from
in front of the chest out and to the side. Responding to this evidence
of play, Teddy chuckled and countered Harriet's move with an extended threat beginning with: "You keep that shit up an' I'm gonna
hafta bring *my wife* down here to take care of you." This ploy
removed Harriet's characterization of him from the center of attention and focused the group instead on the proposed altercation. By
reformulating the relationship from one between him and Harriet to
one between Harriet and his wife, Teddy downplayed the emphasis
on his own sexuality and substituted a fight between two women.
This threatened fight attracted the attention of the patrons, and they
joined in to discuss Teddy's proposal. Faced with group appeal,
Harriet was forced to accept the countermove and deal with the
fighting wife.

From this point on until near the end of the exchange, Harriet and
Teddy, with help from some patrons, described the nature of the
forthcoming battle and provided varying opinions of its inevitable
outcome. This flow of insult and counterinsult and charge and count-
ercharge continued until a patron who had not been present at the
outset interrupted to ask Teddy when he had gotten married. Called
out of frame by the question, Teddy responded: "No, no. We jus'
talkin' shit an' lyin'," and Harriet used this opportunity to turn Teddy's countermove against him and to "cap on" him: "You married all
right. You married to that Seagram's Gin. An' you ain't never gonna
give her up until death do you part." Denied a wife by circumstance, married to the bottle by Harriet, and faced with the
denial of one wife in order to re-establish a wife just denied, Teddy
retired from the fray in defeat.

The exchange, however, had some use. The chaos that had threatened to overwhelm social life had been controlled, and the balance
in social relations had been re-established. By substituting one argument for another and by defining the second clearly as profiling,

Harriet and Teddy developed a context for interaction in which their anger could be safely expressed and within which it was possible for either one to lose without losing face. It was a context that permitted the normal pattern of barmaid-porter exchanges to develop and allowed Harriet to assert her authority and Teddy to submit. From the moment they ceased to fight and began to rap it was inevitable that Teddy should lose. He was in no way as skilled in the use of words as Harriet. Barmaids were generally described as "women who rapped like men"; to survive in their profession, and to survive the way Harriet had, they had to be better talkers than the men they went up against. No such requirement went with the job of porter. There was also a generalized expectation that any barmaid-porter interchange was a programmed routine in which the requirements of playing the role appropriately would overshadow any possible shift in predictable outcome. Teddy would lose this way because his cultural program had supplied him with a lifetime of rules, plans, maps, and directions on just *how* to lose. The social sanctions imposed for such a loss were known and tolerable and, besides, there were points to be gained even in lost battles. It was a context in which real anger was not real, and control could be achieved through expression rather than repression. The consequences of Teddy's and Harriet's actions depended on their adherence to the rules of this "bar game." To have become serious, to have responded seriously to a play communication, to have broken into anger would have been to suffer immediate shame no matter how justified their actions. The context made it impossible for them to be just angry. They could not flail away; they had to become sharp, and their wit became a cutting edge, not a hammer.

What happened in this sequence is a special example of what Erving Goffman [1971] has defined as a remedial interchange, that is, a ritualized renegotiation of a social order threatened with disintegration. It is special because it involves a much larger complex of relations, actions, and desired ends than is normally the case in such events and because it accomplished its various tasks through the creation and performance of the most intense form of play available. Usually a remedial interchange is a simple affair. You step on my toes accidentally; I yell; you apologize, and I say it was nothing. The structure is compact — violation, recognition, remedy, and relief — and the remedial work to restore equilibrium is minimal. The moral rules that link us together and ourselves to society offer convenient avenues for expressions of self-worth without exacting an excessive cost. You are responsible enough to admit fault and I to minimize the gravity of the event; neither of us has lost anything in the process. The needs of social order are not so easily met in the case of Teddy and Harriet. Because they are the source of public order in the bar, the net effect of their argument is to call into question not only their own status but also the patrons' status, the bar's status, and, in one sense, the status of the entire social world; for, when the police of any society are the cause of riot, then all moral standards are in question. Accordingly, the work necessary to reestablish their world is much greater, and it is not theirs alone [see Kirchenblatt-Gimblett, 1975].

This movement to a world that *all* can live with was clear from the outset of the exchange. Harriet's public assertion of Teddy's sexual status within the play world of rapping offered her the safety of "I was only fooling" if Teddy got out of hand and served notice that what was to follow was not a private fight between the two of them but one open to all present. Likewise, Rick's "Ooowee. Teddy gettin' lunch a little early today" not only gave Teddy a clue that a rap had been offered but also that Rick and the other patrons would be more than spectators to the action. Both Teddy and Harriet showed their awareness of these rules by according equal status to Earl's, Rick's, and Jimmy's questions, comments, and cracks throughout the interaction.

The acceptance of this public rapping arrangement brought about a realignment of several necessary relationships. First, it asserted the validity of the new order being established by affirming Harriet's status over Teddy. Remarks addressed to Teddy by patrons were of two types: attacks ("soakin' wet. SEAGRAM'S WET"; "gettin' lunch a little early") or questions ("Lay her out, Ted?"; "you think your wife can take her?"). The former directly characterized Teddy as inadequate, leaving no doubt as to his status as target, and the latter demonstrated his lack of verbal skill by providing opening gambits that he could not follow through on, but Harriet could. On the other hand, no direct attacks were leveled at Harriet and the one commentary ("las' booth, watch yourself, Harriet") was one that she easily picked up and played with. Second, this realignment allowed the boundaries of order to develop and extend so that the patrons were also accorded status above Teddy. They might crack on him, but he would not crack back. To be sure, his attention was focused on Harriet and the depth of his encounter with her, but his inability to cope with both sets of actors in the exchange while she could indicated his still lower place in the hierarchy. Finally, the realignment affirmed the validity of the conclusion of the rap by allowing Teddy to remain silent after Harriet made him out to be a public drunk. This role was the expected characterization of bar porters, and no one, not even Teddy, rose to challenge the description. This is, I think, because everyone recognized that moral order had been achieved again and that everyone could get back to business. Each participant had been returned to his or her rightful place, and Teddy, the only one who might have complained about the result, was silenced by twenty-five seconds of laughter.

In the end, then, not much seems to have really happened. For those involved it was a small event full of a great deal of fun. Everyone, after all, was just profiling. What happened was no different than any other sequence of profiling they had been part of or witness to. Everyone partied tough and got very deep, but no one was all tore up or off the wall at the end. The changes that occurred were real only inside the fight, and only then because they symbolically played out alternative images of the world that could be safely disregarded with the resumption of normal relations. Teddy's gamble and its payoff, for all its personal and social utility, were life as usual, over in a short time and forgotten almost as quickly. Given all of this, what does this interaction mean?

A starting point can be found in Sigmund Freud, who wrote, "There is a path back again from fantasy to reality, and that is *art*" [1922, p. 114]. It is an observation ideally suited to this exchange. It is also unfortunately freighted with an excessive cultural baggage. For some in our culture it conjures up images of self-contained, abstract icons isolated from the real world; for others art represents a qualitatively distinct experience reserved for the gifted few who either because of extraordinary talent are truly creative or because of wealth have the time to acquire taste; for still others art is a rejection of the functionality of experience and an elevation of the impractical, the trivial, and the odd. In suggesting that this event is art, and by extension that profiling is art, I am arguing that, like literature, music, and painting, this interaction and the others like it share the essential qualities of the language of art [Armstrong, 1971]. In particular, these interactions call attention to their existence and their essential structure; they are produced with an awareness of the quality and pattern of their performance, and they display the fundamental moral issues of the community for whom and by whom they are created. They are, like all art, self-reflexive, skillful, and valued [Dewey, 1934; Morris, 1946; Jones, 1971, 1975; Mukarovsky, 1977, 1978].

The reflexivity of this sequence is most obvious in its fictionality.

Among all else that has happened in this interaction, it is clear that
what was occurring was of such intensity that it could only be undertaken as a fiction. Just as clearly, it was not the only choice available. As has been shown, it is possible to rap without becoming as
intense as Teddy and Harriet were, and this level of organization
was, therefore, a conscious choice on the part of all involved. Such a
choice speaks to the quality of moral linkages desired by the patrons
and staff of the bar and the depth to which they will transform experience in order to reintegrate themselves into a whole world. The
fabrication of a new and distinctive world in order to rebuild a threatened one began with Harriet's initial move. Her creativity, however,
was totally within the context of the bar and depended entirely on
the emerging flow of interaction. The organization of experience into that precise arrangement of bodies was luck, and her seizure of
the moment to manipulate the behavioral stream carried with it no
guarantee that her creativity would exist beyond its performance.
Teddy's response, then, added a qualitatively different dimension to
her action when he chose to alter the context of interpretation for
Harriet's actions. By introducing a person whom everyone immediately present knew was nonexistent, Teddy challenged the grounds
for the discovery of meaning and suggested not only that was Harriet playing false but also that she was raising a problem that could
not be dealt with at any other level than fiction. His false wife challenged no one, especially not Harriet, but her presence offered a
level of consciousness that caused everyone to doubt, to play with,
and finally to affirm his state of being. By transforming reality into
fiction, instead of continuing to be angry or lashing out at his tor-
mentors, Teddy created a highly specialized discourse wherein the
communication of significant symbols about himself and the social
order was more useful than personal attack. This artful circle was
completed first by the patrons' acceptance of Teddy's wife and then
by Harriet's legitimization of her and the fictional world she represented. Through their combined acknowledgment of the play and of
the belief that the play should be played, they developed a fictional
web in which everyone became at once and in turn characters, actors, audiences, and texts; all were available for the free use of the
other in the attack of whatever threatened experience.

In this new frame Teddy was brought forth, attacked for his re-
sistance, and safely punished for his transgressions. But his Teddy
was not real; he was a character in a self-generated play, and the
social disorganization of which he was accused was symbolic of
larger issues than simply his refusal to clean a bar. He became a

comic victim estranged by his world so that he could be sacrificed for the common good. For Harriet the gains in this action are self-explanatory. She was angry at Teddy and her actions before, during, and after the play allowed her to express this anger. Teddy's creativity upped the ante, of course, but this merely sweetened the results by adding the pleasure of play to the game. Likewise, the patrons had the pleasure of watching and participating in Teddy's symbolic destruction. They were, for the most part, middle-class blacks, and Teddy threatened them with his challenge of the hierarchy of order. They were angry because Teddy used to be one of them. He was a licensed mortician and had worked for some of the better funeral homes in the city. His assertion of equality placed their senses of self in doubt by showing them other selves they could have become. No one likes to be confronted by an alternative presence when one shares a common past. Their sacrifice of Teddy was one way of asserting their difference and of accenting the personal nature of his failure. What, then, of Teddy? Here he is a complete and classic victim. Though he has been creative and resourceful, in the end he has been the joke, a character played with much too much. He willingly donned the mask for his destruction. He sought out this arena so that he could obligingly fail in each encounter, until, at the end, unmasked and humiliated, he accepted with his own laughter a definition of himself as a real drunk in a real world.

The skill in this scene was reflected both in the particularity of the play created and in its accomplishment. For example, Teddy's choice of a fictional wife to oppose Harriet matched in cultural depth her characterization of his sexuality and challenged her almost as much as she had challenged him. As discussed previously, in the black community the structure of roles can be divided into two rough classes, those based on "respect" and those based on "reputation" [see also Stoeltje, 1972]. The former are marked by adherence to the values and rules of family, church, and home, while the latter are marked by a reliance on skill in verbal competition and contest. Usually respect is associated with women's roles and reputation with men's, and usually each is localized to women's and men's contexts, the house and the street, respectively. Harriet, however, moved between both environments. As a woman she was measured for her respectability, and as a barmaid she was measured for reputation. By threatening her with his "wife," Teddy forced her into a dilemma not unlike his own. If she chose to fight a respectable wife as a respectable woman, then she would lose face in the bar. If she chose to fight a respectable "wife" as a barmaid, then she would cease to be respectable herself. What was established between them, therefore, was an equality of potential: where previously only one of them had anything to lose, now both had. And since both of them had something to lose, both had a reason for playing the event for all that it was worth. Again, the likelihood that Teddy would win was small, but his choice of performance context and content assured him that the battle would not begin with disproportionate states on either side.

From Harriet's perspective Teddy's gambit demanded that she respond in intensity and kind. Recognizing that she had only opened the battle in her initial interchange with Teddy, Harriet was placed in the position of having to continue performing with equal or greater strength in order to maintain her appropriateness in this new field of discourse. Teddy's reaction had turned her initial strength into a disadvantage, and it was necessary for her to recoup by overmatching his rejoinder. In this sense the movement of the rap into profiling had put them into a relationship in which the evaluation of their ability to rap was based on their continued development of ever more complicated and fanciful characterizations of each other. Judged from this perspective, Harriet's final cap on Teddy was a masterful working of an unexpected break in the flow of experience into a social metaphor that both re-established profiling as the mode of performance and denied to Teddy any further possibility that he could continue his rap as he had begun it. By accepting Teddy's marriage Harriet had validated his initial claim and the fictional world that supported it, but by identifying his wife with Seagram's gin she had linked that claim to the real world and to the real Teddy whom everyone knew. Teddy had no escape. The freedom he gained with his fictional flight into marriage was denied as that fiction assumed a too real guise. Harriet demonstrated brilliantly, as Teddy had when he began the encounter, that she knew the essential structure of rapping, the adaptation that particular structure had undergone in their rap, the organization of the real world it had replaced, the peculiar ties that bound their fiction to the real world, and most importantly how to bring them all together in a singularly crushing finale.

But this is not a play; it is only like a play, and individuals are not that willing to suffer public disgrace to satisfy social needs. What had been negotiated by Teddy, at great expense, is not, I think, his own sacrifice, but a carefully wrought restitution of self-esteem. In Teddy's action one can see a continual struggle against self-images imposed by others until the proposed self is the same as his work self in the bar. He begins to rap when experience destroys him; he continues to rap, hoping that the reality inside the "play" will match the one he lost and knowing that such an evolution is problematic and open to doubt; he ceased to fight back only when his new character was achieved. In the often cold and harsh world of black life, to be thought a drunk is better than to be a sexual failure. For Teddy, being thought a drunk was a character he had lived with. It was a character for which he possessed a set of defenses; it was an identity from which he could distance himself at will, and yet it was a conservative choice. Teddy's victory was no great triumph. Certainly he was able to create a play space in which his conflict with Harriet could be acted out inside fairly safe boundaries, but he remained unable to transform reality. Harriet had usurped an authority that was not hers, and when Teddy fought back it was only in terms of that authority structure. At every point Harriet reminded him of his dependence. Teddy's role is a painful stereotype, all the more so because his gain — the restoration of desire and the two rounds of unexpected verbal skill — was only realizable when he was the center of experience. When he was included in the ongoing social world and comedic resolution became the goal, the event changed. Located in this frame, his personal display was transformed into public portrayal, and the sense of what had happened was found in the cost of group integration and conflict resolution. For comedy, especially as it is performed in this exchange, is often conservative in its outlook and savage in its drive for order. Teddy's regaining of his old self was a small price to pay for the self-congratulatory process of putting everyone in his rightful place. That Teddy remained on the bottom beneath a woman and that he was parodied to soothe and soften their fears had little consequence if everyone else was on top where they knew they belonged. When the group as a whole — successes and failures — are located in the profiling enacted, that is, at the intersection of the white and black worlds around them, the sense of the fiction shifts again. Here the play of place and order plays with them ironically as they play with Teddy. They put Teddy in his place in order to affirm their own; the world keeps them in their place. They will not set their wily slave free, and the world will not free them.

It is here in the intersection of these differing, though complementary, systems of position and power that the value of this interaction emerges. What happened in the playing out of this short sequence was related directly to the power struggles of Harriet and Teddy, but their involvement carried a significance far beyond its presentation in this petty squabble. Their battle raised into consciousness not only their own small relations in their own small world but also in the process spoke at several levels to the basic cultural distribution of prestige, role, and status among middle-class blacks. Harriet and Teddy were, after all, concerned with basic identity — with who was who, with how each should act in the presence of each other and the assembled crowd, and with what image this interactive dyad ought to present as it negotiated a solution to its crisis. Their solutions to these questions remained particular, but the underlying structure of action they validated displayed a world view in which clear boundaries of self and other existed. Yet in the beginning this was not an obvious fact. Like the real world which they officially represented, and in which they really lived, Harriet's and Teddy's interaction began in ambiguity.

At the start of their encounter both participants, by common consent, shared a role structure and an unstated system of assumptions that permitted them to interact freely and that permitted the patrons to act unself-consciously in their presence. It was, again, an inversion of the normal organization of male-female relations in the larger world of which the bar was a part and which in its tightly enclosed milieu the bar mirrored for its users. That world held firmly, and almost obsessively, the middle-class American ideal of men's and women's places, of office against home, as visible evidence of its members' successful attainment of the "good life." The male patrons of Brown's did not want their wives to work, and if they did work they wanted everyone to know that their wives worked out of choice and not necessity. Thus, the pattern of role dominance in the bar represented a potential threat to the core beliefs that structured the orderly ways of the local community. For surely, if it was possible to invert the normal world and still have that world survive intact, then the relationship between male and female that the patrons used to make sense of their experiences was not, as they wished, a matter of cultural law but rather was a product of cultural agreement. Like all the threats discussed, this one, too, was minimized by the expectations of the jobs performed and by what the patrons knew of Teddy and Harriet. Still, this threat was a constant undercurrent in their relationship, and its presence did reflect the unspoken boundaries surrounding their actions with and against each other. Thus, when their relationship failed and exploded in anger so, too, did the world they reflected. Where before there had been a secure sense of place and explanation, there were now multiple sets of conflicting signals, each constituting their own sensible languages. The harmony implicit in Teddy's and Harriet's acceptance of their roles and the belief evidenced by their identification with their biographical selves was replaced by a cacophony of discourse and rage. In the vacuum left by their initial interaction, all claims were legitimate and all allegiances were valid.

In its widest sense, therefore, their and their patrons' ability to put the world back together was a reassertion of the social basis of order and of the validity of the world they represented. By recreating the world as it was before it was breached, the participants and particularly the central actors offered up for themselves and the audience a method for dispersing madness. The Humpty-Dumpty qualities inherent in the collapse of the moral ground were banished by a negotiation that created anew what had been lost and that pointed to the possibility that such recreations were themselves fundamental to the structure of action by which the world was brought into being at each moment of time.

Such value, therefore, was not simply the value inherent in all ritualizations. Rather, the order here was at the core of interactive experience for the patrons of Brown's. By their own acknowledgment, what angered and frightened them about their own lives was the illusiveness that wove itself through their daily experiences. Repeatedly in the discussions quoted thus far the patrons of Brown's acknowledged that they were working toward goals that they needed to be real and firm and that, because of their blackness, were neither. Like Teddy and Harriet, their desires and relationships were rendered fragile by a tension over which they had no control but for which they were held responsible. Like Teddy and Harriet, the ordinariness of their struggles and strivings overlay possibilities that threatened far more than just their own place in the world. As one informant rudely said: "If I win it's because I'm a lucky nigga; if I lose it's because I'm a dumb nigga." To which responded another: "Always a nigger, no matter what though." This sequence of profiling offered up the possibility that an integrated self was possible even when the world outside of one's control was demanding and expecting multiple presentations to be played out on an ever-shifting stage. In Teddy's and Harriet's discoveries of themselves and their particular places existed a way to find boundaries where none seemed to exist. That their search led them into an unsatisfying past was perhaps inevitable; that it led them there without destroying them was not. Always the raw edge of reality was blunted by its transformation into fiction. By profiling, by using its artful qualities as the vehicle for replaying experience, all of the participants remained in control of themselves and their world. They were not wholly perfect, nor was their world the way it ought to be, but at least a livable, expressible reality remained to sustain them. Harriet had her revenge, the patrons their place, and Teddy was once again made of "palpable flesh and bone" and not fantasy.

When the examples of profiling presented in the previous chapter are examined in this light, it is obvious that they, too, display the same concern for order and boundaries that dominates this particular example. What distinguished the performances of Brown's Lounge was that they all turned on the question of individual intentions in a shifting universe and, particularly, on the problem of locating self within the context of conflicting demands placed upon lovers, husbands and wives, family, children, and friends. At the center of each performance was a problem of belief and doubt. Should honesty and love override the pain of separation? How can children discover their parents and learn to value their images of them? And are there limits to the acting of self? In each case what was discovered through profiling was the projected wish that problems could be resolved without a loss of integrity or a sacrifice of identity. The plain truth of Billie Holliday spoke to an experience divorced from that formulated by Jimmy. His fiction was not an interpretation of the meaning of the song but an imposition onto the text of a relationship in which the expected rejection of the man because of his implied actions was overridden by the more humane response of acceptance. His result was an assertion that neither participant lost when, in fact, normally something would be lost by both. With Uncle Nick, the question turned on his children's discovery of who he was even though he no longer lived with them. His text sought to use self-awareness and knowledge as a solution to an ignorance imposed from without. His kids came to know him in a crystallized instant by recognizing that his word was absolute and true. In a different way, but no less insistently, the two performances of Rick emphasized the conflicting demands middle-class status placed on the creation and maintenance of a livable and useful self. Like Nick, Rick wanted to be recognized as a man of his word and as a man of words. His use of a street characterization was a method of remaining a part of the widest black community and of identifying himself with the attitudes and beliefs of that world. Its use in the bar world was in some sense a serio-comic attack on the order internalized in Brown's, but even with this as an aspect of his raps he still, like the other profilers, sought in his actions to elevate the black male ability by presenting himself as deserving of respect. Thus, his monologue created a fantasy of a powerful male performance, which by its display of self succeeded in convincing a woman to surrender. In so doing, it displayed a pattern of relationship and dominance in which masculine self, by its presence alone, captured and captivated a woman. Alternately, his rap on Teddy turned on the self-doubt present in the act of interacting itself. Here the question was of control and of appropriateness in the face of an increasingly frenetic involvement in the social life of the bar. His assertion of his success at "flyin'," at not losing control, served to remind his audience and himself of the possibility of power, albeit frenzied, in the face of the destructiveness of partying tough.

At the heart of profiling, in its demands of fictionality and artfulness, lies the clearest expression of the meaning of talking shit. Yet even here, the presentation of cultural fundamentals creates illusive visions that are not easily fixed. They are not illusive, however, because they are subjective. The particular sequence examined and the other examples that it represents are not first meaningful and then nonmeaningful because the perspective of analysis is shifted from one participant to another or from individuals to the group. The meaning shifts because the level of analysis changes, and each new level is added or subtracted from the field of observation and interpretation. Thus, though the contents of each scene were distinctive, the pattern of the journeys for all involved was the same. Each began in fiction in order to regain the real world. Though the gains as perceived by each participant at each level of play were different, the travels of all were as social as was their art — and not simply because the art was negotiated in public but because it created, changed, and even destroyed the entirety of their culture in its performance. Profiling, then, gave the patrons of Brown's a method by which they could test the fundamental assumptions that organized and ordered their lives within and outside the bar. It provided a process wherein the demands of artfulness and fictionality freed those involved from responsibility and accountability and allowed them to act out their own pathways back to the real world. It became, therefore, a way of going deep in order to get back to the orderly surface of their lives. In its most intense, to talk shit was to play freely with the structures and values that made the public and playful lives of the patrons of Brown's possible. It meant to profile in order that the intensity created would allow for things to be said that would otherwise have been lost in silence. It meant, then, not to flee from the world, but to find the world.

What is captured interpretively in profiling is no less at the center of styling and playing. They, too, to paraphrase Clifford Geertz

[1974, p. 448], are black middle-class readings of black middle-class experience, a story they tell themselves about themselves. Their difference is that their illumination of the paradox of self-identity as it is expressed in the experience of being black and middle class is not a commentary on that status but an experiment with that status. They share the focus of play in Brown's, and they also come to be in the nexus of order breached and order restored, but they cannot separate their process of creation from the realities they create. They are the necessary conditions out of which profiling is made, but they do not reach its depth and intensity. In this they share in the intentions and desires most fully translated in profiling; the only difference is their eloquence.

To discover that being black and middle class is at the core of black middle-class play may seem in the end to be a discovery of the obvious, one made no more meaningful by its assertion that this commentary is accomplished through play in its simplest and through the creation and performance of art in its most complex. Play and art, after all, are by definition contexts in which the necessities of practicality and consequentiality are subordinated to the freedoms of *as if* potentialities. Yet it is precisely this paradox that is so important, for it is this obvious function that renders such intensity so important to the continued existence of the world of Brown's Lounge and its patrons. In its performance it not only displays the world as it is but also creates that world anew so that it can continue to be. Its display is not fixed in the materials it uses to create its fictions or its other texts but is perpetually open in the meanings it fashions out of these materials. The art of talking shit makes of all of its texts of profiling, styling, and playing readings of everyday life for those who live it. They are, then, not simply images of the world but pathways for being in the world. They are neither fantasies nor pathologies, but real worlds made more real in order that ordinary lives can remain ordinary. They remain behind the intensities they create, commentaries on each other from profiling to styling to playing to the world outside the bar. Talking shit makes an ordinary world within the bar so that that world can mean something for those who both use it and continue to live in the outside world. It is both a world in its own right and a world within a larger one. Within it the patrons of Brown's can search for themselves and create selves that can carry forward their intentions in the real world. The sense of talking shit is its ability to render ordinary experience sensible by capturing the particular themes of everyday life that challenge, terrorize, and organize the patrons of Brown's into real selves in real worlds. The world it creates and that is recreated by the patrons is not perfect, nor is everything the way it ought to be, but at least in its creation individuals are able to survive.

9   The World from Brown's Lounge

In his *Selected Essays* William Carlos Williams makes the point that "it is in the minutiae—in the minute organization of the words and their relationships in a composition that the seriousness and value of a work of writing exist—*not* in the sentiments, ideas, schemes portrayed. It is here, furthermore, that creation takes place. It is not a plaster of thought applied" [1954, p. 104]. Williams was concerned with an aesthetics of poetry, with establishing the ground on which a language of poetry could be constructed and with devising a set of coordinates for speaking about the organization of poetic language, but his concerns are equally applicable to the ordinary life in Brown's. Here, too, creation was the key. The patrons came to the bar because it was a place where they could make and remake the universe to their own ends, and they stayed and returned because this freedom to construct multiple realities gave them the opportunity to evaluate their lives apart from the ambiguities that surrounded them. And here, too, the value of experience grew out of the arrangements and patterns of communication played by the patrons with and for each other. As the preceding chapters have demonstrated, it was in the small components of space and spacial organization, of social and moral expectations, and of language use and practical action that the intention of Brown's and the complex human activity it contained emerged. The chapters have described the assumptions standing behind normal interaction in the bar; they have discussed the kinds of structures that evolved from these assumptions; they have identified the practical actions that gave rise to these structures; and they have mapped the performances wherein the world was rendered meaningful. At each level of analysis they have shown that the goal of all of these transformations has been the

continuous formation of an arena for interactional play, that is, of
an environment in which it was possible for the patrons to take time
out from the intentions of the serious world outside the bar and to
create a fictional universe in which they could address the fundamental moral and structural issues affecting their lives. In sum they
have shown that the totality of Brown's was the way it was for its
patrons in order that they might have a place to find, to lose, to shat-
ter, and to renew themselves without irreparable harm. That
Brown's Lounge was a world of talking shit wherein through play,
deep play, and sometimes art its patrons could be all that they were
—black, middle class, successful, angry, scared, or proud—is the
thesis of this work. It will stand or fall on the basis of the materials
that have been presented.

There are other, wider issues, however, that Williams's ideas raise
and that are also a part of the intentions of the world of Brown's.
Williams valued works of writing because their contrivance gave
them a special reality. It set them apart from other acts of composition and forced them to be read against other, more enlivened texts
of experience. Distance gave them power to reformulate and resitu-
ate the world. It was the core of their fictionality and the source of
their meaning. Brown's, too, was designed to be a separate experience. Its patrons and its staff consciously sought to distance what
happened there from the ordinary occurrences of the serious world.
And for all of its reality, it was as equally contrived as Williams's
texts. Nothing that happened or was done touched the outside world
half as much as that world dictated the experience of being in the
bar. Life in the bar made sense and was meaningful only as long as it
did not interfere with the experiences of work, family, and business.
It was good fun because it stayed inside behind tightly closed doors.
Like Williams's fictions, its distance was at the heart of its meaning
and at the core of its organization. Yet, to say that Brown's was a
fiction, was only play and nothing more, is to risk transforming it into an empty metaphor. Unlike Williams's poetry, Brown's did not
exist on paper, and it was not the product of an authorial mind. It
was not immutable, and it was not a fantasy writ upon the world.
The world that was created was not a simple displacement of reality, nor was it a replacement or even misplacement of the world at
hand. Brown's was the world. What happened there, whatever else
it was, was ultimately the building of real human lives by real
human beings. Thus, for all their imaginary qualities, the performances that made up the everyday life of the bar were not, in the
strict sense, illusions. They were not escapes from a known world in-

to the safe confines of a controlled, shared symbolism; they were not projections of known expectations on consciously evolved literary languages; and, finally, they were not consistent imaginative experiences. Within the world of Brown's as it was realized from moment to moment by the patrons and staff, there was no room for the retrospection commonly associated with the reading of a literary text [see Iser, 1972, p. 287–95]. After the fact, Brown's performances might be undone, redone, dismissed, or denied, but during their accomplishment they could only be done. Accordingly, they offered no privileged reality against which they could be read. The patrons had no way to watch themselves having an aesthetic experience, nor did they possess the customary sense that artistic processes were the responsibility of a separated artist. Regardless of their involvement in the performance at hand, the patrons were not divided in their attentions, nor were they readers of their own experiences. Being in Brown's meant involvement. It meant a commitment to the program of partying tough and doing it to death, and this, in turn, demanded that all conversational scenes be pushed to the threshold of the imagination. Thus, the more comforting, more typical perception of creativity as a world of finite texts, self-contained authors, and audiences does not hold for the social life of the bar or for the participation of its patrons. The critical difference between Brown's and Williams's fictions and between Brown's and the customary understanding of fictionality is that the construction of its fictional universe involved not the creation of experiences beyond experience but the creation of experience itself, the building of culture anew. In a real sense, then, the world from Brown's attacks the most compelling fiction about fiction we have. What is apparent about the ordinary life of Brown's Lounge is that the imagination is not apart from the practical concerns and consequences of practical actions and that fiction and fiction-making exist not only outside of life or in opposition to it but also at its center.

Moreover, this centering of the imagination in everyday occurrences points directly to what is black about the interactions that made up the world of the bar. Again, for the patrons of Brown's, to be in the bar, to play, to style, and to profile meant to be an active part of the creation of conversation. They did not wait for others to initiate action, and they did not watch from a distance when others performed; instead they articulated a social and moral order that placed the highest value on a total commitment of self to playing, talking, arguing, interacting—to doing whatever was demanded to keep social life vital. As one can see from the extended interactions presented, every participant was constantly monitoring the actions of the others present, constantly looking to see if anyone had left themselves "wide open," in hopes of turning even the simplest of conversation into an occasion for styling or something more. Above all, the connections of content, genre, and context that might have bound the world of Brown's together, the one commonality of performance that most completely tied the interaction together, was the collective intensity of the dramatic structuring of interaction. In Brown's the whole focus of participation was on the opening up of experience and on the inclusion of everyone into the scene being created. Even in the most controlled conversational exchanges, where an intense effort was being made to exclude the others present from the text, those excluded still tried to participate by the creation of commentaries that somehow had to be answered. Accordingly, what was most distinctive about performance was the rejection of the ideas about boundaries in communication that are necessary to the smooth functioning of the serious world outside the bar. Unlike the particular "real" world that they were members of and that they acknowledged was ordered by modes of deference and demeanor determined by whites, the world in the bar specifically rejected the idea that there was "some obligation and some effort on the part of . . . participants to act as if . . . engagement[s] were physically cut off from the rest of the situation" [Goffman, 1963, p. 156]. In place of the normal understanding of the appropriate formalities of social gatherings (wherein participants are expected to be directly involved with those whom they are with and apart from those who are not with them) the patrons of Brown's acted out their business as nigger business. In place of what might have been expected, given their avowed pursuit and valuing of mainstream American goals, the patrons subscribed neither to the formulas of focused attention nor to the patterns of civil inattention. They did not remove themselves from each other, and they did not allow those who acted to create energy, artistic or otherwise, to interpose a silence between themselves and the rest of the group. Rather, they attended to the norms and values of the black community and created contexts of involvement wherein the fundamental expectation placed upon those present was to give of oneself in order to create community [see, Abrahams, 1964, 1970a, 1970b, 1970c, 1972c; Hannerz, 1969; Mitchell-Kernan, 1971; Rainwater, 1970; Reisman, 1970, 1974]. In the presence of each other they kept no distance and respected no one who did not treat experience and its playing as a process of collective action. The patrons came to the bar in order to play with each other, not to perform for each other. Every transcript, every page of talk from which this work has been built, echoes this idea. What is black about the patrons of Brown's is not wholly the color of their skin, for neither language or culture necessarily follow the color line. What is black is that they understood that they might choose to create any style of language in Brown's from all the contexts of speech in which they lived their lives: they could have made it into the outside world of white culture or made it into the inside world of the Nassau Inn simply by changing nothing; they chose, instead, to build a "corner" for themselves and to use it as a place to "talk shit." What is black about the world from Brown's Lounge is that it was a place where performance could happen any time, where no single individual was the ultimate maker of speech and art, and where all present interacted at the threshold of the imagination for their entire stay in the bar. What is black is that expression is at the center of experience, and experience is only real when all are a functioning part of its creation.

Brown's, then, was indeed the world of make-believe that E. Franklin Frazier predicted it would be, but in far different ways than he meant or imagined. It was a fictional world because its patrons and staff wanted and believed that they needed an environment in which they could act and interact without caring about how the outside world would react. But it was a fictional world based in and recreative of a conscious desire on the part of the patrons to have a place where they could be as black as they wanted to be. Those who used the bar did not flee there, and they did not remain at the bar to avoid the challenges of the real world. Brown's was no false reality, no pathological exercise for a group with no ability to cope with reality. Instead, it was a place where those who wanted or needed to ask themselves and others legitimate questions about self and community could ask and answer in a responsible manner. Not everyone "up the hill" needed Brown's, nor was everyone concerned with the reasons for which it existed, but those who came were deeply involved with their personal self-worth and with their places in the world. Central to their concerns was their belief that the ordinary consequences of being in the everyday world allowed them no real time to assess their lives and no real privacy to discover their values. Coming to Brown's was a way of finding such a place and participating in Brown's was a way of testing their values. The distance the bar gave them, therefore, was not a way out of the world that had no place for them but a way into a world that they made for themselves. What can be said with certainty about Brown's Lounge and the men and women who frequented it was that the world therein was not a part of their existence of which they were ashamed and that what they created were not experiences which demanded a state of nothingness to relieve their burdens. Both were parts of their lives, but they were not the only concern that faced them. The patrons were fiercely individual. They wished to be treated as persons, not as representatives of a race or as members of an invisible community. That this was not always the case made them angry and sometimes bitter. Most of all, however, it showed them how fragile life was and how important it was that they have a place where they could create a usable sense of themselves. This they made in Brown's, and the result was a world in which they were able to identify what mattered to them and in which they were able to be what they wanted to be; a world which allowed them to assert to themselves that they were black in the face of the white world's desire that they be something more and the black world's fear that they had become something less.

There are three final points to be made. First, the facts of Brown's Lounge and its social life described in this book present a picture of everyday living that no patron or staff member would recognize in its entirety. The world of Brown's delineated here is more complete than that obtained from the explanations of either single informants or all the participants in the bar life together. Accordingly, no one patron would recognize all of what has been presented nor would every patron agree with what has been said. Ultimately, then, what is presented here are *my* perceptions, *my* record of *my* experiences.

Second, the behaviors and performances described here are restricted, for Brown's is an anachronism that under today's conditions could not in all likelihood come to be. It is a relic of a different neighborhood and of a different way of life. The existence of the bar was premised on the existence of a white working-class set of expectations formulated over thirty years before. Granted, the bar fulfills a legitimate need for the community, but its presence calls attention to that need in a way which is not wholly resolvable with the aspirations of the community. As a result, what happened in Brown's could only happen at the bar. Accordingly, the performances which happened there were more intense than those that have been described as happening in other ethnographies of black culture [see Anderson, 1978; Manning, 1975]. Restricted by its world, the playing and partying tough of Brown's were often harder and deeper than it might have otherwise been. This skewing of the proportions of performance does not necessarily invalidate the findings of this work. If similar interactions are to be sought in other contexts, however, it must be recognized that their frequency and intensity will not necessarily be the same.

Finally, there is the problem of my place in the presentation. There is always the risk that informants will tell the ethnographer what they think he wants to hear. If they believe that I am a friend, they may want to help by altering behavior or conversations; if they believe that I am the enemy, they may tell lies so that I will go away. Because I am white and my informants were black, the latter is a definite possibility in this work. I do not believe it is the case, but there is no way to be completely sure, since the choice was not mine to make. There is also the possibility that I was consciously or unconsciously used by my informants as a way to present information that might otherwise go unheard or unnoticed. Everyone knew that I would be writing a book about my experiences, and my presence provided a forum for self-expression of a fundamental sort. What was said to me would inevitably be said by me to others. Because I was white, and thus for the most obvious and worst reason, it would be listened to in ways different than if I had been black. Accordingly, the overwhelming focus of performance, casual and artistic, on the problem of a self trapped between the conflicting demands of personal desire and public expectations may not be central to the patrons' experiences but may be what the patrons wish the outside world to be most aware of in their existence. If this is the case, I do not object to being the intermediary for such information, and I do not believe that this work suffers as a result. The object of ethnography is not merely to illuminate the lives of others, but it is also to find ways to bridge the distances that exist between ourselves and those we perceive as different. If it is the informants who build those bridges, so much the better. I can only hope that I have said what it was that the patrons of Brown's wanted to be said and that I have shown them to be as they showed themselves to me.

Bibliography

Abrahams, Roger D. Playing the Dozens. *Journal of American Folklore*, 75:209–20, 1962.

_____. *Deep Down in the Jungle . . . Negro Narrative Folklore from the Streets of Philadelphia*. Hatboro, Pa.: Folklore Associates, 1964.

_____. *Positively Black*. Englewood Cliffs, N.J.: Prentice-Hall, 1970a.

_____. Rapping and Capping: Black Talk as Art. In *Black America*, ed. J. F. Szwed, pp. 132–42. New York: Basic Books, 1970b.

_____. Patterns of Performance in the British West Indies. In *Afro-American Anthropology*, ed. N. Whitten, Jr., and J. F. Szwed, pp. 163–79. New York: The Free Press, 1970c.

_____. Creativity, Individuality and the Traditional Singer. *Studies in the Literary Imagination*, 3:5–34, 1970d.

_____. The Black Uses of Black English. Manuscript, 1971.

_____. The Training of the Man of Words in Talking Sweet. *Language in Society*, 1:15–30, 1972a.

_____. Joking: Training of the Man of Words in Talking Broad. In *Rappin' and Stylin' Out: Communication in Urban Black American*, ed. T. Kochman, pp. 215–40. Urbana: University of Illinois Press, 1972b.

_____. A True and Exact Survey of Talking Black. Manuscript prepared for the Conference on the Ethnography of Speaking, University of Texas at Austin, Apr. 20–22, 1972c.

_____. Ritual, or the In and Outs of Celebration. Manuscript, 1973.

_____. *Talking Black*. Rowley, Mass.: Newbury House Publishers, 1976.

_____. Negotiating Respect. *Journal of American Folklore*, 88:12–35, 1977.

_____, and R. Bauman. Sense and Non-Sense in St. Vincent: Speech Behavior in a Caribbean Community. *American Anthropologist*, 73:762–72, 1971.

_____, and John Szwed. *Discovering Afro-America*. Leiden: E. J. Brill, 1975.

Altman, I. Ecological Aspects of Interpersonal Functioning. In *Behavior and Environment*, ed. A. H. Esser, pp. 201–17, New York: Plenum Press, 1971.

Anderson, Elijah. *A Place on the Corner*. Chicago: University of Chicago Press, 1978.

Armstrong, Robert Plant. *The Affecting Presence: An Essay in Humanistic Anthropology*. Urbana: University of Illinois Press, 1971.

Axlerod, M. Urban Structure and Social Participation. *American Sociological Review*, 21:13–18, 1956.

Banton, Michael. *Roles*. London: Tavistock (1965), 1968.

Barker, Roger G. *Ecological Psychology. Concepts and Methods for Studying the Environment of Human Behavior*. Stanford, Calif.: Stanford University Press, 1968.

_____, ed. *The Stream of Behavior*. New York: Appleton-Century Crofts, 1963.

_____, and H. F. Wright. *Midwest and Its Children*. New York: Harper and Row, 1955.

Bascom, William. Verbal Art. *Journal of American Folklore*, 68:245–52, 1955.

Bateson, Gregory, *Naven*, 2d ed. Standord, Calif.: Stanford University Press (1935), 1958.

_____, ed. *Steps to an Ecology of Mind*. New York: Ballantine Books, 1972.

Bauman, R. Differential Identity and the Social Base of Folklore. *Journal of American Folklore*, 84:31–41, 1971.

_____. The Le Harve General Store. *Journal of American Folklore*, 84:330–43, 1972.

_____. Verbal Art as Performance. *American Anthropologist*, 77:290–311, 1975.

Becker, Howard S. Art as Collective Action. *American Sociological Review*, 39:767–76, 1974.

Bell, Michael J. Rapping with the Iron Pimp: Multi-Media Folkloric Communication in an Urban Black Bar. *Working Papers in Culture and Communication*, 1:74–97, 1976.

_____. Tending Bar at Brown's: Occupational Role as Artistic Performance. *Western Folklore*, 25:93–107, 1976.

_____. The Kinesics of Performance: An Example Described. *Southern Folklore Quarterly*, 41:17–31, 1977.

_____. Social Control/Social Order/Social Art. *Sub-Stance*, 22:49–65, 1979.

Ben-Amos, D. Analytic Categories and Ethnic Genres. *Genre*, 2:275–301, 1969.

_____. Towards a Definition of Folklore in Context. *Journal of American Folklore*, 84:3–15, 1971.

_____, and Kenneth S. Goldstein, eds. *Folklore: Performance and Communication*. The Hague: Mouton, 1975.

Berger, Bennet. Black Culture or Lower-Class Culture. In *Soul*, ed. Lee Rainwater, pp. 117–28. Chicago: Aldine, 1970.

Berlin, B., D. E. Breedlove, and Ph. H. Raven. Folk Taxonomies and Biological Classification. In *Cognitive Anthropology*, ed. Steven Tyler, pp. 60–65. New York: Holt, Rinehart and Winston, 1968.

Birdwhistell, Ray. *Introduction to Kinesics*. Louisville, Ky.: University of Louisville Press, 1952.

———. *Kinesics and Context: Essays on Body Motion Communication*. Philadelphia: University of Pennsylvania Press, 1970.

Blacking, John. The Social Value of Venda Riddling. *African Studies*, 20:1–32, 1961.

Burke, Kenneth. *A Grammar of Motives*. Englewood Cliffs, N.J.: Prentice-Hall, 1945.

Burns, Elizabeth. *Theatricality: A Study of Convention in the Theater and in Social Life*. New York: Harper and Row, 1972.

Cavan, S. *Liquor License: An Ethnography of Bar Behavior*. Chicago: Aldine, 1966.

Cicourel, A. The Negotiation of Status and Role. In *Recent Sociology*, ed. H. P. Dreitzel, pp. 4–45. New York: MacMillan, 1970.

———. *Cognitive Sociology*. New York: The Free Press, 1974.

Clinard, Marshall B. The Public Drinking House and Society. In *Society, Culture and Drinking Patterns*, ed. D. J. Pittman and C. R. Snyder, pp. 181–94. New Brunswick, N.J.: Rutgers University Press, 1961.

Collins, R. Lorrance, and G. Alan Marlatt. Social Modeling as a Determinant of Drinking Behavior. *Addictive Behaviors*, 6:233–39, 1981.

Cooke, Benjamin G. Non-Verbal Communication among Afro-Americans. In *Rappin' and Stylin' Out: Communication in Urban Black America*, ed. T. Kochman, pp. 32–64. Urbana: University of Illinois Press, 1972.

Cothran, Kay. Participation in Tradition. *Keystone Folklore*, 18:7–13, 1973.

———. Talking Trash in the Okefenokee Swamp Rim. *Journal of American Folklore*, 87:430–56, 1974.

de Grazia, S. *Of Time, Work and Leisure*. New York: Twentieth Century Fund, 1964.

Dewey, Thomas. *Art as Experience*. New York: Minton Balch and Co., 1934.

Dillard, J. L. *Black English*. New York: Random House, 1972.

Dollard, John. *Caste and Class in a Southern Town*. New Haven, Conn.: Yale University Press, 1937.

———. The Dozens: Dialect of Insult. *American Imago*, 1:3–25, 1939.

Drake, St. Clair, and Horace Cayton. *Black Metropolis*. New York: Harper and Row, 1962.

Duncan, Hugh Dalziel. *Communication and Social Order*. London: Oxford University Press, 1962.

Dundes, Alan. Text, Texture and Context. *Southern Folklore Quarterly*, 28:251–65, 1964.

Firestone, Harold. Cats, Kicks and Color. In *The Other Side*, ed. Harold S. Becker, pp. 281–97. New York: The Free Press, 1964.

Frake, Charles. The Ethnographic Study of Cognitive Systems. In *Anthropology and Human Behavior*, ed. R. Gladwin and W. C. Sturdevant, pp. 72–85. Washington, D.C.: Anthropological Society of Washington, 1962.

Frazier, E. Franklin. *The Negro Family in the United States*. Chicago: University of Chicago Press, 1939.

————. *Black Bourgeoisie*. New York: The Free Press, 1957.

Freud, Sigmund. *Introductory Lectures in Psychoanalysis*. London: Tavistock, 1922.

Gans, Herbert. *The Urban Villagers*. New York: The Free Press, 1962.

Garfinkel, Harold. *Studies in Ethnomethodology*. Englewood Cliffs, N.J.: Prentice-Hall, 1967.

Garvin, Paul, ed. *Prague School Reader in Esthetics, Literary Structure, and Style*. Washington, D.C.: Anthropological Society of Washington, 1964.

Geertz, Clifford. Deep Play: Notes on a Balinese Cockfight. *Daedalus*, 101:1–37, 1972.

————. *The Interpretation of Cultures*. New York: Basic Books, 1974.

Georges, Robert A. Towards an Understanding of Storytelling Events. *Journal of American Folklore*, 82:313–28, 1969.

Gerth, H. H., and C. W. Mills. *Character and Social Structure*. New York: Harcourt, Brace and Co., 1958.

Ginzburg, Eli et al. *The Middle-Class Negro in the White Man's World*. New York: Columbia University Press, 1967.

Gizalis, Gregory. Narrative Rhetorical Devices of Persuasion in the Greek Community of Philadelphia. Ph.D. diss. University of Pennsylvania, 1972.

Glazer, Barney, and Anselm Strauss. *Status Passage*. Chicago: Aldine, 1972.

Goffman, Erving. *The Presentation of Self in Everyday Life*. New York: Anchor Books, 1959.

————. *Asylums*. New York: Anchor Books, 1961.

————. *Behavior in Public Places*. New York: The Free Press, 1963.

————. *Interaction Ritual: Essays on Face to Face Behavior*. New York: Anchor Books, 1967.

————. *Relations in Public*. New York: Basic Books, 1971.

————. *Frame Analysis: An Essay in the Organization of Experience*. New York: Harper and Row, 1974.

Goines, Donald. *Whoreson: The Story of a Ghetto Pimp*. Los Angeles: Holloway House, 1972.

Golde, P., ed. *Women in the Field: Anthropological Experiences*. Chicago: Aldine, 1970.

Goldstein, Kenneth S. *A Guide for Fieldworkers in Folklore*. Hatboro, Pa.: Folklore Associates, 1964.

Gumperz, John J., and Dell Hymes, eds., *Directions in Sociolinguistics*. New York: Holt, Reinhart and Winston, 1972.

Goodenough, Ward. Cultural Anthropology and Linguistics. Report of the 7th Round Table Meeting, ed. P. Garvin, pp. 167–73. Washington: Georgetown University Press, 1957.

Gottleib, David. The Neighborhood Tavern and the Cocktail Lounge. *American Journal of Sociology*, 62:559–62, 1957.

Greer, William H., and Price M. Cobb. *Black Rage*. New York: Basic Books, 1968.

Hall, Edward T. *The Silent Language*. New York: Fawcett Books, 1959.

———. *The Hidden Dimension*. New York: Random House, 1966.

Hannerz, Ulf. *Soulside: Inquiries into Ghetto Culture and Community*. New York: Columbia University Press, 1969.

———. What Ghetto Males are Like: Another Look. In *Afro-American Anthropology: Contemporary Perspectives*, ed. N. Whitten, Jr., and J. F. Szwed, pp. 313–27. New York: The Free Press, 1970.

———. The Study of Afro-American Cultural Dynamics. *Southwestern Journal of Anthropology*, 27:181–200, 1972.

———. Research in the Black Ghetto: A Review of the Sixties. In *Discovering Afro-America*, ed. Roger D. Abrahams and John Szwed, pp. 5–25, 1975.

Hare, Nathan. *The Black Anglo-Saxons*. New York: Collier Books, 1970.

Harper, Fred D. *Alcohol Abuse and Black America*. Alexandria, Va.: Douglass Publishers, 1976.

———. *Alcoholism Treatment and Black Americans*. DHEW Publ. no. ADM 79–853. Rockville, Md.: National Clearinghouse for Alcohol Information, 1979.

———, and M. P. Dawkins. Alcohol Abuse in the Black Community. *Black Scholar*, 8:23–31, 1977.

Heard, Nathan C. *Howard Street*. New York: New American Library, 1968.

Heath, D. B. Anthropological Perspectives on Alcohol: A Historical Review. In *Cross-Cultural Approaches to the Study of Alcohol*, eds. M. W. Everett, J. O. Waddell, and D. B. Heath, pp. 41–101. The Hague: Mouton, 1976.

———. The Sociocultural Model of Alcohol Use: Problems and Prospects. *Journal of Operational Psychology*, 9:55–66, 1978.

———, J. O. Waddell, and M. D. Topper, eds. Cultural Factors in Alcohol Research and Treatment of Drinking Problems. *Quarterly Journal of Studies on Alcohol*, Supplement no. 9, 1981.

Huizenga, J. *Homo Ludens: A Study of the Play Element in Culture*. Boston: Little, Brown and Co., 1950.

Humphreys, Laud. *Tearoom Trade*. Chicago: Aldine, 1970.

Husserl, Edmund. *Cartesian Meditations: An Introduction to Phenomenology*. The Hague: Martinus Nijhoff, 1960.

Hymes, Dell. The Ethnography of Speaking. In *Anthropology and Human Behavior*, ed. T. Gladwin and W. Sturtevant, pp. 15–53. Washington, D.C.: Anthropological Society of Washington, 1962.

———. Introduction: Toward Ethnographies of Communication. In *The Ethnography of Communication*, ed. John Gumperz and Dell Hymes, pp. 1–34. (Special Publication American Anthropologist 66 [6], Part 2). Washington, D.C.: American Anthropological Association, 1964.

————. Models of the Interaction of Language and Social Setting. *Journal of Social Issues*, 23:8–28, 1967a.

————. On Communicative Competence. Manuscript, 1967b.

————. Review: *Language as Symbolic Action* by Kenneth Burke. *Language*, 44:664–69, 1968.

————. Towards Linguistic Competence. *Working Papers in Sociolinguistics*, 16. Austin: University of Texas Department of Anthropology, 1974a.

————. *Foundations in Sociolinguistics*. Philadelphia: University of Pennsylvania Press, 1974b.

————. Breakthrough into Performance. In *Folklore and Communication*, ed. Kenneth S. Goldstein and Dan Ben-Amos, pp. 11–74. The Hague: Mouton, 1975.

Iser, Wolfgang. The Reading Process: A Phenomenological Approach. *New Literary History*, 3:279–99, 1972.

Jakobson, Roman. The Metaphoric and Metonymic Poles. In Roman Jakobson and Morris Halle, *Fundamentals of Language*, pp. 76–82. The Hague: Mouton, 1956.

————. Concluding Statement: Linguistics and Poetics. In *Style in Language*, ed. Thomas Sebeok, pp. 345–59. Cambridge, Mass.: MIT Press, 1957.

Jones, Michael Owen. The Concept of "Aesthetics" in the Traditional Arts. *Western Folklore*, 30:77–104, 1971.

————. *The Handmade Object and its Maker*. Berkeley: University of California Press, 1975.

Keller, Susanne. *The Urban Neighborhood: A Sociological Perspective*. New York: Random House, 1968.

Kepes, G. Design and Light. *Design Quarterly*, 68:1–32, 1968.

Kirchenblatt-Gimblett, B. Multilinguilism and Immigrant Narrative: Code Switching as a Communicative Strategy in Artistic Verbal Performance. Manuscript, 1970.

————. A Parable in Context. In *Folklore: Performance and Communication*, ed. K. S. Goldstein and D. Ben-Amos, pp. 105–30. The Hague: Mouton, 1975.

Kochman, Thomas. Towards an Ethnography of Black American Speech Behavior. In *Afro-American Anthropology: Contemporary Perspectives*, ed. N. Whitten, Jr., and J. F. Szwed, pp. 145–62. New York: The Free Press, 1970.

————. *Rappin' and Stylin' Out: Communication in Urban Black America*. Urbana: University of Illinois Press, 1972.

Korzbski, Alfred. *Science and Sanity: An Introduction to Non-Aristotelian Systems and General Semantics*. New York: Science Press, 1941.

Kronus, Sidney. *The Black Middle Class*. Columbus, Ohio: Merrill, 1971.

Labov, William. *Language in the Inner City: Studies in Black English Vernacular*. Philadelphia: University of Pennsylvania Press, 1972.

————. Rules for Ritual Insults. In *Studies in Social Interaction*, ed. David Sudnow, pp. 120–69. New York: The Free Press, 1972.

————, and Joshua Weltselsky. Narrative Analysis. In *Essays in the Verbal and Visual Arts*, ed. June Helm, pp. 12–44. Seattle: University of Washington Press, 1967.

Lee, Terrence. Urban Neighborhood as a Socio-Spatial Schema. *Human Relations*, 21:241–68, 1968.

Leibow, Elliot. *Tally's Corner: A Study of Negro Street-Corner Men*. Boston: Little, Brown and Co., 1967.

LeMasters, E. E. *Blue-Collar Aristocrats*. Madison: University of Wisconsin Press, 1975.

Lofland, John. *Analyzing Social Settings*. Belmont, Calif.: Wadsworth Publishing Co., 1971.

Lofland, Lyn. Self-Management in Public Settings. Part I. *Urban Life and Culture*, 1:93–117, 1971a.

————. Self-Management in Public Settings. Part II. *Urban Life and Culture*, 2:217–31, 1971b.

Lynch, K. *The Image of the City*. Cambridge, Mass.: MIT Press, 1960.

MacAndrew, C., and R. B. Edgerton. *Drunken Comportment: A Social Explanation*. Chicago: Aldine, 1972.

MacKay, D. M. Operational Aspects of Some Fundamental Concepts of Human Communication. *Synthese*, 9:182–98, 1969.

Macrory, B. E. The Tavern and the Community. *Quarterly Journal of Studies on Alcohol*, 13:609–37, 1952.

Maddox, G. L. Drinking among Negroes: Inferences from the Drinking Patterns of Selected Negro Male Collegians. *Journal of Health and Social Behavior*, 9:114–20, 1968.

————, and J. R. Williams. Drinking Behavior of Negro Collegians. *Quarterly Journal of Studies on Alcohol*, 29:117–29, 1968.

Malinowski, B. *Argonauts of the Eastern Pacific*. New York: Dutton (1921), 1961.

————. *Coral Gardens and Their Magic*, vol. 2. London: Allen and Unwin, 1934.

Manning, Frank E. *Black Clubs in Bermuda: Ethnography of a Play World*. Ithaca, N.Y.: Cornell University Press, 1975.

Mass. Observation. *The Pub and the People*. London: V. Gollanz, 1938.

Mauss, Marcel. *The Gift*. London: Cohen and West Ltd., 1954.

Mead, George Herbert. *Mind, Self and Society*. Chicago: University of Chicago Press, 1934.

————. *The Philosophy of the Act*. Chicago: University of Chicago Press, 1938.

Merleau-Ponty, Maurice. Cezanne's Doubt. *Sense and Non-Sense*, trans. Hubert L. Dreyfus and Patricia Allen Dreyfus. Evanston, Ill.: Northwestern University Press, 1964.

Michelson, W. *Man and His Urban Environment: A Sociological Approach*. Reading, Mass.: Addison-Wesley, 1970.

Mills, C. Wright. Situated Actions and Vocabularies of Motive. *American Sociological Review*, 5:904–13, 1940.

Milner, Christine, and Richard Milner. *Black Players: The Secret World of Black Pimps*. New York: Bantam Books, 1972.

Ming, H. Folkloric Communication in a Philippino-American Community. Ph.D. diss. University of Pennsylvania, 1973.

Mitchell-Kernan, Claudia. Language Behavior in a Black Urban Community. *Monographs of the Language and Behavior Laboratory*, University of California, Berkeley, no. 2, 1971.

Morris, Charles. *Signs, Language and Behavior*. New York: Prentice-Hall, 1946.

Mukarovsky, Jan. *The Word and Verbal Art: Selected Essays by Jan Mukarovsky*, trans. John Burbank and Peter Steiner. New Haven, Conn.: Yale University Press, 1978.

Murray, A. *The Omni-Americans*. New York: Discuss, 1970.

Myrdal, Gunnar. *An American Dilemma: The Negro Problem and Modern Democracy*. New York: Harper and Row, 1944.

Pike, Kenneth. *Language in Relation to a Unified Theory of the Structure of Human Behavior. Part I*. Glendale: Summer Institute of Linguistics, 1954.

Proshansky, H. M., W. H. Ittelson, and L. G. Rivlin. *Environmental Psychology. Man and His Physical Setting*. New York: Holt, Rinehart and Winston, 1970.

Rainwater, Lee, ed. *Behind Ghetto Walls: Black Families in a Federal Slum*. Chicago: Aldine, 1970.

Reisman, Karl. Cultural and Linguistic Ambiguity in a West Indian Village. In *Afro-American Anthropology*, ed. N. Whitten, Jr., and J. F. Szwed, pp. 129–44. New York: The Free Press, 1970.

————. Contrapuntal Conversation in an Antiguan Village. In *Explorations in the Ethnography of Communication*, ed. Richard Bauman and Joel Shezer, pp. 110–24. Cambridge: Cambridge University Press, 1974.

Robins, Lee N., George E. Murphy, and M. B. Breckenridge. Drinking Behavior of Young Urban Negro Men. *Quarterly Journal of Studies on Alcohol*, 29:657–73, 1968.

Rommel, Benjamin, and Mary Rommel. Sociocultural Correlates of Black Drinking: Implications for Research and Treatment. *Quarterly Journal of Studies on Alcohol*, Supplement no. 9, pp. 241–45, 1981.

Roos, Philip D. Jurisdiction: An Ecological Concept. In *Environmental Psychology: Man and His Physical Setting*, ed. H. M. Proshansky, W. H. Ittelson, and L. G. Rivlin, pp. 239–46. New York: Holt, Rinehart and Winston, 1970.

Rose, Dan. Detachment: Continuities of Sensibility among Afro-American Populations of the Circum-Atlantic Fringe. In *Discovering Afro-America*, ed. Roger D. Abrahams and John Szwed, pp. 68–82. Leiden: E. J. Brill, 1975.

Rouch, Jean. On the Vicissitudes of the Self: The Possessed Dancer, the Magician, the Sorcerer, the Filmmaker, and the Ethnographer. *Studies in the Anthropology of Visual Communication*, 5:2–8, 1978.

Ruesch, Jurgen, and Weldon Kees. *Nonverbal Communication: Notes on the Visual Perception of Human Relations.* Berkeley: University of California Press, 1958.

Schectner, R. Towards a Poetics of Performance. In *Ethno-poetics: A First International Symposium*, ed. M. Benamov and J. Rothenberg, pp. 42–64. Boston: Boston University Press, 1976.

Scheflen, Albert. Communication and Regulation in Psychotherapy. *Psychiatry*, 26:126–36, 1963.

———. The Significance of Posture in Communication Systems. *Psychiatry*, 27:316–31, 1964.

———. Stream and Structure of Communicational Behavior: Context Analysis of a Psychotherapy Session. Commonwealth of Pennsylvania: *EPPI, Behavioral Studies Monograph*, no. 1, 1965.

———. *Body Language and the Social Order: Communication as Behavioral Control.* Englewood Cliffs, N.J.: Prentice-Hall, 1972.

Schulz, David. *Coming Up Black: Patterns of Ghetto Socialization.* Englewood Cliffs, N.J.: Prentice-Hall, 1969.

Schutz, Alfred. *Collected Papers: I. The Problem of Social Reality*, ed. M. Nathenson. The Hague: Martinuus N. Nijhoff, 1962.

———. *Collected Papers: II. Studies in Social Theory*, ed. A. Broderson. The Hague: M. Nijhoff, 1964.

———. *Collected Papers: III. Studies in Phenomenological Philosophy*, ed. I. Schutt. The Hague: M. Nijhoff, 1966.

———. *The Phenomenology of the Social World*, trans. George Walsh and Frederick Lehnert. Evanston, Ill.: Northwestern University Press, 1967.

Shklovsky, Viktor. Art as Technique. In *Russian Formalist Criticism: Four Essays*, ed. Lee T. Lemon and Marian J. Reis. Lincoln: University of Nebraska Press, 1965.

Simmel, Georg. *The Sociology of Georg Simmel*, ed. K. Wolff. New York: The Free Press, 1950.

Slim, Iceberg. *Pimp: The Story of My Life.* Los Angeles: Holloway House, 1968.

Sommer, R. *Personal Space.* Englewood Cliffs, N.J.: Prentice-Hall, 1969.

Southworth, Michael. The Sonic Environment of Cities. *Environment and Behavior*, 1:49–70, 1960.

Spradley, James P., and Brenda J. Mann. *The Cocktail Waitress: Woman's Work in a Man's World.* New York: John Wiley and Sons, 1975.

Stewart, William. On the Use of Negro Dialect in the Teaching of Reading. In *Teaching Black Children to Read*, ed. Joan Baratz and Roger Shuy. Washington, D.C.: Center for Applied Linguistics, 1969.

Stoeltje, Beverly. Bow-Legged Bastard: A Manner of Speaking. In *Folklore Annual of the University of Texas Folklore Association*, ed. Tom Ireland et al., pp. 152–78. Austin: Texas Folklore Association, 1972–73.

Strickler, D. P., S. D. Dobbs, and W. A. Maxwell. The Influence of Setting on Drinking Behaviors: The Laboratory versus the Barroom. *Addictive Behaviors*, 4:339–44, 1979.

Sudnow, David, ed. *Studies in Social Interaction*. New York: The Free Press, 1972.

Sundholm, Charles. The Pornographic Arcade: Ethnographic Notes on Moral Men in Immoral Places. *Urban Life and Culture*, 2:85–104, 1973.

Suttles, Gerald D. *The Social of the Slum*. Chicago: University of Chicago Press, 1968.

Szwed, J. An American Anthropological Dilemma: The Politics of Afro-American Culture. In *Reinventing Anthropology*, ed. D. H. Hymes, pp. 153–81. New York: Vintage Books, 1974.

————, ed. *Black America*. New York: Basic Books, 1970.

Thiel, Philip. Notes on the Description, Scaling, Notation and Scoring of Some Perceptual and Cognitive Attributes of the Physical Setting. In *Environmental Psychology: Man and His Physical Setting*, ed. H. M. Proshansky, W. H. Ittelson, and L. G. Rivlin, pp. 593–619. New York: Holt, Rinehart and Winston, 1970.

Thompson, Robert. Aesthetic of the Cool. *African Arts VII*, 1(Autumn), 1969.

Tiger, Lionel. *Men in Groups*. London: Panther Books, 1970.

Tumin, Melvin M. Some Social Consequences of Research on Race Relations. In *Recent Sociology*, no. 1, ed. H. P. Dreitzel, pp. 242–62. New York: MacMillan, 1969.

Turner, Victor, *Dramas, Fields, and Metaphors*. Ithaca, N.Y.: Cornell University Press, 1974.

Valentine, BettyLou. *Hustling and Other Hard Work: Life Styles in the Ghetto*. New York: The Free Press, 1978.

Valentine, Charles A. Deficit, Difference and BiCultural Models of Afro-American Behaviors. *Harvard Educational Review*, 41:137–57, 1971.

————. Black Studies and Anthropology: Scholarly and Political Interests in Afro-American Culture. *Addison-Wesley Modular Publications*, 15:1–53, 1972.

Vander Zanden, James W. Sociological Studies of American Blacks. *Sociological Quarterly*, 14:32–52, 1973.

Vitols, M. N. Culture Patterns of Drinking in Negro and White Alcoholics. *Diseases of the Nervous System*. 29:391–94, 1968.

Wallace, Anthony F. C. *Culture and Personality*. New York: Random House, 1961.

Walsh, David. Sociology and the Social World. In *New Directions in Sociological Theory*, ed. P. Filmer et al., pp. 15–36. New York: MacMillan, 1973.

Warringer, Charles. The Nature and Function of Official Morality. *American Journal of Sociology*, 63:165–68, 1958.

Watson, O. Michael. *Proxemic Behavior: A Cultural Study*. The Hague: Mouton, 1970.

————. Symbolic and Expressive Uses of Space: An Introduction to Proxemic Behavior. *Addison Wesley Modular Publications*, 20:1–8, 1972.

Weaver, Warren. The Mathematics of Communication. In *Communication and Culture: Readings in the Codes of Human Interaction*, ed. A. G. Smith, pp. 15–24. New York: Holt, Rinehart and Winston (1944), 1966.

Weber, Max. *Economy and Society: An Outline of Interpretive Sociology*, ed. Guenther Roth and Claus Wittich, trans. E. Fischoff et al. New York: Bedminister Press, 1968.

Whitten, Norman E., Jr., and John Szwed, eds. *Afro-American Anthropology*. New York: The Free Press, 1970.

Wilden, Anthony. *System and Structure: Essays in Communication and Exchange*. London: Tavistock, 1972.

Williams, William Carlos. *The Selected Essays*. New York: Random House, 1954.

Wilson, Peter J. Respect vs. Reputation: A Suggestion for Caribbean Ethnology. *Man*, 4:70–84, 1970.

_____. *Crab Antics: The Social Anthropology of English-Speaking Negro Societies of the Caribbean*. New Haven, Conn.: Yale University Press, 1973.

Winter, G. *Elements for a Social Ethic*. New York: MacMillan, 1966.

Wittgenstein, Ludwig. *Tractatus Logico-Philosophicus*. London: Routledge and Kegan Paul (1921), 1971.

Yerkovitch, Sally M. Gossiping; or the Creating of Fictional Lives, Being a Study of the Subject in an Urban American Setting Drawing Upon Vignettes from Upper Middle Class Lives. Ph.D. Diss. University of Pennsylvania, 1977.

Young, Katherine. Indirection in Storytelling. *Western Folklore*, 34:46–55, 1978.

Young, Virginia H. Family and Childhood in a Southern Negro Community. *American Anthropologist*, 72:269–88, 1969.

A Note on the Author

Michael J. Bell is an associate professor of English and Folklore at Wayne State University, Detroit, Michigan, and director of the Center for Urban Folklife. He received his A.B. from Saint Joseph's College and his M.A. and Ph.D. from the University of Pennsylvania. He has published articles on urban folklore in such journals as *Southern Folklore Quarterly*, *Western Folklore*, and *Sub-Stance*.